THE WEAPONS STATE

THE WEAPONS STATE

Proliferation and
the Framing of Security

David Mutimer

LYNNE
RIENNER
PUBLISHERS

BOULDER
LONDON

Published in the United States of America in 2000 by
Lynne Rienner Publishers, Inc.
1800 30th Street, Boulder, Colorado 80301
www.rienner.com

and in the United Kingdom by
Lynne Rienner Publishers, Inc.
3 Henrietta Street, Covent Garden, London WC2E 8LU

Library of Congress Cataloging-in-Publication Data
Mutimer, David, 1964–
    The weapons state : proliferation and the framing of security /
David Mutimer.
        p. cm.
    Includes bibliographical references and index.
    ISBN 1-55587-787-7 (alk. paper : hc)
    1. Nuclear nonproliferation. 2. Nuclear arms control.
3. Biological arms control. 4. Chemical arms control. 5. Security,
International. I. Title. II. Series.
JZ5675.M88   2000
327.1'747—dc21   99-37489
                                                                    CIP

British Cataloguing in Publication Data
A Cataloguing in Publication record for this book
is available from the British Library.

Printed and bound in the United States of America

The paper used in this publication meets the requirements
⊗ of the American National Standard for Permanence of
Paper for Printed Library Materials Z39.48-1984.

5 4 3 2 1

Contents

Prologue

We had seen it all before. U.S. carrier battle groups were making their way to the Gulf, there to be joined by the forces of their allies. U.S. troops were gathering under a hot Arabian sun, contemplating the pleasures of rubber suits sealed against the possible use of chemical weapons. The chemical weapons were those of Iraq, and this time it seemed biological weapons might be added—the smart money was on Anthrax.

The first time we watched, the United States was joined by an impressive coalition of states—most of which provided only political or financial support but support nonetheless. In a very real sense, we all joined them through the magic medium of the Cable News Network. We watched as carefully selected images of the U.S.-led coalition were beamed around the world, bringing the remarkable might of modern military technology to bear on Iraq. Iraq faced this barrage because it had invaded Kuwait, a tiny neighbor with which Iraq shared a disputed boundary—disputed primarily because it cut across one of the world's largest oil fields. Surely no state had ever behaved so reprehensibly, invading a neighbor and then declaring it to be part of the invading state? Well, perhaps so, but this was 1990, and the world community was determined to show that it was not done these days. We elected the United States our leader, or at least we saluted smartly when the United States selected itself to be our leader, and off we all trooped—most of us virtually—to win a war against "naked aggression" in the name of a "new world order."

In 1991 the world community won and, better yet, won at a very low cost, at least in terms of the only currency that seemed to be of interest—the lives of allied servicemen and servicewomen. The fear throughout the fighting had been that Iraq would use the store of weapons of mass destruction we all assumed it had hidden away. Each time a Scud missile was apparently destroyed en route to Saudi Arabia, we worried that some deadly chemical had been scattered inadvertently over the desert. Every time the air raid siren sounded in an Israeli city, we held our breaths to see if the people would need their gas masks—or worse yet, if they wouldn't, because gas masks don't do much against a nuclear attack. In the end, though, the war proved entirely conventional. Only later did Gulf War Syndrome raise the possibility that some weapons had been used about which we had not been told or, more likely, that the protection against these weapons' use that our troops had been given had proven almost as harmful as the weapons themselves.

What was to be done about these Iraqi weapons? They might not have been fired, but it was likely, if not certain, that they were still there. The nearly global alliance the United States had assembled had won that particular war but had not (quite) destroyed Iraq or even driven out its government (although not for want of trying). So there sat Iraq—led by the same government that had just so blatantly flouted the (oh, so new) rules of nonintervention and that probably still had a frightening collection of chemical weapons; it might have some even more horrifying biological weapons, and the odds were that it was close to building at least one nuclear weapon. Fortunately, Iraq had just lost a conventional war, and convention dictates that victors can write the terms of a cease-fire. What was written was UN Security Council Resolution 687, which ordered Iraq to disarm, and the United Nations created a special organ, the United Nations Special Commission (UNSCOM), to make sure Iraq complied. Compliance proved a bit of a problem, which is why we were back watching a familiar story in autumn 1998—UNSCOM's inspectors had packed up and left Iraq, and the United States (after a last-minute intervention by the UN Secretary-General seemed to have averted military action yet again) launched a massive military strike to punish Iraq for failing to follow the rules.

Much had happened in the intervening years, because that first visit to the Gulf came at a crucial moment in international history. The Cold War, which had defined the problematic of international security for forty years, had just ended. States in general, and the United States in particular, were trying to come to terms with the implications of the peace that follows the end of a cold war. Although there had been much talk of a peace dividend, it was difficult to believe no threats were out there somewhere; it was just not clear exactly what they were or how to respond to them. Into this breach stepped Iraq—the Soviet Union may have gone, and its successors and former allies might now even be on the same side as the United States and its allies, but Iraq made the world look as if it were still a dangerous place. Unfortunately, Iraq by itself could not pose the sort of threat the Soviet Union and the United States posed to each other; nor could it provide the kind of orientation necessary to replace the security compass provided by the Cold War. However, what if Iraq were only one of a number of similar threats? Then perhaps the dangers of the post–Cold War world could be more clearly apprehended, and the leaders of the new world order could begin to think about how to respond. But what would make other threats "similar"? What kind of threat did Iraq pose?

Charles Krauthammer provided an answer in a widely cited article in *Foreign Affairs* even as the Gulf War was unfolding:

> Iraq, which (unless disarmed by Desert Storm) will likely be in possession of intercontinental ballistic missiles within the decade, is the prototype of this new strategic threat, what might be called the "Weapon State.". . .
>
> The danger from the Weapon State is posed today by Iraq, tomorrow perhaps by North Korea or Libya. In the next century, however, the proliferation of strategic weapons will not be restricted to Weapon States. Windfall wealth allows oil states to import high technology weapons in the absence of a mature industrial base. However, it is not hard to imagine maturer states—say Argentina, Pakistan, Iran, South Africa—reaching the same level of weapons development by means of ordinary industrialisation. (Today most of these countries are friendly, but some are unstable and potentially hostile.)[1]

Krauthammer's argument provided a solution to the problem of generalizing Iraq. Iraq was a "Weapon State"—or, to adopt the label that has become more common, a rogue state. More formally, Iraq was the prototype threat of the contemporary world, created through the proliferation of strategic weapons. Iraq was dangerous, but dealing with Iraq did not eliminate that danger, because Iraq was only the first in what might be a series of threats to international security produced by the proliferation of strategic weapons. Here was something that could be dealt with in a general fashion, that might even provide an organizing framework for security in the vaunted new world order for which the Gulf War was supposed to have been fought.

At least one member of the coalition seemed to think this form of generalization regarding Iraq could orient security in the new world order, for Canada made a bold proposal toward the end of the Gulf War. Canada suggested a UN gathering to condemn the proliferation of weapons of mass destruction, their means of delivery, and "massive build-ups of conventional weapons." A program of action would be initiated at the meeting, designed to produce a follow-up conference in 1995 to "celebrate completion of the comprehensive network of specific nonproliferation regimes."[2] Canada was not alone. Britain and Japan announced that they would jointly sponsor a resolution at the United Nations to create a Register of Conventional Arms, an idea that had been raised before but that lacked support until we were confronted by Iraq's conventional arsenal. On 29 May 1991 U.S. president George Bush picked up the proliferation theme in a speech at the U.S. Air Force Academy:

Nowhere are the dangers of weapons proliferation more urgent than in the Middle East.

After consulting with governments in the region and elsewhere about how to slow and then reverse the buildup of unnecessary and destabilizing weapons, I am today proposing a Middle East arms control initiative. It features supplier guidelines on conventional arms exports; barriers to exports that contribute to weapons of mass destruction; a freeze now, and later a ban on surface-to-surface missiles in the region; and a ban on production of nuclear weapons material. Halting the proliferation of conventional and unconventional weapons in the Middle East, while supporting the legitimate needs of every state to defend itself, will require the cooperation of many states, in the region and around the world.[3]

In the accompanying fact sheet released by the White House, the connection between Bush's proposal and the more general problems of proliferation, addressed particularly in the prior actions by the UK and Canada, was drawn explicitly:

Since proliferation is a global problem, it must find a global solution. At the same time, the current situation in the Middle East poses unique dangers and opportunities. Thus, the president's proposal will concentrate on the Middle East as its starting point, while complementing other initiatives such as those taken by Prime Ministers John Major [of the United Kingdom] and [Canada's] Brian Mulroney.[4]

The Gulf War had been fought in the name of a new world order, but only after it had ended did we begin to see what the fight had been against. Although Iraq had clearly been the enemy, it was just the most visible example of a much wider problem: the proliferation of weapons of mass destruction, their means of delivery, and even what Canada called "massive build-ups of conventional weapons."

This is a book about that wider problem. The book does not detail the dangers of weapons proliferation or even test the various measures that have been taken in response to the problem of proliferation—at least not directly. Rather, it is about the way in which weapons proliferation was made a problem and how that making has shaped and been shaped by the measures taken in response to it. At least as important, this book is about the effects of making a problem of weapons proliferation in the way it was made. Why were we again watching the United States go to war with Iraq in autumn 1998, just as it had almost done at the beginning of the year and indeed as it had done once or twice a year since 1991? This book suggests an answer to that question, but not by asking what caused this particular event or even the sequence of similar events but rather by showing how the production of weapons proliferation as a problem made possible just such a cyclical series of "crises."

By asking about the world that is effected by imagining the problem of weapons proliferation in a particular way, the book assumes that security problems, like weapons proliferation, are produced from the way in which the world is seen and acted upon rather than found preformed in the world out there. It is therefore unlike most books about weapons, arms control, proliferation, or even war, because it is rooted in the postpositivist turn in the discipline of international relations. At the same time, the book tries to grapple with the politics of a contemporary issue that is clearly of concern to those who make and analyze international security policy as it is conventionally understood. My hope is that those who think about problems of military security in general, and weapons proliferation in particular, will see some of the political implications of their chosen subject that might not have occurred to them before.

* * *

What follows is the working out of an argument that has been a number of years in the making. As with the problem of weapons proliferation, which is its focus, the argument is a social product, emerging from a series of interactions. I have been fortunate to be able to engage with some tremendously gifted people in the varied interactions that have resulted in this book. The ideas found here began to take shape in the two years I spent as principal researcher on a project for the Verification Research Programme, as it was then, of the Canadian Department of Foreign Affairs. I am grateful to the department, and to Ron Cleminson and Alan Crawford in particular, for the opportunities that association provided. I was also fortunate to have two supportive and stimulating academic environments in which to work while the argument of the book took shape. The York Centre for International and Security Studies housed me during my work for Foreign Affairs, and I cannot say enough about the York Centre's welcoming and supportive research environment—other, perhaps, than to point out that it is again my professional address. The majority of the book was written while I was a lecturer in the Department of International Relations at Keele University, and I express my deepest gratitude to all of the members of the department for making my all too short time there a terrific personal and professional experience. I would also like to thank Keele University more generally for the semester's research award in 1997, which gave me the concentrated time required to draft the manuscript of the book.

Parts of the argument have previously appeared as "Reimagining Security: The Metaphors of Proliferation" in Keith Krause and Michael Williams, eds., *Critical Security Studies* (Minneapolis: University of Minnesota Press, 1997), pp. 187–221, and "Reconstituting Security: The Practices of Proliferation Control," *European Journal of International*

Relations 4 (1) 1998, pp. 99–129. A number of people have provided invaluable assistance in the development of this argument by commenting on and discussing drafts of the manuscript, the original proposal, and the other forms in which the central argument has been presented; they include Andreas Behnke, Ken Booth, David Campbell, Alex Danchev, Alexandra Gheciu, Bradley Klein, Andrew Latham, Andrew Linklater, Debbie Lisle, Jennifer Milliken, Matthew Paterson, Richard Purslow, and Hidemi Suganami, as well as the anonymous reviewer for Lynne Rienner Publishers. In addition, my parents, Brian Mutimer and Eleanor Mutimer, have not only provided help and support throughout this and all of my professional endeavors but are the most accommodating and thorough proofreaders I could ever hope to find. I also express my deepest gratitude to Keith Krause; I cannot begin to list all he has done for me but will note only that he has always been the fiercest critic of my work, in all the best senses of the term. Knowing the kind of people they are, I expect that these friends and colleagues would happily accept responsibility for the errors and omissions in the final text, but that responsibility is mine alone.

This book is a work, first and foremost, about meaning, and it is Anne who gives my life and work its meaning. Thank you all.

—*David Mutimer*

1

Introduction

The 1991 Gulf War was fought to create a new world order to replace the order that had been defined by the Soviet-U.S. rivalry of the Cold War. The interpretation of the threat Iraq posed in the Gulf, once generalized, would come to stand as the primary threat to peace in this new order. This interpretation held that the Iraqi threat had been produced by the proliferation of weapons of mass destruction and the excessive and destabilizing accumulations of conventional arms. Thus the problem of weapons proliferation was articulated as a serious new global security problem, demanding global solutions. The new world order to be created by the Gulf War was to be a world order centered on the United Nations; so if global solutions to a security problem were needed, they would begin to be found at the United Nations. Just under a year after the war in the Gulf, the UN Security Council met at the level of Heads of State and Government for the first time in its history in an attempt to begin charting the order for our new world. In its final declaration, the Security Council stated, "The proliferation of all weapons of mass destruction constitutes a threat to international peace and security. The members of the Council commit themselves to working to prevent the spread of technology related to the research for or production of such weapons and to take appropriate action to that end."[1]

When the UN Security Council determines that something is a threat to international peace and security, it is a serious matter because the council can then take any action, up to and including the use of force, to combat that threat. The Security Council determined that the Iraqi invasion of Kuwait constituted a threat to international peace and security, and the consequences of that determination were very serious.

It is important to recognize the significance of the Security Council's determination that proliferation is a threat to international peace and security. The language is that of Chapter VII of the UN Charter, the chapter on

1

the collective security function of the UN, and it is a language that has rarely been invoked. With few exceptions, all of which have followed the end of the Cold War, Chapter VII powers have been used by the Security Council only in response to fairly clear instances of interstate violence—such as the Iraqi invasion of Kuwait. This means that in January 1992, weapons proliferation was authoritatively stated to be a serious security problem in the contemporary world, comparable to interstate aggression. The spread of weapons themselves was seen as caused by "the spread of technology related to the research for or production of" weapons of mass destruction, their means of delivery, and even advanced conventional weapons.

At the same time it stated that proliferation constitutes a threat, the Security Council committed itself to take "appropriate action" to prevent its occurrence. Having pointed to the movement of technology as the key to producing the problem in the first place, the members' action would likely focus on that movement. This is precisely what has happened. The term *weapons of mass destruction* (WMD) refers to nuclear, chemical, and biological weapons, which in particular have been the focus of attention as an agenda of proliferation control has been constructed following the end of the Gulf War. Iraq's use of Scud missiles, combined with the fear that some might be tipped with one of these weapons of mass destruction, added ballistic missiles to the list of proliferation concerns. Finally, even so-called conventional weapons were considered part of the problem—Iraq had the fifth-largest conventional arsenal in the world at the time of the Gulf War. What actions have been taken by the international community to combat the threat posed by weapons proliferation since the end of the Gulf War?

Combating Proliferation, 1991–1998

A fairly robust regime for the control of the spread of nuclear technology was believed to exist at the time of the Gulf War. The regime was anchored by the nuclear nonproliferation treaty (NPT), which had aimed to prevent the acquisition of nuclear weapons by states other than those that had tested a nuclear weapon by 1968. These five nuclear weapon states (NWS)—the United States, the Soviet Union, the United Kingdom, France, and the People's Republic of China (PRC)—were permitted to retain their nuclear weapons as parties to the NPT. Any other state that became a party joined as a nonnuclear weapon state (NNWS) and thereby pledged "not to receive the transfer from any transferor whatsoever of nuclear weapons or other nuclear explosive devices or of control over such weapons or explosive devices directly, or indirectly; not to manufacture or otherwise acquire nuclear weapons or other nuclear explosive devices; and not to seek or receive any assistance in the manufacture of nuclear weapons or other nuclear explosive devices."[2] If a state had a nuclear power program, however, it would be able to develop a nuclear weapons program, if it so chose.[3] The NPT therefore was supplemented by two additional measures. The first was the requirement that all NNWSs party to the NPT must put their civilian nuclear programs under the full-scope safeguards administered by the International Atomic Energy Agency (IAEA). The second was the creation of two supplier control groups to coordinate controls over the movement of nuclear technology.

These two additional elements of the nuclear nonproliferation regime aim to "prevent the spread of technology" for the purpose of building nuclear weapons. The IAEA safeguards constitute a system of international inspections for materials accountancy; they aim to ensure that no "significant quantity" of nuclear material goes missing as it moves through a power plant. Full-scope safeguards require that a state's entire nuclear program be placed under IAEA safeguards.[4] In theory, the IAEA has access to all nuclear material and facilities in the territory of all NNWSs party to the NPT and can thereby account for the movement of nuclear material through those facilities to ensure that none is diverted to a nuclear weapons program. A noted student of nuclear nonproliferation was able to report in 1991 that "since its implementation, no significant quantity of nuclear material has been detected and no nuclear explosion originating from nuclear material subject to IAEA safeguards has been observed. From this point of view, the result could not have been better."[5]

As a support measure for the NPT and its system of safeguards, the major nuclear suppliers have also formed two bodies to coordinate controls placed on the export of their nuclear material and technology. The first of these was called the Zangger Committee and comprised those suppliers that were party to the NPT. The problem was that, until 1992, neither China nor France was party to the NPT; thus if a supplier control group were limited to states party to the NPT, some fairly significant suppliers would be excluded. In response to the test of an Indian nuclear device in 1974, a second group was formed, known as the London Club after its first meeting place or more formally as the Nuclear Suppliers Group (NSG). The NSG was not limited to states party to the NPT and so could cover much more of the potential supply with its controls. Both groups operated in much the same fashion, with members agreeing to the technologies to be controlled and to the standards that should be met for a potential recipient to be permitted to receive nuclear material or technology from a member state. The implementation of these rules was left to the individual members through their systems of national export controls.

The aftermath of the Gulf War demonstrated convincingly that the nonproliferation regime was not as robust as had been believed. Iraq was an NNWS party to the NPT and had been a party since the treaty's entry into force in 1970. The first phase of UNSCOM inspections that followed the end of the Gulf War included seven IAEA inspections of Iraq, designed to assess that country's nuclear weapons capabilities. The first two reports revealed evidence of uranium enrichment, and by the seventh "the existence of an Iraqi weaponization program [had] been acknowledged and confirmed."[6] In other words, an extensive nuclear weapons program had been uncovered in Iraq that included the development of technology to produce weapons-grade fissile material at one end to the development of an actual weapon at the other.[7] All of this technology had been built while Iraq was subject to "full-scope" IAEA safeguards.[8]

Clearly, the nuclear nonproliferation regime needed to be strengthened if states were to combat the threat posed by the proliferation of weapons of mass destruction. What is more, the nuclear regime was the most fully developed of any technology now of proliferation concern. Appropriate action to prevent the spread of military and related technology would therefore require not only the reinforcement of the nuclear nonproliferation regime but the creation of similar regimes for chemical and biological weapons, for missile technologies, and perhaps even for conventional weapons. Finally, the nuclear nonproliferation regime itself was under some threat, because the original treaty contained a small time bomb on a twenty-five-year fuse: twenty-five years after the NPT entered into force, a conference of states party had to be convened to decide whether to extend the treaty indefinitely or for one or more additional fixed periods. The NPT had entered into force in 1970, and so the Extension Conference was to be held in 1995.

In the years following the Gulf War and the Security Council's determination that proliferation constitutes a threat to peace and security, a remarkable amount of action has been taken in response to the threat posed by the potential development of weapon states through proliferation—although I defer judgment on the degree to which this action has been appropriate. In each area identified as a proliferation concern—nuclear, chemical, biological, and conventional weapons, as well as missile delivery systems—some attempt has been made to strengthen controls on the spread of technology related to the research for or production of such weapons. I summarize those developments briefly as follows.

- The largest number of developments has concerned the strengthening of the nuclear nonproliferation regime. The NPT was extended indefinitely in 1995, and both France and the PRC joined in 1992. In 1996 a treaty banning the testing of nuclear weapons was opened for signature, and another, banning further production of fissile material for explosive purposes, was under negotiation in Geneva. The

IAEA reviewed its safeguard procedures and has begun to strengthen them so they should be less easily circumvented in the future.

- A convention banning the production, transfer, and use of chemical weapons (the Chemical Weapons Convention [CWC]) has been negotiated, and it entered into force in 1997. The CWC also created an international inspectorate, the Organization for the Prohibition of Chemical Weapons (OPCW), to monitor commitments made under the CWC. The monitoring made possible by the CWC is perhaps the most extensive and intrusive ever established, as OPCW inspectors have the right to conduct inspections anywhere on the territory of states party to the CWC and can do so on very short notice. Finally, the Australia Group, a suppliers' group similar to the NSG, which had been formed in 1984 to coordinate export controls on chemical weapons technology, was greatly expanded.

- Biological weapons had been banned by an international convention, the Biological and Toxin Weapons Convention (BTWC), in 1972. At the time, however, conventional wisdom held that biological weapons had little military value, so no provisions were included to monitor compliance with the BTWC. The states party have established a working group to prepare possible verification procedures, and they expect to approve a package of such procedures at a review conference scheduled for the year 2001. Earlier, the Australia Group had added controls over biological weapons technology to its initial concern with chemical weapons, and so the expansion of its membership also provides extended control on the supply of that technology.

- The Missile Technology Control Regime (MTCR) began as a procedure to coordinate export controls on missile technologies among the members of the Group of Seven (G-7). With the articulation of missile technology to the new proliferation agenda, the membership of the MTCR has also greatly expanded and now stands at 29. One MTCR member, Canada, even suggested that the regime serve as the basis for a global convention—a CWC for missile technology. Nothing came of the suggestion, and it has been dropped.

- Even conventional weapons have come to be seen as proliferation problems following the Gulf War, and a number of actions have been taken to prevent the spread of technologies related to conventional arms. In 1992 the UN General Assembly established a Register of Conventional Arms, calling on UN members to submit data annually on their transfers of major conventional weapons. A treaty modeled on the CWC has been negotiated banning the production and transfer of antipersonnel land mines. Finally, a new suppliers' group has been created by the Wassenaar Arrangement, which coordinates export controls on technologies related to conventional arms.

Following the Security Council's call to arms—or, perhaps more appropriate, its call away from arms—considerable action seems to have been taken to prevent the spread of technology related to research for and production of arms. Proliferation has become a primary security concern of the post–Cold War era. Proliferation is a threat, however, because it has been stated authoritatively to be a threat. More than that, weapons proliferation has itself been constructed as a problem of contemporary security. As with the creation of a threat by its being stated as a threat by the United Nations and other authoritative speakers, proliferation is a construction that begins with what is said and continues with how that saying is embedded in the actions it makes possible. Because of the privileged position of the state in international relations, what is stated by the state—or by states when they gather as something like the Security Council—often has the greatest importance. The weapon state and the state of weaponry, as well as the weapons and states themselves, are made possible by being stated by the state.

An Overview of the Argument

By invading Kuwait and triggering the spectacular response that was the Gulf War, Iraq has done the international community an unwitting service. All of the old truths about security seemed to have crumbled along with the Iron Curtain. In 1990 both practitioners and students of security needed a new set of guidelines for a new world order. Most of all, they needed a good new threat against which security could be organized. Iraq provided one, and with a little ingenuity it proved possible to generalize from Iraq to Krauthammer's weapon state. The weapon state was the product of a process that could be called proliferation, the spread of military and related technology to possible future Iraqs. To stem proliferation and prevent the creation of new weapon states, the international community needed to examine its systems for managing the movement of military technologies, as well as the conditions of the production and flow of those technologies. The experience in Iraq pointed to the state of weapons in order to prevent the weapon state. The state of weapons was found wanting, so much international action has taken place to gain a measure of control. The United States almost went to war with North Korea again because of that state's (possibly nuclear) weapons. All in all, we have gotten ourselves into quite a state over weapons.

Throughout 1998 the prospect of another war with Iraq over its weapons programs loomed before finally being realized at the end of the year. After seven years of international action the prototype weapon state was still proliferating. It is perhaps necessary to look again at all of that action to see just how "appropriate" it has been. The actions taken to control proliferation have certainly been effective, not because they have achieved the goals states have identified for them—or another war with Iraq would not have been necessary in 1998—but because they produce very real *effects*. To see whether the actions are appropriate, it is necessary to ask questions about the effects of these actions. In this book I investigate the effects of the actions reviewed in this chapter to judge, ultimately, how appropriate they have been.

I begin from the premise that social practices effect the creation of a world of a particular kind rather than reflect a world that is there for them to find. In the chapters that follow I demonstrate the world that is created by the practices of proliferation control, the kinds of objects that populate that world, the identities of the actors who inhabit it, and the interests those actors pursue. I show it to be a contingent and created world, effected in practices that—ultimately and ironically—prove ineffective within the world they create. In Chapter 2 I defend this initial premise and set out the terms in which the substantive examination of the practices of proliferation control will proceed. Central to this examination is the argument that the social world is produced through intersubjective interpretations that *frame* parts of social life in terms of a particular *image*. It is through the construction of this image that an area of social life, and therefore of social action, is created and is populated with objects and with actors. "Proliferation" is one such image that frames problems of weapons, military technology, and security in a particular fashion.

In Chapter 3 I set out the resources at the disposal of states by the time of the Gulf War to allow them to imagine problems of the relationship between arms and security. It was out of these resources that the image underlying the practices of proliferation control was constructed. In Chapters 4, 5, and 7, I conduct a detailed examination of this image, and the practices to which it has given rise and in which it is instantiated. In particular, I examine this image to see what world it has produced; what objects are created by thinking and acting in terms of "proliferation"? This question leads me to conclude in Chapter 4 that the object of the "proliferation" image is an autonomous technology that *will* spread if left unchecked, with potentially devastating consequences. In turn, this framing enables certain practices that aim to check this autonomous technological diffusion. The foundations of these practices are the supplier control groups, similar to the London Club: small collections of states that coordinate their own export controls over technologies now identified as "proliferation" concerns.

What actors are produced to act within these practices and on these objects? That is the question I tackle in Chapter 5. I argue that the world of proliferation control is populated with three classes of states—suppliers and recipients as well as rogues—known by their relationship to the circulation of technologies concerned with the production of military equipment. Security problems emerge when the circulation of these technologies produces undesirable effects that range from the production of weapons of mass destruction by certain states through the amassing of "excessive and destabilizing" conventional arsenals in particular locations to the creation of another rogue state. To prevent these things from happening, suppliers take it upon themselves to police the circulation of technology to prevent undesirable consequences—consequences they have also taken upon themselves to define. Recipients are expected to accept these policing measures in the name of global security and at the risk of being identified as the final actor produced by these practices: the rogue state. Rogues are those states Krauthammer attempted to label weapon states, a label I have resuscitated to enable certain connections hidden by the rogue label and by way of resistance to the dominant "proliferation" discourse.

Actors not only act within practices and on objects, their actions are informed by the interests they pursue. Interests, of course, are central to the traditional stories told about world politics by students of international relations. The argument I am pursuing here, however, suggests that those interests are not fixed but are formed in practice together with the objects and identities. In Chapter 7 I look at the way in which the "proliferation" discourse constitutes the interests of those who act within it and the way in which those interests intersect with those constituted in other areas of international life. I show that the practices of proliferation control presume a series of universal interests that overshadow a number of particular interests, which the practices also produce. I also show that proliferation practices intersect with key interests produced in other areas of international life, in ways often profoundly contradictory.

There are alternatives to the world of "proliferation" control. The creation of a "proliferation" image has drawn selectively on a rich set of discursive resources to form the world the practices it enables are in the process of effecting. Those same resources are available to opponents of the "proliferation" image to contest its practices. The nonaligned movement in general, and India in particular, have sporadically attempted to engage in such a contest, notably in terms of an image of "disarmament." In Chapter 6 I explore this contest, looking not only at what opponents of a proliferation agenda have done but at how the terms in which they have tried to conduct the contest could be extended for a more successful contestation of "proliferation." In this chapter I begin to sketch one possible alternative representation of the relationship among weaponry, technology, and security—beginning with the preferred language of disarmament employed by those outside the privileged suppliers of the "proliferation" image and suggesting the resources available to articulate a successful alternative image. Such an image, drawing on features of the preproliferation discourses of military technology I discuss in Chapter 3, as well as contemporary discourses of technology and economy, would effect a rather different world from that of "proliferation."

Before I can talk of a world different from that created by the practices of proliferation control and of why it might be sought, however, I must explore the nature of the world those practices are effecting. To begin, I set out the terms in which that exploration will be conducted.

2

Imagining Security

The prevailing view of the weapons proliferation problem sees Iraq as the harbinger of a wider security problem in the twenty-first century, a problem produced by the proliferation of weapons and related technologies. That view looks on the actions I outlined in Chapter 1 as the sensible response of an international community to a threat it has recognized only just in time, if not a little late. It is a view neatly presaged by Charles Krauthammer in the same article in which he introduced the weapon state:

> The post–Cold War era is thus perhaps better called the era of weapons of mass destruction. The proliferation of weapons of mass destruction and their means of delivery will constitute the greatest single threat to world security for the rest of our lives. That is what makes a new international order not an imperial dream or a Wilsonian fantasy but a matter of the sheerest prudence. It is slowly dawning on the West that there is a need to establish some new regime to police these weapons and those who brandish them.[1]

I want to draw attention to several aspects of this quotation, because they reveal the assumptions on which it, and the proliferation agenda more broadly, are based.

The first key aspect of this short text is Krauthammer's claim that weapons proliferation will constitute the greatest single threat to world security for the rest of our lives. I do not want to contest or qualify the claim but instead to ask what it means—and perhaps as important, what is necessary for the claim to be meaningful. It would seem initially that the meaning of the sentence in question is self-evident: the process of weapons proliferation, of the spread of weapons of mass destruction to more countries in more parts of the world, threatens the world's security. Indeed, the meaning seems so apparent that explanation of its meaning are more difficult to read than the sentence itself. But is the meaning indeed so simple or, more to the point, so unproblematic? First, Krauthammer's claim assumes a single, identifiable phenomenon that is "the proliferation of weapons of mass destruction and their means of delivery." The way in which the weapons proliferation agenda was advanced following the Gulf War seems to suggest that this has not always been the case. As I will show in more detail in Chapter 3, for much of the Cold War period, issues related to weapons of mass destruction and their means of delivery were not commonly assumed to be part of a problem known as proliferation.

Krauthammer's claim also rests on the assumption that there is an un-problematic whole known as *world security* that can be threatened. He assumes, that is, that at some level the security of the world (whatever that may mean) is indivisible. But what of the last sentence of the quotation? Krauthammer argues that "it is slowly dawning on the West that there is a need to establish some new regime to police these weapons and those who brandish them." Within the space of a few lines, the "world security" with which Krauthammer appeared to be concerned has become a problem con-fronting "the West." Who are "those who brandish" these weapons after proliferation? They are not individuals or even groups of organized crimi-nals, as his use of "police" might seem to suggest. Rather, it is "what might be called the 'Weapon State'"[2] that is holding and brandishing these weapons. Weapon states are members of the international community— Krauthammer cited Iraq, North Korea, and Libya but suggested that it is possible for Argentina, Pakistan, Iran, and South Africa to achieve this sta-tus. World security is perhaps less universal than first imagined.

It is also worth considering the implications of Krauthammer's sug-gestion that the problem of proliferation, and the attendant growth of weapon states, is "slowly dawning" on the West. For this assertion to be meaningful, there must be a problem in the world somewhere (or in many places at once) that, for whatever reason, is hidden from the view of "the West." There must, in other words, be a rigid separation between the ob-ject in question—in this case, the proliferation of weapons of mass de-struction—and the viewing subject—in this case, the West. What is more, there must also be a clear, unproblematic subject. The West is taken as a subject that can view, on which something can "dawn." Phrased in this way, perhaps the meaning of Krauthammer's short quotation is less obvi-ous. Although we conventionally speak of something called "the West," it is not readily apparent that it is sufficiently singular for problems to "dawn" on it.

What ties much of this together, what makes the passage coherent, is suggested by Krauthammer's use of *prudence,* the watchword of the tradi-tional study and practice of international security, a study founded on po-litical realism. In his classic statement of the principles of political realism,

Hans Morgenthau writes, "Realism, then, considers prudence . . . to be the supreme virtue in politics."[3] Realism has been increasingly criticized in recent years in ways that resonate with the questions I have posed regarding Krauthammer's quotation. Realism, particularly the security study that forms a central element of its view of international relations, has been accused of serving Western—particularly U.S.—policy in the name of the international. What allows this political effect to pass unnoticed has been realism's claim to objectivity—to the separation of subject and object. Again, as Morgenthau puts it so succinctly, "Political realism believes that politics, like society in general, is governed by objective laws that have their root in human nature."[4] If international politics is governed by objective laws, then security is a neutral state of affairs rather than politically biased. This objectivity also requires that both the objects of study and the subjects who study or who view those objects are also objectively knowable. Realism takes the objects of social life and the subjects of social action to be constituted prior to their entry into that action.

Charles Krauthammer's short summation of the problem of weapons proliferation is much richer in its meaning than it might first appear. His quotation is founded on a series of assumptions, which seem at least problematic once exposed to view. Michel Foucault has written that "practicing criticism is the art of making facile gestures difficult."[5] By making difficult what seems at first blush so simple, not just in Krauthammer's formulations but in the general understanding of the agenda of proliferation control, I am joining a growing body of scholars who aim to practice criticism on questions of security. This scholarship begins by suspending what is commonly taken as given: the objects of international security (and security policy), the identities of the subjects of international actions, and even the interests these actors pursue. Each of these—the objects, identities, and interests—is assumed to be self-evident in Krauthammer's quotation, as in security studies in general. In the rest of this chapter I will question their self-evidence and suggest a way of thinking about how the *formation* of the objects, identities, and interests of weapons proliferation can be investigated rather than assumed.

Proliferation and Security Studies

Ken Booth has characterized the traditional study of security as follows:

> The dominating security questions were: Is the Soviet threat growing? What is the strategic balance? And would the deployment of a particular weapon help stability? In that period of looking at world politics through

a missile-tube and gun-sight, weapons provided most of the questions, and they provided most of the answers—whatever the weapon, whatever the context, and whatever the cost.[6]

Security concerned the disposition of weapons and the use of those weapons to protect the state—in particular the United States and, somewhat more generally, its (European) allies but at root the state as an institution and an actor in international relations. With security considered in this way, through the missile tube, the development of a proliferation control agenda following the breakup of the Soviet Union is not overly surprising. The Soviet threat was no longer an issue, but weapons still exist. Krauthammer's suggestion that the weapon state might supplant the Soviet state as the source of threat is a direct response to this change within the context of security as traditionally conceived.

Nevertheless, the idea that security is provided through the acquisition of weaponry, that security is what is achieved when you look at world politics through a missile tube or a gun sight, has come in for sustained criticism in recent years. This criticism was originally motivated by a recognition that it was more than just the potential for interstate violence that rendered people insecure—even during the Cold War with its ever-present possibility of nuclear annihilation. The edifice of traditional security, or strategic, studies proves much less stable than it might have appeared at its Cold War height. Once questions were asked about the adequacy of an exclusive focus on weapons as a source of security, the very foundations of that building needed to be reformed.[7] As with any conceptual building, security study rested on a set of foundational assumptions, which were usually unstated and unremarked. Once you probe a little into the sources of threat, you run into these assumptions, and it becomes difficult to the point of impossible to leave them unexamined. When you look a little more closely, they turn out to be the same set of assumptions I revealed in discussing the short passage from Krauthammer.

Strategic studies has taken as given a number of important aspects of its field of study, of which the nature of the subject—the military nature of security—is first and foremost. Strategic studies also takes as given the referent object of that security and the subjects of security practice, which turn out to be one and the same. It is *states* that are to be secured through the deployment of particular weapons (or through their elimination, or some other alteration in the general disposition of the arsenal). It is also states that are to do the securing through the "threat or use of military force."[8] At the deepest and least examined level, strategic studies takes as given the interests pursued by states in seeking security. It is generally recognized, even by those who adhere to a traditional understanding of security, that problems other than military problems exist in international relations—they are just not to be considered problems of security.[9] Similarly, most would accept that there are actors other than the state and even that the reason for providing security for the state is ultimately to provide security for those who live in that state. Interests, however, are sacrosanct.

These crucial aspects of the study of security can be restated using the same formulation I adopted earlier. Traditional approaches to security take as given the objects, the identities of those who act, and the interests they have. The critique of security studies began with the first of these, suggesting that the object of study in security was, at the least, too narrow. Once that was opened to question, however, identities of the actors could no longer be assumed. If, for example, as Ken Booth has argued, security *is* emancipation, then thinking of identities defined solely in terms of the state is nonsensical.[10] Similarly, although perhaps less obvious, the nature of interests is also changed as the object at issue and the identities of the actors involved change—a point to which I return in some detail later. The critique of traditional security studies has therefore opened to question the objects of security study—and, by extension, the practices through which security is sought—as well as the identities of those who act to secure and, finally, the interests these actors pursue. In doing so, critical security studies connects with currents of critique that have been developing in the discipline of international relations and, more broadly, within social theory generally.

Critique and Interpretation

To say that strategic studies and the political realism from which it grows take aspects of their study as given means they are assumed to exist in an unproblematic fashion and that they are accessible to study and manipulation: there *are* states, they *have* interests, these interests *are* threatened. The goal of security studies is to identify threats and to develop means by which states can safeguard their interests in the face of those threats. This is true of the academic study of security and of the study that takes place within the apparatuses of states with a view to formulating security policy. Indeed, in many instances and particularly in the mainstream of security studies in the United States, these two activities are inextricably related.[11] The trouble is that as solid as they may appear, states and interests, threats and problems are not unproblematically presented to the scholar's or even the policymaker's gaze. At the beginning of *Writing Security,* David Campbell made this point in reference to the Gulf conflict, which plays so central a role in the present story:

> On August 2, 1990, Iraq became a danger to the United States. For many, this was obvious—nothing could be more real and less disputable than an

invasion of one country by another. . . . Yet, without denying the brutal-
ity of such an action, the unproblematic status with which this episode is
endowed deserves analysis. After all, an event of this kind (particularly
one so distant from America) does not in and of itself constitute a danger,
risk or threat. . . . Indeed, there have been any number of examples in
which similar "facts" were met with a very different American reaction:
only a decade earlier, the Iraqi invasion of Iran (an oil-producing state
like Kuwait) brought no apocalyptic denunciations or calls to action—let
alone a military response—from the United States.

   Danger is not an objective condition. It is not a thing which exists
independently of those to whom it may become a threat.[12]

Campbell's point is that danger, threat, this central concept in the study of
security does not slowly dawn on those who are threatened but rather is
created through their interpretive acts.

   A further point is to be made concerning Campbell's work. The focus
of *Writing Security* is not, in fact, on the way in which danger is interpreted—the manner by which the interpretation of risk and the consequent
creation of threat occur. Rather, Campbell's argument shows the way in
which the interpreting subject—in this instance the United States—is *itself
created by those acts of identifying danger.* If we can accept that both the
threats and the subjects of international security are created in acts of interpretation, it should be clear that the interests those subjects pursue are
also consequences of these same acts. It would be difficult to argue that interests remain fixed when the bearer of those interests does not. Jutta
Weldes has made the case with respect to interests:

> In contrast to the realist conception of "national interests" as objects that
> have merely to be observed or discovered, then, my argument is that na-
> tional interests are social constructions created as meaningful objects out
> of the intersubjective and culturally established meanings with which the
> world, particularly the international system and the place of the state in
> it, is understood. More specifically, national interests emerge out of the
> *representations . . . through which state officials and others make sense
> of the world around them.*[13]

   These "representations through which state officials and others make
sense of the world around them" are central to my argument in this book.
Rather than take the objects of study as given, I ask questions about the
construction of a particular object, a particular set of identities and interests, and the specific practices through which proliferation is confronted.
The key to answering these questions is to identify the way in which the
problem is represented or, to use the language I deploy later, the image
that is used to frame the issue in question. This image serves to construct
the object of analysis or policy, to identify the actors, and to define their

interests. It is therefore the image that enables the practices through which these actors respond to the problem of proliferation.

Practice and Interpretation

Terry Nardin has provided a useful starting point for thinking about international practice. Nardin argues that there is ambiguity in the use of *practice,* which in some instances refers to people's conduct and in others to standards that inform that conduct or by which that conduct is judged. For Nardin these standards—what he calls the "ideal conception" of conduct— rather than the conduct itself, should be seen as practice, and he provides a series of examples: the virtuoso performance, the just war, the responsible parent, the perfect ambassador.[14] Although it is useful to note this duality within the term *practice,* Nardin is mistaken in suggesting it is possible to separate the conduct itself from the ideal conception of that conduct. He reinforces this separation by adding adjectives to his examples of practices: the virtuoso performance is knowable only in the context of the standards by which all performance is judged. Each example he gives is just as meaningful when the adjective is removed. If you refuse to accept the separation Nardin's formulation implies, you can see practices as both the embodiment of a set of standards for conduct and, crucially, the *source* of standards for future conduct. When people engage in practice, they govern their conduct according to standards they derive from previous instances of the same practice.[15]

Acts of interpretation are indispensable to the reproduction of practices, understood in this fashion. First, before a person can engage in a practice, he or she must determine that previous examples of conduct are part of a single pattern—that is, that they are instances of a single practice rather than multiple practices or random activity. Even having recognized that these prior instances of behavior form a practice, she must formulate a guide to her own activity from these prior instances. Of course, such interpretive acts are often unconscious and are rarely, if ever, entirely individual. We are not often in the position of trying to engage in an unfamiliar practice without assistance. Rather, we share these crucial interpretive acts with others in our society. We recognize collectively that certain patterns of behavior are parts of the same practice, and we teach others, in more or less formal ways, the standards of conduct that govern these behaviors.

In a short book published in 1956, Kenneth Boulding outlined a similar conception of social life around the concept of *the image:* "The image not only makes society, society continually remakes the image. This hen and egg process is perhaps the most important key to the understanding of the dynamics of society. The basic bond of any society, culture, subculture, or organization is a 'public image,' that is, an image the essential characteristics of which are shared by the individuals participating in the group."[16] Practices are stable patterns of behavior produced by acting in terms of the image; on the other hand, the image is seen in those same patterns of behavior, and thus it is reproduced. What Boulding calls *the image* is necessarily social; it is a public image shared by members of a society. Thus the acts of interpretation that produce practices are not subjective, as they appear in the previous paragraph, but *intersubjective*.[17]

Charles Taylor has provided a clear example of the nature of constitutive intersubjective meanings in practices: "Take the practice of deciding things by majority vote. It carries with it certain standards, of valid and invalid voting, and valid and invalid results, without which it would not be the practice that it is."[18] All those who participate in the practice must share an image of the practice in which they are engaged. They must share a certain collection of rules for fair and unfair voting, as well as knowing what essential behaviors they are expected to perform. They must also understand that they are independent agents but also parts of a collective who can decide as a whole through the aggregation of independent decisions. As Taylor concludes, "In this way, we say that the practices which make up a society require certain self-descriptions on the part of the participants."[19] The image of majority voting constitutes the practice of voting by enabling the actors and actions necessary for the practice and defining the relationships between the actors and those between the actors and the practice.

The same is true for the practices in which states engage, which are the object of study in international relations. A practice such as waging war, perhaps the definitive practice of the traditional study of international relations, is conducted in terms of certain standards, as is voting.[20] Intersubjectively held meanings establish the conditions under which war may or may not be waged, as well as establishing which violent conduct is and which is not to be counted as war. The image constitutive of war is socially held, adjudged, contested, and taught. Thus, when the United States went to war in Vietnam, it was recognized by the society of states to be waging war, despite its subjective labeling of the violence as a police action. On the other hand, the U.S. War on Drugs was recognized by those same states to be metaphorically warlike rather than an instance of the practice of waging war, despite the use of military and paramilitary violence.

If intersubjective meanings constitute practices, engaging in practices involves acting toward the world in the terms provided by a particular set of intersubjective meanings. Practices can therefore be said to carry with them sets of meanings. If we investigate state action in terms of practices, we can ask questions about the constitutive intersubjective meanings, about the world these practices make through reproducing meaning. As Roxanne Doty has argued, "Policy makers . . . function within a discursive space that imposes meanings on their world and thus *creates* reality."[21] At this point I reconnect to the argument with which this chapter began, because the reality that is created in this discursive space involves the identification of the objects of action, the actors, and the interests that are pursued. The intersubjective understandings that constitute practices can be thought of, adapting Boulding's usage, as images that frame a particular reality. This framing is fundamentally discursive; it is necessarily tied to the language through which the frame is expressed.

A problem—for example, that of the proliferation of weapons—is not presented to policymakers fully formed. Weapons proliferation as a problem does not slowly dawn on states but rather is constituted by those states in their practices. What is more, this practically constituted image of a security problem shapes the interests states have at stake in that problem and the forms of solutions that can be considered to resolve it. To understand how an image shapes interest and policy, it is useful to consider the place of metaphor in shaping understanding.

Language, Metaphor, and Understanding

It is not entirely common to think that metaphor has much to do with the making of policy in general and of security policy in particular. Security policy concerns the serious matter of war; its subject is troops, not tropes. Nevertheless, it would seem even policymakers bent on waging war recognize the occasional utility of an apt metaphor. Hidden in a footnote is a report by Chris Hables Gray on a small change in the language surrounding the war in the Gulf: "Originally, the attack on Iraq and occupied Kuwait was to be called Desert Sword, but it was decided to portray the war as more of a natural force."[22] Gray's contention rings true, as Desert Sword fits more obviously with the prior operation, Desert Shield, than does Desert Storm. Somebody in the Pentagon, however, recognized that swords are wielded by hands whose owners can then be held responsible; storms are acts of nature or of God, not of people. Although the clear intention of this use of metaphor is political in the narrowest sense—we might even say it is meant as public relations—the *means* by which metaphors function is independent of such intention. Swords and storms carry different meanings; that is, they have different entailments and as such shape a labeled object, such as a military action, in different ways.[23]

Paul Chilton recently used metaphor as an analytic starting point to examine the heart of Cold War security discourse. In the conclusion to *Security Metaphors,* Chilton explains how metaphor relates to policy:

> Metaphor is an element in the discourse of policymaking; it does not
> drive policy. . . . It would be absurd to reduce the Cold War to the influ-
> ence of metaphor. However, both cognitive analysts of policymaking and
> historians of the Cold War have noted the part played by analogical rea-
> soning and by metaphor. Whatever distinctions might be drawn between
> the two terms "analogy" and "metaphor," they can both be treated as
> manifestations of the cognitive process whereby one thing is seen in
> terms of another.[24]

The common understanding of metaphor is that it is a literary tech-
nique, allowing an author to provide descriptive depth and allegorical
commentary by establishing a relationship between two separate objects or
ideas. Chilton argues that metaphors are much more than this, that
metaphor is "an indispensable ingredient of thought itself."[25] Policymakers address problems by means of what I have called images—that is, the
student or policymaker constructs an image of a problem, of an issue, or
even of other actors. This image relates the thing imagined to another, in
terms of which the first is understood. This act of relation is crucial both
to understanding and to the scholarly act of interpretation that follows.
Metaphors compose the images used to structure and support our understanding of a problem and therefore our response to that problem. The
choice of Desert Storm over Desert Sword is designed to foster political
support for a policy problem by imagining the operation in terms of a
force of nature it would be nonsensical to oppose. We might decry the devastation caused by weather, but we would look a bit foolish marching on
Washington to bring an end to hurricanes. The general relationships—
among the image of a policy problem, the condition of the problem itself,
and the policy solution to that problem—however, allow these ideas to be
given a much wider scope than they would receive as a form of public
relations.

In *Security Metaphors* Chilton provides a detailed and rigorous examination of the role of metaphor in Cold War security. Specifically, he explores the way in which three metaphors were central to the understandings that gave rise first to the Cold War and later to its end. He looks first
at how the metaphor of security and then the related metaphor of containment emerged from attempts within the U.S. state to make sense of the
postwar era. In the final part of his book, Chilton turns to the end of the
Cold War and to the place of architectural metaphors, particularly the common house, in producing the Cold War's end. The metaphors of security,
containment, and the common house did more than simply support a policy choice; they structured the way in which we can think about problems
and thus shape that choice in the first place.

I am not a professional linguist, and I do not intend to provide the
kind of detailed analysis of metaphor in political discourse Chilton gives

of the opening and closing phases of the Cold War. I am concerned, however, with the way in which discursive images frame security problems, constituting them as problems of a particular kind and thereby making possible certain policy options while precluding others. This productive function of frames is most readily seen through the role of metaphor in producing understandings and actions. To show how this happens, I will consider an example provided by George Lakoff and Mark Johnson in a work that has been central to the use of metaphor as an analytic tool in the social sciences, which forms an important basis for Chilton's later work.[26]

The image and the metaphors contained within that image frame a problem in a particular way, so as to highlight certain possibilities while precluding others. Lakoff and Johnson argue:

> Every description will highlight, downplay, and hide—for example:
> I've invited a sexy blonde to our dinner party.
> I've invited a renowned cellist to our dinner party.
> I've invited a Marxist to our dinner party.
> I've invited a lesbian to our dinner party.
> Though the same person may fit all of these descriptions, each description highlights different aspects of the person. Describing someone who you know has all of these properties as "a sexy blonde" is to downplay the fact that she is a renowned cellist and a Marxist and to hide her lesbianism.[27]

It is not difficult to imagine a similar set of descriptors of direct relevance to international relations:

> I have invited a Nobel Prize winner to the discussion.
> I have invited a prime minister to the discussion.
> I have invited a noted freedom fighter to the discussion.
> I have invited a former terrorist to the discussion.

These four descriptors could all be applied to a single individual, and indeed they have been applied to at least one individual. Just as each of the epithets Lakoff and Johnson apply to their hypothetical dinner guest highlights and downplays or hides various parts of the person in question, so do those of my discussant. The description, given to another member of the group, forms a key part of the image of her fellow discussant. Indeed, having no other image on the basis of which to frame behavior toward this person, she will base her actions on the image created by that description. The first epithet downplays the high political office of the individual in question and hides her former terrorist activity. Similarly, the epithet *terrorist* downplays or hides the person's prime ministerial role, as well as her status as a Nobel laureate. Not only will the image of the other discussant be altered in relation to each descriptor, but so will that person's conversational strategies and interests. Indeed, it is not difficult to imagine that someone who would happily sit at a table with a person described as a Nobel Prize winner might refuse the invitation to sit with a former terrorist.

There is a fairly serious concern with Lakoff and Johnson's formulation of the role of metaphor in our understanding. They speak of "grounding" our conceptual system in terms of simple elements of our everyday lives that we can experience directly, without social mediation. Thus, for example, spatial metaphors of "up" and "down," "in" and "out" are based on our experiences of the world—we have an inside and an outside, we stand erect, we sleep lying down and rise when we awaken.[28] Lakoff and Johnson have been criticized for betraying a biological bias, and although they clearly want to ground metaphors in part on our unmediated physiological experience of the world, they also allow for social rather than biological grounding: "In other words, these 'natural' kinds of experience are products of human nature. Some may be universal, while others will vary from culture to culture."[29] Nevertheless, the very idea of grounding tends to assume a hierarchy of knowledge and the possibility of preconstituted experience that is not socially mediated. We do not need to accept this possibility of presocial knowledge, however, to make use of their insights into metaphor.

Earlier I quoted Paul Chilton to the effect that "'analogy' and 'metaphor' . . . can both be treated as manifestations of the cognitive process whereby *one thing is seen in terms of another.*"[30] This formulation of the relationship between metaphor and cognition precisely echoes a passage from David Campbell's *Politics Without Principle,* in which he argues that "as understanding involves rendering the unfamiliar in terms of the familiar, there is always an ineluctable debt to interpretation such that there is nothing outside discourse."[31] Both Chilton and Campbell argue that we confront new phenomena by establishing relationships to old phenomena that we understand, or at least understand in a particular way. Campbell's further point is that these relations are relations between discourses—that is, the familiar is not preconstituted but rather enters into knowledge through its discursive construction. There is therefore no possibility of grounding our understanding in the manner Lakoff and Johnson suggest, because no hierarchy of truth exists to provide a ground for metaphorical reference. Nevertheless, the role of metaphor cannot be discounted but rather must be slightly refigured. Instead of being seen as the linguistic link between levels of experience (or between the literal and the figurative),[32] metaphor becomes a bridge between realms of discourse. Metaphor is a central tool for the act of rendering to which Campbell refers: the unfamiliar is related to the familiar, in part, through the creation of metaphorical links.

Consider again the earlier example I derived from Lakoff and Johnson: the individual described as a Nobel Prize winner, a prime minister, a freedom fighter, or a terrorist. We might expect that this example means there *is* a person who *is* each of these things, that her characteristics are prediscursive. Even if we reject the possibility of the prediscursive, however, in other words, if we accept that nothing exists outside discourse, we can retain all that is important in this argument. Each epithet relates to a particular discourse or set of discourses and can be seen as an indicator of a discursively constituted identity. This is most obvious in the relation between terrorist and freedom fighter. These labels are identity markers constituted in particular discourses rather than in any particular features of the individual in question or her activities. In other words, we can think of the distinctions among highlighting, downplaying, and hiding in terms of the evocation of particular discursive representations.

To use the epithet *terrorist* is to evoke one discourse with a certain set of entailments that go along with it, whereas using the epithet *freedom fighter* evokes a different discourse and a different set of entailments. Generally, the use of freedom fighter downplays the role of the individual in perpetrating acts of violence, a role highlighted by the entailments of terrorist. This is not always the case, however. The use of freedom fighter by the Reagan administration in the 1980s meant that in certain circles the term has come to be a pejorative and not only entails the role of the individual so named in perpetrating acts of violence but marks those acts as violence in the cause of a reactionary politics. This difference in the entailments of the same label in different circumstances is important, because it demonstrates that not only does metaphor link discourses but that the production of those links depends on the discursive context in which the metaphor is evoked. Metaphors are not grounded in a real or literal experience; further, even the discursive connections they create are never entirely stable.

Clearly, such a conception of understanding, and of the discursive construction of knowledge, carries its own problems. The most commonly raised concern is with the conclusion Campbell stated earlier as "there is nothing outside discourse." Certainly, to a community of security scholars and practitioners, the idea that there is only language is anathema. As Stephen Walt warned in a noted article, "Issues of war and peace are too important for the field to be diverted into a prolix and self-indulgent discourse that is divorced from the real world."[33] The implication is obvious: there is a real world out there with which security scholars must be concerned because it gives rise to war if we are not careful. However, Campbell does not say there is nothing *but* discourse but rather that there is nothing *outside* discourse. Although the difference between the two phrases might seem insignificant, it is far from it.

If we want to assert a real world entirely divorced from discourse, our own bodies are a likely place to start. Those who argue for unmediated access to the real world, argue, in fact, for access through our bodies—

whether that is sight, touch, or smell. To continue with the example I have been using, although it might be accepted that Nobel laureate, prime minister, freedom fighter, and terrorist refer to socially constituted roles or identities, surely there is still a person's body on which these labels are hung and that exists without and prior to the labels. Judith Butler has examined the way in which the body is constituted in discourse. She argues that the body is no more outside discourse than anything else, but that does not deny the materiality of the body: "to claim that discourse is formative [of the body] is not to claim that it originates, causes, or exhaustively composes" the body.[34] Butler is not arguing that there are no bodies or that our material bodies come into being only when they are named in discourse; her argument is that any reference to that material body in discourse constructs it in a particular way. To refer to a particular body as "terrorist" or "prime ministerial" is to situate it in a particular discourse. Importantly, to refer to that same body as "man," "woman," or, indeed, even as "body" is to situate it in a particular discourse and to construct it as that object. Butler makes this case in its strongest possible terms by arguing that any attempt to identify the extradiscursive in order to ground discourse is to construct a boundary between the discursive and the extradiscursive. This boundary, however, is a product of our act of identification; that is, the so-called extradiscursive is also created through discourse.[35]

This point causes considerable confusion, and so the argument is worth stating at some length. The point is that any reference, even reference to the label *body,* is an act of classification, of saying that the object is this kind of thing and not that kind of thing—but the "kinds" in question are always ultimately conventional. Consider, for instance, the limits that define a particular body as a *woman's* body. The most obvious convention is that defining the lower age limit: at what point does a body cease being a *girl's* body and become a *woman's* body? It is impossible to answer this question without reference to a set of malleable norms. In some societies a woman's body is determined by the capacity to reproduce. In contemporary British society that body emerges in stages, depending on the context in which the question is posed. For the purposes of consensual sexual relations, the body emerges at 16; however, in terms of its capacity to exercise political franchise, the body becomes a woman's body when it is 18 years old. For a male body the situation has been even more strange; until 1999 in terms of its sexual capacity the body became a *man's* body instead of a *boy's* body at different ages depending on the sex of its partner—the body was a *man's* body for purposes of sexual relations with women at age 16 but only at age 18 for sex with another man. We can ask similar questions about the limits between women's and men's bodies: What sort of body is that of the transsexual or the hermaphrodite? It is even possible to see the discursive limitations of the body itself, without considering it as a sexed body of any kind. Are prostheses parts of the body? In the case of eyeglasses, I expect most of us would say no. In the case of artificial limbs, I expect we would be less likely (and less inclined) to say no automatically. In the case of artificial organs, we would be hard-pressed to say no. None of these answers is certain, however, and none can be answered with reference to some extradiscursive "truth."

There is therefore no need to deny the materiality of bodies, or of any other object, to assert that there is nothing outside of discourse. Rather, we must recognize that to know an object or to act on it or in relation to it, that object must enter into discourse. Arguing from a rather different position from that of Campbell or Butler, George Lakoff comes to remarkably similar conclusions in his more recent work:

> Categorization is not a matter to be taken lightly. There is nothing more basic than categorization to our thought, perception, action and speech. Every time we see something as a *kind* of thing, for example, a tree, we are categorizing. Whenever we reason about *kinds* of things—chairs, nations, illnesses, emotions, any kind of thing at all—we are employing categories. Whenever we intentionally perform any *kind* of action, say something as mundane as writing with a pencil, hammering with a hammer, or ironing clothes, we are using categories. . . . Without the ability to categorize, we could not function at all, either in the physical world or in our social and intellectual lives.[36]

It is through this act of categorization, or naming, that an object is constituted as an object for the purposes of engagement. How we act toward an object depends on what *kind* of object it is. How we act in such a relationship also depends on what *kind* of "we" we are. That is, our identity is crucial to understanding that engagement. The way in which other discussants will engage with the prime ministerial terrorist will vary just as much by how each identifies herself as by which epithet is used to characterize the other. It is important to recognize, however, that identity is also the result of categorization, of grouping those "like" as self and those "different" as other. If we want to understand a particular form of engagement—for example, international engagement with weapons proliferation—we need to look at the way the objects and identities of those engaged have been constructed: What kind of thing is weapons proliferation, and what is it not? Who is involved in the proliferation agenda, and of what kind are they? How are the various elements of the proliferation agenda referred to, and therefore into what discursive contexts are they set? These are questions I address in the remaining chapters of this book.

Conclusion

This chapter's primary claim is that threats or policy problems do not dawn on states, as Charles Krauthammer would have us believe the problem of proliferation dawned on the West. I argue, by contrast, that these problems are produced through acts of interpretation and, what is more, that the states or other actors that threaten or are threatened are also produced in these same interpretive acts. To make use of these claims to examine the contemporary concern with weapons proliferation, I argue that social life is *framed* in terms of a particular *image*. That image identifies the objects of social action and the identities of the relevant actors as objects and subjects of a particular kind. Only in terms of this image can policymakers or analysts know an international policy problem, and therefore only in terms of this image can action be taken. Therefore, the actions being taken by states and others in response to the problem of weapons proliferation are founded on an image that has constructed that problem in the first place. This means, in turn, that practices can be seen to instantiate the images that enable them and thereby become a central object of study in an analysis such as this, which seeks to reveal the images constitutive of international life. The images that frame policy problems and thereby produce those problems, the actors and practices of security, draw on discursive resources to tie the things imagined within the frame to other discursive frames—linking that which is framed to other things we understand in particular ways. Images therefore tie discourses together; by creating certain links and not others and by creating these links in particular ways, metaphors highlight, downplay, and hide other images that are operative in any given area of social life.

The concepts I have developed in this chapter form the analytic basis for the rest of the book. I will show the emergence of a relatively coherent discourse centered around the image of "weapons proliferation." The coherence is revealed across a series of formerly distinct issue areas—the spread of nuclear technology, chemical and biological arms, antipersonnel land mines, major conventional weapons systems, and nuclear weapons testing, for example. In detailing this image I reveal the resources from which it is built and thus the discourses it highlights, downplays, and hides. An important means of revealing what is hidden by the emergent proliferation discourse is to tease out the alternatives that were immanently possible but that were not tried. Counterfactual arguments are always difficult to make, but I hope to show where the possibilities lay for such alternatives, how they were possible, and how they were made impossible by the proliferation discourse.[37]

By detailing what was highlighted in the proliferation discourse, as well as what was hidden and downplayed, my overarching goal is to show the effects of the proliferation image. Throughout, it is important to recognize the political nature of the image-making process. As Paul Chilton noted: "Concepts do not exist as determinate essences, but are produced and contested. The formulation and reformulation of metaphors is a crucial part of the production and contestation of mental models. This process can occur because image schemas have an inherent 'logic' which provides potential metaphorical entailments that speakers may or may not specify."[38] The entailments of images can therefore provide resources for the political contestation of international practices. I intend to show not only the entailments of the "proliferation" image, which are productive of the practices of proliferation control, but also to draw attention to these discursive resources and to the possibilities for contestation.

3

Before Proliferation

The object of study in this text is the "proliferation" image, which has come to define a considerable portion of contemporary international security study and practice. Images, however, do not appear de novo, and in the case of weapons proliferation the various technologies that are of concern have been the object of international practice for much of the twentieth century. What *is* novel about the "proliferation" image is the way it ties these various technologies together into a single international problem. It is an image, however, that is built out of the raw material provided in the first instance by the images that have constituted the practices through which these varied technologies, conceived as different problems into the 1980s, have been framed. In particular, one of these earlier images, that of nuclear proliferation, has dominated the reframing of these varied technologies by a single image.

In this chapter I take a look at the technologies of concern to "proliferation": weapons of mass destruction—that is nuclear, chemical, and biological weapons—and excessive and destabilizing accumulations of conventional weapons. My interest is to reveal the images that framed each of these technologies before they were assembled into a single, "proliferation" image. To do this, I examine a series of sites in which these technologies were constituted, show what sort of object or objects each of these images produced, and sketch the forms of practice the frame enabled. This task requires a partial and selective reading of the history of weapons and their regulation in the twentieth century.

Multiple Images of the Ultimate Weapon

The first attempts to gain some control over the nuclear genie, which had been so dramatically released from its bottle in 1945, foundered on the

29

failure of the United States, the Soviet Union, and the United Kingdom to agree on the 1947 Baruch Plan. The plan called for the international control of nuclear energy, centered on the creation of a UN agency that would have control over all aspects of the field. The United Nations would also hold in trust the only legal arsenal of atomic weapons in the world. The Acheson-Lilienthal report, which is the basis of the Baruch Plan, pointed out the benefit of this arrangement over contemporary proposals for the elimination of atomic weaponry:

> When the news of the atomic bomb first came to the world there was an immediate reaction that a weapon of such devastating force must somehow be eliminated from warfare; or to use the common expression, that it must be "outlawed." That efforts to give specific content to a system of security have generally proceeded from this initial assumption is natural enough. But the reasoning runs immediately into this fact: The development of atomic energy for peaceful purposes and the development of atomic energy for bombs are in much of their course interchangeable and interdependent. From this it follows that although nations may agree not to use in bombs the atomic energy developed within their borders the only assurance that a conversion to destructive purposes would not be made would be the pledged word and the good faith of the nation itself. This fact puts an enormous pressure upon national good faith. Indeed it creates suspicion on the part of other nations that their neighbors' pledged word will not be kept. This danger is accentuated by the unusual characteristics of atomic bombs, namely their devastating effect as a surprise weapon, that is, a weapon secretly developed and used without warning. Fear of such surprise violation of pledged word will surely break down any confidence in the pledged word of rival countries developing atomic energy if the treaty obligations and good faith of the nations are the only assurances upon which to rely.[1]

Thus for Dean Acheson and David Lilienthal, although the expressed goal was to eliminate nuclear weapons, the best that could reasonably be achieved was a form of regulation. As it turned out, even this form of control was more than could reasonably be achieved in the early days of the Cold War. The report, however, articulated and linked the elements of two images that would frame the nuclear weapons problem and around which practices would develop: a "disarmament" image and an "arms control" image.

With the failure of the Baruch Plan, nuclear weapons became integrated into the arsenals of the leading states of the international system. Although there was a recognition that these weapons should perhaps be subjected to some form of international control or even elimination, for the time being they were elements of functioning national militaries at a time of pronounced international tension. Nuclear weapons therefore developed within an additional, strategic, frame, as well as within a pair of management frames—specifically, they were framed within strategic practice in terms of deterrence. Each of these three images—"disarmament," "deterrence," and "arms control"—gave rise to a different set of practices that were institutionalized in different locations but never entirely divorced from each other. This connection results in part from their common origin in the interpretation of the new atomic devices in the Acheson-Lilienthal report, along with a precursor document, an Agreed Declaration of the three participating states in the Manhattan Project released three months after Hiroshima.

In this section I examine the three principal images that constituted nuclear weapons in the Cold War, using the Acheson-Lilienthal report and the Agreed Declaration as starting points. The present "proliferation" image shows a debt to all three of these predecessors. Such a mixture can have potentially interesting results, for, as we shall see, these three images are by no means necessarily compatible.

Deterrence

The military developed atomic weapons in the context of a war and with the expressed intention of using them as part of a campaign of strategic bombardment. Although the remarkable destructive power demonstrated over Japan led to calls for their elimination or for tight international control, atomic weapons were never removed from the preserve of the militaries in states that developed them. They were therefore thought of, in the first instance, as weapons.[2] Although this may appear little more than a statement of fact, it is a categorization or a representation, and one with considerable power. By labeling nuclear explosives as "weapons," those with the initial access to them categorized them as devices of a particular kind.[3] They understood the devices in terms of discourses that constituted the range of technologies with which people had killed each other *in certain circumstances*. This latter point is important, because not all technologies of killing were discursively constructed as weapons: exceptions include poisons administered through food, for example, or the hangman's noose.

Jonathan Schell appeared to recognize the contingency of these devices' labeling at the beginning of *The Fate of the Earth:* "These bombs were built as 'weapons' for 'war,' but their significance greatly transcends war and all its causes and outcomes. They grew out of history yet threaten to end history. They were made by men, yet they threaten to annihilate man. They are a pit into which the whole world can fall—a nemesis of all human intentions, actions and hopes."[4] The images Schell suggests, a pit and a nemesis, would entail a very different set of containing practices from those entailed by the image of weapons for war. Both images suggest dangers that must simply be avoided, not managed so they can somehow be lived with and certainly not put to the kind of use that carries the high value placed on providers of security or peace. There were possibilities for framings of nuclear weapons less extreme than Schell's but that would still have denied any notion of their being weapons for use in a practice as instrumental as war. Atomic explosives have been conceived, for example, as doomsday devices—human creations that allow us to exercise the power of God in ending creation—an image that would still have entailed potential use but not a military-strategic use. Having been imagined as weapons, however, atomic explosives were further constituted as particular weapons to fulfill particular functions through their articulation in strategy.

The development of a strategy, or, more properly, a series of strategies, within which to place nuclear arsenals was a drawn-out, hotly contested process that saw the development of strategy from an arcane military practice to a widespread (if still arcane) civilian, academic practice. A core of strategic concepts emerged from the early civilian strategists, centered mostly at the RAND Corporation. These strategists—notably Bernard Brodie, Herman Kahn, and Thomas Schelling—thought about the unthinkable in ways that profoundly influenced the making of U.S. strategic policy.[5] There is no need to rehearse the strategy debates that largely constituted strategic studies throughout the Cold War; rather, I will sketch the way in which nuclear weapons were constituted by the heart of strategic discourse that emerged from these debates: the theory of deterrence.

The central feature of mature nuclear deterrence theory is the notion of mutual assured destruction (MAD), which makes a virtue out of features of atomic explosives first articulated in the Agreed Declaration: "The Agreed Declaration cites three reasons for seeking international control. This Declaration recognizes that the development of atomic energy, and the application of it in weapons of war, have placed at the disposal of mankind 'means of destruction hitherto unknown.' . . . The second point recognized in the Agreed Declaration is that there can be no adequate military defense against atomic weapons."[6] Given almost unlimited destructive potential and the inability to provide a defense against this destruction, nuclear weapons made possible *mutual* deterrence.[7] The argument is that if each side in a potential conflict holds sufficient weapons to destroy the other and there is no "adequate military defense," both sides will be deterred from launching a nuclear war. Mutually assured destruction from nuclear weapons would result in mutual deterrence and the avoidance of nuclear war.

Strategy debates were thus concerned with the correct means to ensure deterrence—what mix of weapons, in what sorts of configuration, and governed by which operational plans. For all of the output of the strategy industry, the answers provided to these questions can essentially be reduced to two: ensure a capability to use nuclear weapons to retaliate against an attacker even after a nuclear attack (deterrence by punishment), or use nuclear weapons in battle to prevent an enemy from achieving its objectives (deterrence by denial). Indeed, Michael Williams has argued convincingly that these are the only two possible answers to questions of strategy, posed within the confines of deterrence.[8] What was common to all of the positions within the various nuclear strategy debates was that nuclear strategy, whatever its form, was to be a deterrent strategy.

A considerable contradiction is implied in the dual framing of nuclear explosives as weapons and as instruments exclusively for deterrence. This contradiction is seen in a number of ways throughout the strategy debate, most notably in the odd position of nuclear weapons being accepted as weapons whose only use is in their nonuse. Williams cites a wonderful example of the result of the contradictions of deterrence. "This is a conclusion that even Hoag himself seems to find difficulty in believing, to say nothing of justifying: 'Such a policy,' he argues, 'suffers from the political defect, but analytic virtue, of explicit bizarreness.' Explicit bizarreness would seem to be a peculiar attribute to consider as an 'analytic virtue.'"[9] The contradiction between weapons and deterrence with regard to nuclear weapons has also led Robert Jervis to make one of the most trenchant critiques of nuclear strategy: that it suffers from what he calls "conventionalization." For Jervis, thinking of nuclear weapons in conventional terms—as weapons—leads to dangerous strategies because it ignores the lessons of the nuclear revolution, which produced the possibility of strategies of mutual deterrence in the first place.[10] These contradictions, the conventionalization critique in particular, point directly to the constructed nature of the weapon framing of nuclear weapons. The central characteristic of nuclear explosives—that they are extremely powerful explosives— seems to deny their coherent consideration as weapons at all, yet this is how they are primarily conceived.

The crucial features of the strategic context within which nuclear explosives were constituted are that it produced nuclear weapons, as opposed to some nonweapon object, and that it produced these weapons as instruments of deterrence rather than, for example, simply developing larger bombs to destroy military targets.[11] The radically unfamiliar—explosives based on previously unimagined physical principles and with inconceivable power—was rendered in terms of the familiar by means of the weapon metaphor. These devices were placed into a military strategic context and were enmeshed in the practices for making and avoiding war. Given the circumstances of their birth, it is unlikely that nuclear explosives could have escaped all military framing, but the particular framing of "deterrence" shaped the practices of employment and control. Paradoxically, indeed perversely given the possible effects of their use, nuclear weapons qua weapons were seen to be a source of security. Nuclear weapons were also imagined in other ways, however, than simply as strategic weapons.

Nuclear Arms Control

Through the late period of the Cold War, that time identified by détente and the descent into a second Cold War, the focus of attempts to rein in the arms race was the practice of arms control between the two superpowers. This practice had developed out of the failed attempts at international control and in the context of the articulation of the "deterrence" image. Only when the mechanisms of deterrence and an understanding of the routes to possible war that underlay deterrence were accepted was "arms control" as it emerged possible.

Emmanuel Adler has traced the development of a theory of nuclear arms control and its acceptance by policymakers first in the United States and then in the Soviet Union.[12] Adler shows how the central concepts of arms control were developed in the last few years of the 1950s, principally by a relatively small group of civilian strategists and scientists. By 1960 the bulk of this conceptual work had been accomplished, and its results were published in a special edition of *Daedalus,* the journal of the American Academy of Arts and Sciences.[13] For my purposes, Adler's account has two crucial elements. First, he makes clear that arms control thinking was dependent on the prior formulation of strategies of deterrence.[14] Second, arms control was seen as clearly distinct from disarmament; Adler quotes Thomas Schelling, a leading figure in the development of both deterrence and arms control: "Whatever the prospects for successful negotiations with the Soviet Union during the coming months and years, on the subject of strategic weapons, there could not be a greater contrast between the serious and businesslike prospects for realistic negotiations in 1969 and all the fantasy and pretense about 'general and complete disarmament' that characterized the beginning of our decade."[15]

The negotiations to which Schelling referred were instances of the practice that developed from the successful articulation of arms control, as Adler puts it, as "a politically *viable* alternative both to disarmament and to military superiority."[16] The principal achievements of this practice—at least until the denouement of the Cold War—were the hot line agreement, the antiballistic missile (ABM) treaty, the interim agreement (strategic arms limitation treaty [SALT I]), and SALT II.[17] Because these agreements are the products of a practice—a practice constituted by a set of intersubjective meanings including an image of the problem the practice was aiming to solve—I can read the texts of these agreements for those constitutive understandings and, in particular, for the way in which nuclear weapons were imagined within the practice of "arms control." Thus instead of recounting the history of arms control, I will provide such a reading both to reveal the "arms control" image and to give an example of the method of argument I adopt in much of the rest of the book.

The first of these major achievements of the "arms control" practice was the hot line agreement of 1963. This memorandum of understanding between the two governments created the famed red phones which have been so widely represented in popular culture. The actual hot line was rather more prosaic, as the memorandum put in place a dedicated Telex line between the two capitals.[18] An official narrative on the memorandum, published by the U.S. Arms Control and Disarmament Agency (ACDA), explains the purpose of the hot line: "The need for ensuring quick and reliable communication directly between the heads of government of nuclear-weapons states first emerged in the context of efforts to reduce the danger that accident, miscalculation, or surprise attack might trigger a nuclear war."[19] The goal of the hot line agreement was to create the conditions in which the two countries could live with nuclear weapons. Each would hold nuclear arsenals, but both would endeavor to manage the relationship between themselves and those arsenals in such a way that nuclear war would be avoided.

The ABM treaty and the two SALT agreements continued to develop the context in which nuclear weapons could be held but not used. For example, in the preamble to the ABM treaty the states wrote: "Considering that effective measures to limit anti-ballistic missile systems would be a substantial factor in curbing the race in strategic offensive arms and would lead to a decrease in the risk of outbreak of war involving nuclear weapons."[20] Similarly, the SALT II treaty preamble, following from the limitations introduced in SALT I to which it refers, states: "Convinced that the additional measures limiting strategic offensive arms provided for in this Treaty will contribute to the improvement of relations between the Parties, help to reduce the risk of outbreak of nuclear war and strengthen international peace and security."[21]

Taken together, the goals of the two SALT agreements and the ABM were to cap the development of each side's nuclear holdings at a point where a rough symmetry existed between the two arsenals and to restrict greatly the ability of either side to defend against a nuclear attack by the other. Thus the ABM treaty limited the states to two antiballistic missile sites and outlawed the development of wide-area defenses against ballistic missiles. SALT I was an interim agreement that froze the development of both sides' arsenals pending the conclusion of a final, balanced limitation agreement. This second agreement, SALT II, provided for numerical limits on each state's arsenal, with sufficient flexibility to allow each to organize its numbers differently for its own purposes. The principles on which the agreement was based were set out simply in the preamble: "Guided by the principle of *equality* and equal security; Recognizing that the strengthening of *strategic stability* meets the interests of the Parties and the interests of international security."[22] The agreements were designed to provide stability in the strategic relationship by creating conditions of equality—and, with the ABM treaty, vulnerability.

The problem arms control confronted was that of a military relationship between potential enemies that could lead to war. Arms control represented nuclear weapons as weapons, although of a different character from others, as ACDA recognized: "These risks, arising out of conditions which are novel in history and peculiar to the nuclear-armed missile age, can of course threaten all countries, directly or indirectly."[23] Although the threat is general, the possibilities for control rest with the two superpowers. In most points, the image of the problem embedded in the practice of arms control echoes the 1946 Acheson-Lilienthal report.[24] The major difference between the later practice and the earlier report, of course, is the resort to a bilateral rather than a multilateral system of control.

The practice of arms control is comprehensible only in terms of the particular weapon constructed by the "deterrence" image. For example, "deterrence" suggests that a rational nuclear power, in a condition of MAD, would not start an all-out nuclear war, but it does not rule out that such a war could happen by mistake.[25] Hence, the first concrete outcome of the arms control practice was a communication system designed to insure against accidental nuclear war. More important, the strategic context of deterrence was essential to agreements based on equality, strategic stability, and vulnerability. So important, in fact, is this particular context that U.S. arms control negotiators saw it as their task to educate their Soviet counterparts in deterrence.

The importance of this discursive context is most easily seen with reference to the ABM treaty. It is counterintuitive to argue that a system for defending against an enemy attack is dangerous, yet the ABM treaty clearly states that an agreement between the United States and the USSR held that "effective measures to limit anti-ballistic missile systems . . . would lead to a decrease in the risk of outbreak of war involving nuclear weapons."[26] When framed in terms of deterrence resting on mutual assured destruction, however, it makes perfect sense. Effective defenses against nuclear attack eliminate the destruction on the threat of which deterrence rests. Even if the defense is not necessarily effective, it removes the *assurance* of destruction, which is central to deterrence arguments. Once nuclear weapons are framed in terms of mutual deterrence resting on assured destruction, *defense* against nuclear attack becomes *dangerous*.

The mutuality of deterrence gives rise to the symmetry, or principle of equality, on which the SALT process was predicated. The danger built into the "deterrence" image arose from asymmetry, or strategic superiority, which is why deterrence (and then arms control) worked for equality. This is best illustrated with U.S. hawks' nightmare scenario: If the Soviet Union had superiority, it could launch an all-out attack and destroy the U.S. strategic arsenal. The Soviet Union would then have a nuclear monopoly. Realizing it was capable of doing this, the Soviet Union would no longer be deterred. Although there are any number of problems with such thinking, the argument is neatly derived from the premises of deterrence theory and so puts a premium on equality. This principle, derived from the strategic discourse in which nuclear weapons were located and constituted, found expression in the equal ceilings of SALT II.

Finally, underlying all of the practice of arms control is the notion of strategic stability, another derivative of deterrence theory. Again, mutual assured destruction ensures that one of the states will avoid launching a nuclear war if it is confronted with a simple choice: nuclear war or no nuclear war. Wars do not always begin so neatly, however, and some form of protection from the "back door" into war is needed. The hot line agreement addressed one such back-door route by attempting to prevent a misunderstanding from resulting in a war neither side wanted. It was also considered possible, however, that a crisis would escalate into a nuclear war—particularly because nuclear deterrence was supposed to deter all sorts of things other than nuclear war. To prevent a tumble into war, which could then escalate into a nuclear war, strategic discourse counseled maintaining strategic stability.[27] A condition is stable if changes to that condition are unlikely to cause it to topple into war. The notion of stability, and the consequent need to maintain balances, is a crucial element of the "arms control" framing, and has important implications for the "proliferation" image of the post–Cold War era. Although arms control depended very specifically on the understandings of stability in deterrence theory, those understandings have much deeper roots in international relations.[28]

Strategic Stability and Balance

The *balance of power* is generally used to refer to the system of interstate relations created in Europe following the defeat of Napoleon.[29] The mechanism of power balancing—stabilizing relations among states by maintaining power equivalences—was progressively naturalized by theorists of international relations. Hedley Bull argues that both an objective and a subjective balance are necessary for a balance of power to operate. Nevertheless, he clearly places primacy on the objective conditions of the balance: "But if the subjective element of belief in it is necessary for the existence of a balance of power, it is not sufficient. . . . A balance of power that rests not on the actual will and capacity of one state to withstand the assaults of another, but merely on bluff and appearances, is likely to be fragile and impermanent."[30] This naturalization of the balance of power reached its zenith with Kenneth Waltz's *Theory of International Politics:*

> The theory, then, is built up from the assumed motivations of states and the actions that correspond to them. It describes the constraints that arise from the system that those actions produce, and it indicates the expected outcome: namely, the formation of balances of power. Balance-of-power theory is microtheory precisely in the economist's sense. The system, like a market in economics, is made by the actions and interactions of its units, and the theory is based on assumptions about their behavior.[31]

Thus the balance of power is not only a desired outcome; power balancing is the natural outcome of the behavior of states. There is thus strong incentive to maintain balances and to avoid anything that could destabilize them.

Our common experience with balancing is that of two masses offsetting one another—rendered visually by the classic scale, or balance.[32] Two masses—or in the case of international relations, two states—offset each other in a stable fashion. The introduction of a third mass greatly complicates the problem of balancing.[33] Although the classic balance-of-power system in Europe is generally considered to have five states (Russia, Prussia, Austro-Hungary, France, and Britain), the actual mechanism of the balance was the creation and maintenance of stably balancing dyads. Britain's famed role as a balancer involved its changing sides to ensure that one grouping did not overbalance the other. Bull indicates the dyadic basis of the balance of power in a discussion of simple (dyadic) and complex (three or more) balances: "Whereas a simple balance of power necessarily requires equality or parity in power, a complex balance of power does not. In a situation of three or more competing powers the development of gross inequalities in power among them does not necessarily put the strongest in a position of preponderance, *because the others have the possibility of combining against it.*"[34]

Martin Wight also argued that regardless of the form of a system of balance, the concept was infused with a dyadic understanding of balance: "But the distinction between multiple and simple balance is immaterial to the conception of the balance of power as an even distribution. In both the multiple and the simple balance there is the idea of equipoise."[35] Indeed, Waltz took this feature of metaphor and history and raised it to the status of law, arguing that the ideal—that is, the most stable—balance is that between two roughly equivalent states: "International politics is necessarily a small-number system. The advantages of having a few more great powers is at best slight. We have found instead that the advantages of subtracting a few and arriving at two are decisive."[36]

The theoretical moves that produced a balance-of-power theory privileging systems of two over other systems is not unconnected from a global system imagined as bipolar. The work of Bull, Wight, and Waltz both reflected and informed the production of an international balance-of-power system of two primary poles. The relationship between the United States and the Soviet Union was therefore imagined in terms of a balance of power, which needed to be stabilized to avoid the collapse of order and the attendant possibility of nuclear war.[37] This balance was considered not only the normal condition between the two superpowers and their blocs but also, according to leading theorists of international relations, the ideal international system. The need to maintain stability meant that changes—usually new weapon systems—were evaluated in terms of their potential to introduce instabilities, either arms race instabilities or crisis instabilities.

Arms race instabilities resulted from the acquisition of weapons seen to trigger a new round of arms building by the other side. The U.S. "Star Wars" proposal was arms race destabilizing, for it tended to prompt both an increase in the Soviet arsenal to overwhelm any U.S. defense and the development of countermeasures. Crisis instabilities were even more dangerous, as they were changes that increased the likelihood of nuclear war in the event of a crisis—that is, changes that could lead to the dangerous tumble into war and then to nuclear war. Multiple independently targetable re-entry vehicle (MIRV) technology, for example, was criticized for introducing crisis instabilities. On the ground, a missile with 10 MIRVed warheads—the US MX, for example—could be destroyed by a single incoming warhead. Once launched, however, that single missile could strike 10 targets—Soviet missile silos, for instance. In a crisis, the argument ran, a greater incentive would exist to launch a MIRVed missile than one with only one warhead because of this unfavorable ratio.

The practice of "arms control" relied heavily on this understanding of balance and the need to maintain stability. Arms control agreements aimed to create stable balances between the arsenals of the two poles and to establish mechanisms that would prevent crises from destabilizing the central balance of power. It is no exaggeration, I think, to maintain that without an understanding of balances privileging stability, the practice of arms control would have been impossible. Their centrality, both to the theory of deterrence and to the practice of arms control, made the notions of balance and stability important resources in the reimagination of security following the end of the Cold War. This use of balance and stability has two important implications. First, relying on these resources when framing other security problems tends to reproduce the dyadic structure of the Cold War and of balance-of-power theory in international relations. Second, notions of balance and stability were crucial in differentiating "arms control" as a practice from those practices warranted by the "disarmament" image.

Multilateral Images of Nuclear Weapons

Although the superpowers took it upon themselves to control nuclear arms, a wider international community continued to seek the elimination of this new weapon. The practices that grew around nuclear disarmament were institutionally separate, but never entirely detached from those of arms control. The focus for these efforts was an ongoing multilateral conference, most recently called the Conference on Disarmament (CD) and loosely affiliated with the United Nations.[38] Both the Soviet Union and the United States have been members of this conference since its formation, which has served to connect the discourse and practice of "disarmament" to those of "arms control"—indicated by the evocation of the goal of disarmament in the various products of the arms control practice.

Despite these gestures in the direction of disarmament, the superpowers generally, and the United States in particular, showed a marked preference for the practices of arms control throughout the Cold War. Part of this preference might be explained by the centrality of balance and stability to strategic thinking. Disarmament—understood as the elimination of weapons, particularly nuclear disarmament as the elimination of all nuclear weapons—was seen to be destabilizing. Although zero on both sides produced an equivalence, it was an equivalence considered arms race unstable. The argument was that the advantages of any nuclear monopoly— even one characterized by only a few weapons and one that could last only a short time—were potentially so great that any crisis would be likely to trigger nuclear arms building, either to create a monopoly or to avoid the opponent's creating one.

A "disarmament" image of the problem of nuclear weapons also carried some unfortunate entailments. Nuclear disarmament had been articulated early on to the program of general and complete disarmament.[39] This program was largely discredited within the hard-headed strategic studies and strategic policy community in the United States in particular. General and complete disarmament was seen as a soft, utopian idea that, at best, could not possibly work in the dangerous real world in which we live and that might not be desirable even if it were possible. What is perhaps worse, in a system that places high value on power and symbolizes power most potently through weaponry in general and nuclear weaponry in particular, disarmament carried entailments of vulnerability and weakness. Disarming is something winners do to losers, not something the strong do to themselves.

Nevertheless, the idea of disarmament, particularly nuclear disarmament, had both a popular political potency and an appeal to the many states that were not nuclear armed. (This latter appeal, unfortunately, tends only to reproduce the connection of disarmament to weakness.) Disarmament therefore found an institutional home in the multilateral Conference on Disarmament, and the "proliferation" image emerged in this multilateral practice. The first two points of the 1945 declaration, repeated as starting points for Acheson-Lilienthal, had been translated into the twin discourses of arms control and deterrence.

> The third point, and again we quote from the Agreed Declaration, is that these are weapons "in the employment of which no single nation can in fact have a monopoly." Of the three, this is perhaps the most controversial. Strong arguments have been brought forward that the mass of technical and scientific knowledge and experience needed for the successful development of atomic weapons is so great that the results attained in the United States cannot be parallelled by independent work in other nations.[40]

On this point the diplomats who framed the Agreed Declaration were more astute than their committee of experts. The Soviet Union paralleled the development of atomic weapons within four years and then took only three to follow the United States in developing hydrogen (fusion) weapons. By the 1960s the United Kingdom had built a nuclear arsenal from its participation in the Manhattan Project, France had an independent nuclear capacity, and the People's Republic of China had become the fifth member of an expanding nuclear club. This situation led members of the Eisenhower and Kennedy administrations in the United States to believe that by 1980 there would likely be over 20 nuclear weapon states.[41]

The principal reason for the apparent ease of becoming a nuclear power was the intimate relationship between nuclear energy and nuclear weapons. As Frank Barnaby put it, "A country with a nuclear-power programme will inevitably acquire the technical knowledge and expertise, and will accumulate the fissile material necessary to produce nuclear weapons."[42] In the 1960s nuclear energy was seen as a cheap, clean, and efficient way to generate the electricity needed for global industrial development. U.S. President Dwight Eisenhower's Atoms for Peace proposal in December 1953, for instance, called for the creation of an international agency to safeguard nuclear material while making it available for the peaceful uses of humankind.[43] This served as the foundation of the International Atomic Energy Agency (IAEA) and, ultimately, for the nonproliferation treaty (NPT).

Beginning from the assumption of a necessary link between nuclear energy and nuclear weapons, the NPT attempted to create a structure through which the former could be generally available while the latter were tightly restricted. The principal undertakings are spelled out in the first two substantive articles:

> *Article I.* Each nuclear-weapon State Party to the Treaty undertakes not to transfer to any recipient whatsoever nuclear weapons or other nuclear

explosive devices or control over such weapons or explosive devices directly, or indirectly; and not in any way to assist, encourage, or induce any non-nuclear weapon State to manufacture or otherwise acquire nuclear weapons or other nuclear explosive devices, or control over such weapons or explosive devices.

    Article II. Each non-nuclear-weapon State Party to the Treaty undertakes not to receive the transfer from any transferor whatsoever of nuclear weapons or other nuclear explosive devices or of control over such weapons or explosive devices directly, or indirectly; not to manufacture or otherwise acquire nuclear weapons or other nuclear explosive devices; and not to seek or receive any assistance in the manufacture of nuclear weapons or other nuclear explosive devices.[44]

There were, however, two trade-offs in the treaty, so the nonnuclear weapon states (NNWSs) were not simply renouncing a possible strategic advantage for no return. The first is found in Articles IV and V, which provide for the full dissemination of the benefits of the peaceful uses of nuclear energy.[45] Most important, Article IV (ii) articulates the importance of nuclear energy in providing for the needs of industrial development, as well as placing an obligation on states with nuclear programs to assist in that development.[46] NNWSs were to be provided with access to nuclear technology for nonweapons purposes in exchange for renouncing the weapons. Because of the close links between weapons technology and other forms of nuclear technology, NNWSs party also agreed to place all of their nuclear facilities under international safeguard (Article III).

    The second trade-off in the NPT is found in Article VI, which reads: "Each of the Parties to the Treaty undertakes to pursue negotiations in good faith on effective measures relating to cessation of the nuclear arms race at an early date and to nuclear disarmament, and on a Treaty on general and complete disarmament under strict and effective international control."[47] The NPT was to be a stepping-stone on the (admittedly long) road to nuclear disarmament, recalling in its language early attempts at international control. The reference to good-faith negotiations on stopping the arms race explicitly linked the NPT and the multilateral disarmament practice out of which it grew to the increasingly bilateral attempts by the superpowers to control arms.

    By constructing the problem in terms of the relationship between nuclear energy and nuclear weapons, the NPT enabled a series of control practices that focus on the movement of technology. IAEA safeguards, which are applied to all parts of NNWSs' nuclear programs and to the civilian aspects of NWSs' programs, track the movement of nuclear material to detect diversion to a weapons program. In addition, increasingly extensive export controls have been placed on nuclear technology and material, particularly since the 1974 Indian test explosion. Restrictions on the testing of nuclear weapons were also sought in the multilateral disarmament practice, particularly in an ongoing attempt to conclude a comprehensive test ban treaty (CTBT) that would outlaw nuclear testing. Each of these control practices—safeguards, export controls, and test bans—plays an important part in the central story of this book, and I defer detailed treatment until later chapters.

The image of nuclear weapons on which the NPT was built is rather different from that which constituted the practices of "deterrence" and "arms control," despite the fact that all three emerged from the first interpretation of atomic explosives in the 1945 Agreed Declaration. The NPT constructs nuclear weapons as an inevitable outgrowth of a broader technology, a technology prone to proliferation. The other two practices take the weapons as given, as artifacts with particular characteristics that need to be embedded in management practices. The problem posed by each construction is unique. The nuclear nonproliferation regime confronted as a problem the spread of nuclear weapons technology to more and more states. The problem produced in the "arms control" image was the growth in the numbers and sophistication of existing arsenals. Finally, the "deterrence" image produced nuclear weapons with the potential for extreme destruction. Given that these images constructed different objects and different problems in relation to those objects, the practices enabled by the images, although related, were also somewhat different. Taken together, these three images and their attendant practices provided a rich collection of resources for the construction of the security problem posed by weaponry in the 1990s. Nuclear weapons, however, are not the only technology now gathered into the "proliferation" image, and the others also provide varied resources for the political and practical imagination.

Poisons, Toxins, and Taboos

At the end of the nineteenth century, the states of Europe gathered in The Hague in an attempt to outlaw the use of what we now call chemical weapons (CW). Since then, chemical and, later, biological weapons have been the object of a number of forms of control—some constructed in a fashion rather different from their later nuclear counterparts. This is not to say that these weapons were not inserted into the practices of both "arms control" and "disarmament"; they were, and they were constituted in particular ways within those practices. A further, uncodified, normative restraint was placed on their use, however: in common phrasing a taboo was placed on the use of chemical weapons. The taboo frame and its formation provide an interesting contrast to the technological frame of "proliferation" or even the military frame of "deterrence," as well as additional resources for imagining military technology.

Formal constraints were placed on the use of CW in warfare, first by the Hague Convention of 1899 and, because the use of gas had been widespread in World War I, by the Geneva Protocol of 1925. This protocol, in the words of its title, enacted "the prohibition of the use in war of asphyxiating, poisonous and other gases, and of bacteriological methods of warfare."[48] The Conference on Disarmament then negotiated a prohibition on developing, producing, stockpiling, and transferring biological and toxin weapons, which entered into force in 1975.[49] The CD also attempted to negotiate a similar convention for chemical weapons, but the negotiations were fruitless until the early 1990s. It was only as part of a "proliferation" frame, following the end of the Cold War and the war in the Gulf, that the chemical weapons convention (CWC) was achieved. Operating together with these formal constraints was an apparently strong normative constraint, or taboo.

Richard Price explores the taboo on CW use in a noted article in *International Organization*.[50] Price begins with the general agreement among students of CW that a normative constraint exists:

> There is a virtual consensus in this literature that the nonuse of CW in World War II is attributable to three major factors: as summarized by one study, "the two sides warned each other not to use chemical weapons at the risk of strong retaliatory action in kind; a general feeling of abhorrence on the part of governments for the use of CB (chemical/biological) weapons, reinforced by the pressure of public opinion and the constraining influence of the Geneva Protocol; and actual unpreparedness within the military forces for the use of these weapons."[51]

The study to which Price refers is Frederic Brown's 1968 work, *Chemical Warfare: A Study in Restraints*. Brown examines the three factors to which Price points and argues that it is the last of the three that was crucial in explaining the nonuse of CW in World War II. Law and public opinion, he argues, proved unreliable and generally ineffective. Although there was evidence of deterrence, it was less important than the nonintegration of CW into the militaries of the period.[52] As Price persuasively argues, however, this nonintegration itself needs to be explained. Militaries had used CW in World War I, and other technologies—not the least, nuclear weapons—had received initial moral opprobrium, only to be quickly integrated into states' arsenals. From this Price argues "not that the CW prohibition was an all-powerful norm that by itself determined the outcomes of nonassimilation and nonuse. Rather . . . the existence of a stigma against using CW was a necessary condition for the nonuse of CW."[53]

The most important aspect of Price's treatment of the taboo is his explicit adoption of a genealogical method. He argues that the taboo emerged and survived because of the particular history of CW. For instance, the set of features that he argues combined to make the use of CW taboo—"the portrayal of CW as a weapon against which there is no defense, its symbolic connection with a notion of civilized conduct, the castigation of CW as a weapon of the weak akin to poison, the genealogical legacy of the institutionalized form of the taboo promoted and practiced by political leaders"[54]—applies almost as well to nuclear weapons, yet no similar taboo exists against nuclear use. Indeed, in a more recent work Price and Nina Tannenwald compare the CW taboo with the nonuse of nuclear weapons, concluding that "the nuclear non-use norm was initially *uninstitutionalized* (in fact, 'use' is what was institutionalized), while the anti-CW norm was *institutionalized* from its earliest origin."[55] This conclusion suggests that the fact that chemical weapons are taboo although nuclear weapons are not is a contingent outcome of a particular practice rather than the result of some inherent property of either technology.

The taboo frame constitutes rather a different object than the military and arms control frames within which nuclear weapons were generally constituted. In the former frame it is *use* of the weapons that is constructed as the problem, whereas in the latter it is various aspects of their *existence* and *deployment*. There are a number of ways to illustrate this difference. For instance, both the Hague Convention and the Geneva Protocols prohibit the use of CW, whereas all of the various treaties concerned with controlling nuclear weapons consider issues of possession. The three SALT agreements, including the ABM, restrict what nuclear weapons may be held. The NPT divides the world between those allowed to hold nuclear weapons and those not so allowed. Even the dramatic agreements of the late 1980s focus on possession: the intermediate-range nuclear forces (INF) treaty shapes the arsenals of nuclear powers by eliminating certain types of weapons, and the strategic arms reduction treaties (START) place SALT-style limits on these arsenals, but they are limits that involve the destruction of certain weapons rather than ceilings on the addition of new weapons. The framing of the problem posed by a particular weapon in terms of its use enables very different practices than does a frame producing possession as the problem. Both ways of framing military technology have a part to play in the later production of the "proliferation" image.

Having discussed nuclear arms control extensively earlier, I will illustrate the difference between possession and use framings with reference to a text that appeared in 1978 entitled *Chemical Weapons and Chemical Arms Control,* which included the proceedings of a 1977 conference to examine issues of CW control following U.S. ratification of the Geneva Protocol in 1975. Two of the three papers around which the text is organized deal explicitly with issues of use. The first looks to military planning for chemical warfare, and the second examines the chemical requirements of the North Atlantic Treaty Organization (NATO). Only the last paper mentions the problem of a growing number of arsenals, and even there it is placed in the context of means of "Preventing Chemical Warfare." The discussion that surrounds these papers is concerned entirely with prospects for a chemical arms control agreement between the United States and the Soviet Union.[56]

As I noted earlier, the agreement between the United States and the USSR on a chemical weapons convention was not reached for more than a decade after this conference. The agreement resulted from a shift in the framing of the CW problem from one of "use" to one of "proliferation." With such a shift, CW control changed "from the ban on use to a ban on possession."[57] What is more, the discursive alterations that gave rise to the new "proliferation" agenda were triggered in part by a perceived potential for the collapse of the taboo constraining CW. With reports of chemical use by Iraq in its war with Iran and consistently circulating stories of the use of CW by the United States in Vietnam and the Soviet Union in Afghanistan, concern was growing in the 1980s that the taboo was failing. For instance, one strategic think tank in the United States began a 1987 report on CW by noting that there was growing cause for concern that the CW taboo was breaking down and that, consequently, proliferation had become a new threat.[58]

The way CW was treated provides another possible frame for considering military technology. Here was a weapon that in terms of its destructive potential paled in comparison not only to nuclear weapons but to sophisticated conventional weapons as well but that earned the label *weapon of mass destruction*. Despite CW being the subject of international control longer than any other weapon category, the control did not focus on possession or production until the development of the new "proliferation" agenda. In its place was a weapon constructed as "beyond the pale," a technology it was simply not permissible to use in civilized society.[59] The difference between this and nuclear technology is instructive. CW technology is as intimately tied to civilian technology as is nuclear weapons technology, if not more so. As we shall see later, this feature of CW became extremely problematic in the context of the CWC. Although the CW problem was framed in terms of use rather than of possession, its relationship to the civilian chemical industry was not an issue. In other words, a frame that imagined CW as a weapon whose use was taboo downplayed or even hid the relationship between the weapons and the chemical industry out of which they grew.

Conventional Weapons and the Commercial Frame

One of the more remarkable features of the new "proliferation" image is the way in which it encompasses both conventional arms and weapons of mass destruction. As with chemical weapons, conventional weapons had been constituted within "arms control" and "disarmament" practices as well, obviously, as strategic military practices. There is, however, another important framing of conventional arms. I call this the "commercial" image of conventional weapons and argue that it is the most important frame within which conventional weapons have been constituted, one that has considerable significance in the story that follows.

Following the carnage of World War I, the production and sale of what we now call conventional weapons came in for outraged attack. The mood is perhaps captured most famously in the title of a noted work on the issue, *Merchants of Death*.[60] Concern over the merchants of death resulted in the Covenant of the League of Nations, seeking to outlaw the role of private capital in the production and sale of arms and stating in Article 8: "The Members of the League agree that the manufacture by private enterprise of munitions and implements of war is open to grave objections. The Council shall advise how the evil effects attendant upon such manufacture can be prevented."[61] In addition, "Members of the League . . . will entrust the League with the general supervision of the trade in arms and ammunition with the countries in which the control of this traffic is necessary in the common interest."[62]

The practical results of the covenant were two publications produced by the league. The first was the *Armament Year-Book,* published first in 1924 and continued until 1939, which drew on public sources to provide a compendium on arms policies. From 1925 until 1938 the league also produced the *Statistical Year-Book of the League of Nations*, which reported arms trade data supplied by member states. To implement the trust of Article 23(4), the members of the Paris Peace Conference also concluded the St. Germain Convention, which placed a general prohibition on the export of arms (although it allowed for exceptions through export licenses) and called for full publicity in the arms trade to be enforced by the league. The United States refused to ratify the convention, and it never entered into force. The league convened a conference in 1925 to try to develop alternatives. That conference produced another convention limited to publicity measures, which also failed to enter into force.[63]

I wish to make two points about these efforts. The first is that the focus on publicity, or what is now called *transparency,* is indicative of how similar the image of conventional weapons is now to the way it was then. Consider this statement by the president to the first session of the 1925 conference: "The direct purpose of our Conference is therefore not the reduction of armaments, a problem reserved for a future which we hope is not far distant, nor even a reduction in the trade in arms. This Conference recognizes that there is a legitimate trade in arms."[64] The sentiments expressed are echoed almost exactly in the UN resolution that established the Register of Conventional Arms in 1991:

The General Assembly . . .
Considering that increased openness and transparency in the field of armaments could . . . contribute to restraint in military production and the transfer of arms.
Realizing the urgent need . . . to accelerate efforts towards general and complete disarmament under strict and effective international control.

• • •

3. *Reaffirms* the inherent right to individual or collective self-defence . . . which implies that States also have the right to acquire arms with which to defend themselves.[65]

In both periods disarmament and even severe restriction of the transfer of weapons were seen as desirable but future goals, and production and transfer of arms were recognized as legitimate; thus the immediate goal was to increase information about production and transfer as a way to foster restraint.

The second point is the content of the image itself, in addition to its stability. Conventional arms have been framed by a commercial image as an industry parallel in most ways to any other commercial venture. The league covenant talks about the manufacturing of arms, private enterprise, and the trade in arms even when seeking international regulation. Arms manufacturers are *merchants* of death—or, conversely, the merchants of death are arms *manufacturers*. The reciprocal statements are extremely important in this case, because they indicate how deeply rooted this image is in our discourse on weapons. It is almost impossible to talk about the creation and acquisition of conventional arms without lapsing into the language of industry. We talk about the arms industry, about arms production and trade, and about the arms market. The global (conventional) weapons state is framed very powerfully in commercial terms.

In a contemporary critique of the arms industry in the vein of *Merchants of Death,* Anthony Sampson repeatedly attacks the image of this business as just like any other:

Coming up from this carefree underworld [of a helicopter sales convention], the bright images lingered in my mind over the next days, between discussions about arms sales in the Pentagon and the State Department. The arms industry, I realised, had a verve and drive which made their own logic beyond any arguments about strategy and diplomacy, and it refused to accept that it was different in kind from other industries: it was only more adventurous and inventive. This was, after all, just another salesmen's convention.[66]

• • •

It is the small arms which have been the instruments of most of the hundred wars since the Second World War, from Lebanon to Biafra, from the Yemen to Katanga; and which have been the cause of most loss of life. And it is the trade in rifles, machine-guns or mortars which reveals the cold heart of a business in which diplomacy and wars are translated into orders, balance-sheets and profits. It is here that the day-to-day juxtaposition of death and commerce seems most casual, and the sale of guns looks as banal as any other business.[67]

Sampson makes clear that those involved in the production and transfer of conventional arms see themselves as involved in a business just like any other—an interpretation with which he clearly disagrees. What is perhaps more interesting, however, is that even as he disagrees, Sampson is unable to escape from the commercial frame. The image of the helicopter sales convention haunts him as he discusses arms *sales* with U.S. government officials. The *trade* in small arms seems particularly brutal to the author. We literally have had no frame *other* than the commercial with which to imagine conventional arms; even as we contest the claim that arms production and sales is a business like any other, we do so in a language that implicitly recognizes it as a business.

It is important to recognize that there is nothing necessary about this particular framing, nothing essentially commercial or even industrial about conventional arms. It is true that modern conventional arms are produced by industrial processes and that close connections exist between so-called civilian and so-called military industries—Boeing is not only the world's largest manufacturer of civilian aircraft but is one of the largest military producers in the world as well. The same is true, however, of any of the other military technologies reviewed in this chapter. It is extremely difficult to distinguish between a civilian chemical factory and a chemical weapons plant, and it is essentially impossible to distinguish a biological weapons laboratory from an advanced biotechnology laboratory. Even in the case of nuclear weapons, the close connection between civilian and military uses of the nuclear fuel cycle means the line between them must be actively policed. Nevertheless, only the production and transfer of conventional arms are imagined in terms of an industry, giving rise to trade.

The commercial frame has produced a particular way of analyzing conventional arms and a particular set of practices of state intervention (even if we include the 1991 UN Register, it would be foolhardy to call these practices of control). The analysis takes the commercial nature of the creation and movement of arms as its starting point. A small sample of the literature on various aspects of conventional arms production and transfer yields these references in the titles alone: *Arms Production, Arms Sales, Arms Trade, Arms Supermarket, Arms Bazaar, Commerce International des Armes, Lethal Commerce, Deadly Business, Gun Merchants,* and *The Globalization of Defense Production.*[68] This commercial discourse is reproduced in popular press reports on arms; for instance, a full-page analysis in Britain's *Guardian* in 1997 was titled "The Arms Trade: The Profits of

Doom."[69] The metaphors that structure the discourse of conventional weapons tie that discourse to those through which modern business is imagined—even when an author wishes to make a somewhat subversive point, the chosen metaphor is still commercial, if not necessarily modern; hence arms bazaar and gun merchants.

The analysis the commercial discourse produces is tied to those produced by analyses of other aspects of global capitalism. In its most popular moments, this sort of analysis produces texts of investigative reportage that reveal the insides of corporate (and state) boardrooms.[70] In newspapers it produces texts that read like those found in the Business section—and, indeed, they often are. In the *Guardian* article to which I just referred, the authors write, "Britain, according to figures released this week, now accounts for almost a quarter of the global arms market—22.1 per cent, to be precise . . . and worth over £5 billion a year."[71] At its most sophisticated, this work applies various approaches from economics and political economy to issues of arms creation and distribution. Consider this excerpt from Keith Krause, *Arms and the State: Patterns of Military Production and Trade:*

> Since state power is often equated with military power, and since possession of the most powerful weapons available has long been a driving influence behind foreign policy, demand from states that do not possess weapons based on the new technologies will produce a rapid expansion of the arms trade. On the supply side, the relatively great profits to be realised in the early stages of the product cycle result in increased and rapid incremental innovation. This, plus the chance to lower unit costs (by realising economies of scale and spreading R&D [research and development] costs), will drive producers to export arms, especially if local demand cannot absorb all increases in output. As a consequence of these demand-pull and supply-push factors the arms transfer pipeline is filled with technology I transfers of weaponry and associated skills.[72]

The passage is revealing because it begins by locating arms at the heart of the system of international power—as the basis of state power and the "driving influence behind foreign policy." Nevertheless, the analysis of the spread of weapons is made in terms of industry dynamics—of supply-push and demand-pull factors, economies of scale, profits, and the product cycle; of R&D, unit costs, and local demand absorbing output.

The "commercial" image, with its collection of metaphors imagining conventional arms creation in terms of any other industrial process, underlies the forms of state intervention that have been tried as well. Essentially, the most common form of state involvement in the arms trade has been that of promoter. As a commercial activity it tends to be highly profitable, and so even governments, which make some claims to seek restrictions on this form of trade, run headlong into these economic benefits. The new Labour government in the United Kingdom, for instance, faced the trade-offs involved in its first months in office. In September 1997 Foreign Secretary Robin Cook announced that he was canceling £1 million in sales to Indonesia in protest of its human rights record; the next month he approved 11 new contracts with that state.[73] In keeping with so many other government statements from arms-exporting countries, Cook explained his approach to the arms industry soon after taking office: "The Government is committed to the maintenance of a strong defence industry, *which is a strategic part of our industrial base* as well as of our defence effort."[74]

One notable attempt to impose some form of restriction on this industry was that of the Carter administration in the United States. Jimmy Carter attempted to impose unilateral restraints on U.S. overseas sales of arms and launched a set of multilateral talks aimed at producing internationally agreed constraints. Both sides of this effort produced little in the way of results.[75] At least one point, however, is worth making about Carter's efforts. One of the guidelines he introduced was the prohibition on the state's aiding commercial salespeople in their efforts. A 1982 report on U.S. arms sales explains what happened to this guideline when Ronald Reagan replaced Carter:

> The Carter administration attempted to reduce commercial arms sales by discouraging American officials abroad from assisting US arms salesmen. In a directive popularly named "the leprosy letter," US government officials were barred from helping US arms manufacturers abroad without express authorization from Washington. The Reagan administration has taken the opposite view: in April 1981 the Carter directive was rescinded, and US officials overseas were instructed to extend *the same courtesies to American firms selling arms as to other business representatives.*[76]

For the Reagan administration, as for Blair's government in Britain 15 years later, the arms trade is primarily trade.

Conclusion

The various technologies now included in the weapons proliferation agenda—nuclear, chemical, and biological weapons and excessive and destabilizing accumulations of conventional arms—have been imagined in very different ways throughout the twentieth century. Nuclear weapons have been framed in terms of at least four images: "deterrence," "disarmament," "arms control," and, of course, "proliferation." Chemical and biological weapons, although at times framed within the practices produced by these four images, have also been framed in terms of a "taboo." Finally, conventional weapons (a framing in itself and one that requires weapons of mass destruction for its meaning) have additionally been framed by a "commercial" image, as industrial products traded in markets. These varied images, which constituted their particular weapons as such and were embedded in a set of practices that contained those weapons, provided a rich set of interpretive resources on which policymakers and others could draw in constructing a new security agenda following the Cold War. I argue that one of these images—the "proliferation" image—came to dominate that construction, but the new "proliferation" image draws on these resources in interesting ways to create a particular security problem in the contemporary world.

4

The Proliferation Image

On 29 April 1997, 180 days after Hungary deposited its instruments of ratification, the chemical weapons convention entered into force. This marked the culmination of almost 30 years of negotiation and followed by more than 20 years the convention controlling biological weapons, with which chemical arms are so often paired.[1] The result is one of the most comprehensive and complex treaties devised for the international control of armaments, and it contains the most extensive, intrusive, and expensive set of verification procedures ever attempted. Indeed, the scope of what had been agreed almost prevented the United States from ratifying the convention, as the U.S. Senate almost balked at the prospect of enabling such extensive verification practices.

The principal obligation to which the states party agree is that they will not "develop, produce, otherwise acquire, stockpile or retain chemical weapons, or transfer, directly or indirectly, chemical weapons to anyone."[2] In addition, the convention obliges its parties to destroy existing stockpiles on their own or other states' territories and to destroy any CW production facilities. In an extensive set of schedules appended to the convention, the CWC sets out the various chemical agents and CW precursors to be controlled to ensure complete elimination of these weapons. These schedules divide chemicals into three groups: those banned from any commercial use, and those that may be used but must be reported, with the latter divided by the threshold at which reporting must take place.[3] Schedule 2 and 3 chemicals are widely used in industry, so to monitor CWC compliance the extensive verification regime established by the convention was considered necessary.

To administer that regime, the convention established a Technical Secretariat as part of the Organization for the Prohibition of Chemical Weapons (OPCW), the executive body of the convention. The Technical Secretariat may carry out two forms of inspection. The first is to monitor the declarations of the states party; although potentially extensive, this function is not particularly intrusive. The inspectorate, however, is also required to carry out challenge inspections. Under the terms of Article IX of the CWC:

> Each State Party has the right to request an on-site challenge inspection of *any facility or location in the territory or in any other place under the jurisdiction or control of any other State Party* for the sole purpose of clarifying and resolving any questions concerning possible non-compliance with the provisions of this Convention, and *to have this inspection conducted anywhere without delay* by an inspection team designated by the Director-General and in accordance with the Verification Annex.[4]

Put simply, the CWC allows any state to accuse another of violations and to have that accusation tested by an international inspection *anywhere* and *without delay.* It is without doubt the most intrusive measure of international inspection ever agreed, far outstripping the powers of the IAEA under the terms of the NPT.

Questions of verification, particularly the power to conduct on-site inspections, played a central role in the history of arms control throughout the Cold War. The Soviet Union repeatedly refused to agree to on-site inspections of any kind, let alone inspections that could be carried out anywhere without delay on the demand of any other state. The United States repeatedly refused to accept any agreement that did not allow for on-site inspections if it considered them necessary for the verification of that agreement's provisions. (This was an easy stance for the United States to adopt, given Soviet refusals to countenance on-site inspection. The difficulty the CWC had in gaining U.S. Senate approval suggests that U.S. negotiators took advantage of their opponent's position.) Indeed, the requirement for extensive verification if a global ban on chemical weapons were not also to be a global ban on the chemical industry is generally cited as the reason for the long stalemate in negotiating a CWC.

The Eighteen Nation Disarmament Conference (ENDC, a precursor to the CD) began discussions of a global ban on chemical and biological weapons (BW) in 1968. At this point, biological weapons were not included in any state's arsenal, and there seemed no immediate prospect of their being developed as useful weapons. The discussions were thus able quickly to conclude a convention outlawing the production and use of BW, which included no particular provisions for verification.[5] Chemical weapons, on the other hand, had been used and were considered militarily important. In particular, both the United States and the Soviet Union held extensive chemical arsenals. The importance of this difference was that negotiations for a CWC, despite being formally housed in the Conference on Disarmament, were in practice bilateral negotiations between the United

States and the Soviet Union. Thus from 1977 to 1980, the focus of the CWC negotiations was a bilateral working group of the two superpowers. By 1980 superpower relations had deteriorated into what is generally termed the Second Cold War; consequently, the bilateral working group and the possibilities for a CWC ended. As the Stockholm International Peace Research Institute (SIPRI) reported in 1982, "The prospects for a successful outcome of these negotiations have fluctuated over the years, the present situation of resurgent Cold War giving little cause for optimism."[6]

By 1986 there seemed more cause for optimism but still no immediate prospect of a CWC. Again, SIPRI's annual report is useful: "A host of problems still remains to be dealt with before a chemical weapons convention could be finalized. . . . The crucial obstacles are of a political nature. Among the latter central issue is inspection on challenge."[7] Throughout the intervening period, in fact, the question of verification had retarded negotiations, pitting East against West and particularly the Soviet Union against the United States.[8] The conclusion to the CWC was also determined by agreements between the superpowers: a 1989 agreement that provided for joint challenge inspection exercises to test the provisions of a CWC verification regime and a June 1990 agreement to stop producing CW and to reduce stockpiles to 5,000 tons each by the year 2002. It was in this context that the CWC negotiations were finally concluded, whose provisions supersede the reductions envisaged in the 1990 agreement.

What made this change possible? More than 20 years of negotiations from 1968 to 1990 yielded little progress on a CWC, then the next three years produced a final text of breathtaking scope. Clearly, part of the reason is the end of the Cold War and the capacity that produced for agreement between the Soviet Union/Russia and the United States. The importance of the 1989 and 1990 agreements clearly indicates that the end of the Cold War contributed positively to the conclusion of the CWC, although there is more to it than that. In 1990 the United States and the USSR agreed to reduce their stockpiles of chemical weapons to 5,000 tons over the following 12 years. Three years later the United States and Russia signed a treaty obliging them to eliminate those weapons entirely. What happened during this period was a shift in the imagining of chemical weapons—a reframing of the chemical weapons problem from one of "arms control," in which the superpowers dominated and disagreements over verification were central, to a problem of "proliferation."

Framing Chemical Weapons

As I demonstrated in Chapter 3, an "arms control" frame in the context of the Cold War enabled a set of practices that focused on bilateral negotiations between the Soviet Union and the United States but were not necessarily exclusive to the two superpowers. Thus although the SALT and START talks were bilateral, the conventional arms control process—mutual and balanced force reduction (MBFR) and later conventional forces in Europe (CFE)—was housed in a multilateral forum but with the lead clearly taken by the Soviets and Americans. The frame not only shaped the form of negotiating practice but defined the problem and ordered the sorts of solutions that were sought. Essentially, "arms control" problems concerned the relationship between superpower arsenals or, in the case of conventional weapons, their two alliances' arsenals. "Arms control" constructed an image of weapons as counters to be balanced against other identifiable counters.

The notions of balance and counting were central to "arms control" practices; for years conventional arms control negotiations were named with reference to balance. More centrally, a substantial part of both the negotiation processes and—even more extensively—the preparatory debates over arms control in the United States involved determining how the arsenals were to be counted so balances between the two could be determined. In the case of strategic nuclear weapons, this debate centered on whether to count launchers or warheads or yields or throw weight.[9] The euromissile talks, which resulted in the INF agreement, centered on which missiles held by either side counted and even on whether missiles that had not yet been built should be counted. Similarly, in the conventional arms control talks, most of the years of negotiation centered on the question of how to count the different arsenals of the two superpowers and their alliance partners.

Having constituted a problem of numerical equivalences that needed to be balanced, "arms control" naturally gave rise to solutions involving equal numbers of particular categories of weapons to be allowed on each side. Thus the SALT agreements set overall limits on warheads, with various subceilings for particular types of launchers. Those ceilings were identical for each side, therefore allowing for only the smallest variations in the mix among the various components of strategic nuclear arsenals. When the START agreements reduced strategic nuclear arms rather than just limiting their numbers, the pattern was repeated. A numerical ceiling was applied to the arsenals of the United States and the Soviet Union, with each side agreeing to destroy enough weapons to balance off at 4,250 warheads each.[10]

Similarly, because "arms control" was a problem of creating and maintaining numerical equivalences between two potential enemies, assuring those equivalences was seen to be crucial to maintaining any agreement. In other words, verification was central to a negotiation framed in terms of "arms control," and intrusive, on-site inspection came to be the litmus test of acceptable verification. This is not to say that intrusive on-site inspection would always be necessary, even by the standards set in the

United States, but rather that it acquired both iconic status and political value. Such inspection also became, as with human rights in the practices of the Conference on Security and Cooperation in Europe (CSCE), a useful rhetorical weapon to deploy against the Soviet Union.

"Arms control" practices, then, were characterized by a central bilateral negotiation between the Soviet Union and the United States. The primary issue of that negotiation was the determination of a means by which the weapons that were the focus of that negotiation could be counted and the number to which each side would reduce or limit its arsenal. Generally, the most contentious feature of this negotiation involved agreeing to a verification process by which each side could see for itself that the other was adhering to the agreed limit. Such a generic description applied to the SALT I and II talks, the START talks, the MBFR and CFE talks, and the INF talks during the 1980s. Crucially for the present argument, the description also applies to discussions around chemical weapons up to the early 1990s.

Although there was ongoing multilateral negotiation over chemical weapons in the Conference on Disarmament, it was the bilateral discussion between the Soviet Union and the United States that determined what, if any, progress was made in the larger forum. The issue that dominated the on-again, off-again discussion was that of verification—how to ensure that *any* limit agreed between the two superpowers (even a zero limit, as was finally agreed in the INF) would be verifiable by the other side in conditions in which chemical production for industrial purposes was permitted. When the two superpowers finally reached agreements, they were agreements of a classic "arms control" nature. First, the two agreed to mock inspection exercises to become used to the idea of intrusive on-site inspections of chemical facilities. Second, they agreed to reduce their own arsenals to an agreed level—5,000 tons each—within an agreed time frame.

As these negotiations were reaching their conclusion, however, a reframing of the chemical weapons problem was occurring. Chemical weapons were beginning to be imagined as part of a "proliferation" problem. This reframing began around allegations of CW being used by Iraq in its war with Iran. There had been allegations of use before, but they were largely confined to the Soviet Union (in Afghanistan) and the United States (in Vietnam). In the early 1980s it was a Third World state that was alleged to be employing chemical weapons. Suddenly, the normative restraints against the use of CW seemed to be weakening. The *SIPRI Yearbook 1987,* for instance, noted: "In the absence of a universal ban on the possession of chemical weapons, the international taboo against their use is being eroded. In 1986 Iran submitted new complaints of use of chemical weapons by Iraqi forces (previous complaints having been made and investigated in 1984 and 1985), and a UN team of specialists found the allegations to be well-founded."[11] With reference to the 1985 allegations, Iran was reported to have responded by moving its own chemical weapons to the front lines.[12]

With the normative restraint on use seemingly under threat and the appearance of chemical arsenals outside the East-West security system, the problem came to be articulated in the language of proliferation, echoing that of nuclear proliferation. Thus, for example, in 1986 the British representative to the CD announced, "World-wide there may be more than 20 nations which now either possess chemical weapons or are looking at the option of acquiring them."[13] Furthermore, the CD considered the possibility of a chemical nonproliferation treaty explicitly modeled on the NPT but rejected it because of the legitimation of "haves" and "have nots" in the NPT.[14] Despite the rejection of a simple copy of the NPT for chemical weapons, the CWC as it was concluded is the result of a "proliferation" framing of the problem and represents a practical replication of the nuclear nonproliferation regime. This tentative consideration of chemical weapons as a proliferation problem marks the first step in expanding the "proliferation" image to frame weapons other than nuclear weapons and so in some ways is the beginning of the central story of this book. To see how the reframing of CW as a "proliferation" problem enabled the CWC and also what is entailed by reimagining any weapons technology in terms of "proliferation," it is necessary to examine the "proliferation" image in more detail.

The Proliferation Image

To this point I have discussed the various images through which weapons technology has been framed in general terms. The central argument of this book is that these technologies have been reframed in terms of "proliferation," and that this has had particular practical and political consequences. To make this argument and to explore those consequences, it is necessary to fill in the "proliferation" frame in much more detail. This image joins together a number of discursive links to create a particular discursive construction of an international security problem. The central element of the image, the one that draws the others together into a single image, is proliferation itself.

Before its appropriation by those concerned with the development of nuclear weapons following World War II, proliferation was commonly used (when it was *commonly* used) to talk of the reproduction of animals and plants. Animals—even human animals—proliferated by having children, usually a lot of children. Rabbits were particularly proliferous. This meaning is clearly reflected in the *Oxford English Dictionary*'s definition of proliferous: "Producing offspring; procreative; prolific." Initially, analysts and policymakers adopted the language of proliferation for the problem of an increase in the number of states with access to nuclear technology after controlled fission was developed in 1945. This act of discursive imagination yielded nuclear proliferation as a policy problem in the Cold War. Nuclear technology would "reproduce," spawning an ever-growing "family" of nuclear nations. This image of nuclear proliferation underpinned the various solutions that were devised: the NPT and its attendant supplier groups, the Nuclear Suppliers Group (NSG) and the Zangger Committee. We can see what sort of "thing" is made of nuclear proliferation by its being imagined as "proliferation" if we look more closely at the earlier use of proliferation—the familiar referent in terms of which this new and unfamiliar nuclear technology came to be understood.

Animals produce offspring; they are procreative, that is, they are proliferous. To say that an animal proliferates is to say that it has young. Often, particularly when used for humans rather than for other animals, proliferation carries the connotation of excessive reproduction—humans proliferate when they have noticeably more than the accepted number of children rather than just when they have children. This implication is suggested in the *Oxford English Dictionary*'s use of prolific in the definition I quoted earlier. Thus proliferation has two important entailments as the metaphor chosen to imagine the development of nuclear weapons. First, proliferation is a *natural* process that requires external intervention not to proceed but rather only for prevention (e.g., various forms of birth control). Second, the result of unchecked proliferation tends to be *excessive* growth in the originating organism. Both of these entailments are captured nicely in a use of the term *proliferation* in a discussion of metaphor by literary theorist Paul de Man: "Worse still, abstractions [tropes] are capable of *infinite proliferation.* They are like *weeds*, or like *cancer*; once you have begun using a single one, they will crop up everywhere."[15]

De Man's reference to cancer is rather ironic. Cell biologists have also adopted the language of proliferation to talk about the way in which cells in organisms multiply.[16] In particular, the language of proliferation is central to the study of cancers. The connection between cell proliferation and cancer throws the entailments of proliferation into stark relief. By itself, cell proliferation is a harmless, natural process—indeed, it is essential to life as we know it. This proliferation is managed by a series of biological control mechanisms that regulate the growth of cells so they faithfully reproduce what is coded into their genetic material. Once these mechanisms fail and the cells reproduce without control, cancers, often deadly to the organism as a whole, result. As Andrew Murray and Tim Hunt write in introducing the study of cell proliferation, "Without knowing the checks and balances that normally ensure orderly cell division, we cannot devise effective strategies to combat the uncontrolled cell divisions of the cancers that will kill one in six of us."[17] Proliferation, as appropriated within the study of cancer, refers to an autonomous process of growth and spread, internally driven but externally controlled. Danger arises when the controls fail and the natural proliferation of cells produces excessive reproduction.

When the language of proliferation was used in thinking about the development of nuclear technology after the discovery of controlled fission in the U.S. Manhattan Project, a process similar to that which produces cancer was imagined as a result.[18] The U.S. nuclear program was the original technology that would multiply and spread. Such spread, when imagined as "proliferation," is a natural process and is inevitable without active outside intervention. Once the development of nuclear technology is imagined as "proliferation," this entailment of a natural process of spread leads to the expectation of inevitable growth in the number of nuclear powers. This, of course, is precisely what was expected. Because such a condition was considered dangerous and undesirable, attempts were made to establish external controls over the proliferation of nuclear weapons. Again, this follows from imagining the problem in terms of "proliferation." Some form of external control is necessary to prevent the prolific growth of nuclear weapons outside the United States. Attempts to place such external, international controls on nuclear proliferation resulted in the NPT of 1970, which remains the principal mechanism of proliferation control. What are the implications of this image—with its understandings of autonomous, natural growth and external control—for the policy response to the development of nuclear technology?

The first implication is that something imagined in terms of "proliferation" is seen to grow or multiply from a single source. Although animal reproduction involves two individuals, the father is quickly forgotten, and it is the mother who is proliferous. The budding of cells, which gives rise to the proliferation of some plants and, of course, cancers, begins with a single, or source, cell and spreads from there—in the case of a cancer, both to produce a single tumor and to create a number of separate tumors throughout the host body. Similarly, the problem of weapons proliferation is one of a source or sources proliferating, that is, reproducing by supplying the necessary technology to a new site of technological application. This form of imagining highlights the transmission process from source to recipient. Hence, the dominant response to nuclear proliferation has been the creation of supplier groups—the Zangger Committee and the NSG—that seek to control the spread of nuclear technology. In other words, to paraphrase Murray and Hunt, they attempt to provide the checks and balances that normally ensure orderly transfer and prevent the spread of nuclear technology resulting in the "cancer" of a prolific number of nuclear weapons.

The second implication of the proliferation metaphor for the problem of nuclear weapons spread is an extreme technological determinism. Animal reproduction is an internally driven phenomenon, and so the metaphor of proliferation applied to the development of nuclear technology highlights the autonomy in the growth of that technology and its problematic weapons variant. It is worth recalling Frank Barnaby's words: "A country with a nuclear power program will inevitably acquire the technical knowledge and expertise, and will accumulate the fissile material necessary to produce nuclear weapons."[19] In fact, the text from which this quotation is drawn presents an interesting example of the autonomy of the proliferation metaphor. The book is entitled *How Nuclear Weapons Spread: Nuclear-Weapon Proliferation in the 1990s.* Notice that the *weapons themselves* spread; they are not spread by some form of external agent—say, a human being or a political institution. Under most circumstances such a title would be unnoticed, for the implications are so deeply ingrained in our conceptual system that they are not recognized as metaphorical.

This image, by highlighting the *technological* and *autonomous* aspects of a process of *spread,* downplays or even hides important aspects of the relationship of nuclear weapons to international security. To begin with, the image hides the fact that nuclear weapons do not spread but *are* spread—and, in fact, are spread largely by the Western states. Second, the image downplays—to the point of hiding—any of the political, social, economic, and structural factors that tend to drive states and other actors both to supply and to acquire nuclear weapons. Finally, the image downplays the politics of security and threat, naturalizing the security dilemma to the point that it is considered an automatic dynamic. The image of "proliferation" thus privileges a technical, apolitical policy by casting the problem as a technical one. The NPT controls and safeguards the movement of the technology of nuclear energy. The supporting supplier groups jointly impose controls on the supply—that is, the outward flow—of this same technology. The goal in both cases is to stem or at least slow the outward movement of material and its attendant techniques.

These entailments suggest that to reimagine another problem of weapons technology in terms of "proliferation" is to construct that problem as technologically autonomous and to privilege solutions that attempt to control this natural growth by means of interventions aimed at the constituent technologies. This is precisely the strategy institutionalized within the chemical weapons convention. The general obligations of the states party to the CWC—set out in its first article—are to refrain from developing, producing, or holding any CW; to refrain from using CW or making military preparations for their use; and to refrain from assisting anyone else from doing anything prohibited by the convention.[20] These obligations are usefully compared with those assumed by states in the first two articles of the NPT.[21] In both cases the obligations of states party are to refrain from producing or procuring the weapon in question and to forego transferring the weapon to others. The difference—and it is an important difference—is that in the case of the NPT, five nuclear weapon states do not have to renounce their nuclear weapons capability. Otherwise, the obligations are identical.

More to the point than the initial obligations, however, are the practices each treaty institutionalizes to prevent the spread of weapons. In both cases direct international supervision and control are placed on precursor technologies to ensure that they do not "spread" to weapons. The NPT obliges all NNWSs party to place their nuclear industries under IAEA safeguards, and the NWSs party to the NPT have also placed their non-military nuclear facilities under international safeguard.[22] These safeguards are an internationally monitored material accountancy, designed to ensure that all fissile material used to produce nuclear energy is accounted for throughout the nuclear fuel cycle—and thus has not been diverted to produce nuclear weapons. Similarly, the CWC establishes an extensive machinery to verify that chemicals from the chemical industries of the states party are not used to produce CW. The mechanics of the CW system vary from those of the nuclear safeguards, but the essentials do not. In both cases potential industrial sources of technological spread are declared to the international agency, which can then monitor those industries to ensure that the declarations are accurate and that the material of concern is properly accounted for.

The CWC is therefore a "proliferation" control instrument, in the same way the 1989 and 1990 bilateral agreements between the Soviet Union and the United States over chemical weapons were "arms control" agreements. The centrality to the CWC regime of the practices monitoring chemical industries to ensure they are not used to spread chemical weapons marks it as an instrument to control proliferation, not one designed to achieve disarmament, for instance. Only in the context of a reimagining of the problem of chemical weapons from one of "arms control" or "disarmament" to one of "proliferation" did the CWC become possible. As chemical weapons came to be imagined as a "proliferation" problem in the late 1980s, the CWC as a nonproliferation agreement for chemical technology (but without the overtly discriminatory features of the nuclear NPT) became realizable. The end of the Cold War not only produced a limited arms control agreement between the superpowers concerning chemical weapons but, more important, created the conditions for realizing what reimagining in terms of the "proliferation" image made possible.

A "proliferation" image produces a particular kind of object. It imagines a technology that reproduces naturally and autonomously, moving outward from an identifiable origin by relentlessly multiplying. The image imagines this technology as essentially benign but with the possibility of excess—reproduction is natural, expected, and even desirable, but prolific reproduction is dangerous. To permit the benign spread of technology while preventing the dangerous conclusion to that spread, external controls are required. Because the object of "proliferation" is imagined in this fashion, the forms of control that can be applied are constrained. Put another way, the particular imagination of the object of "proliferation" enables a specific series of control practices. The reverse is also true: creating given practices will construct the object of those practices in particular ways. The result is a neatly closed circle it is simple to reify—we face this particular problem with these practices; these practices are employed, so we are facing this problem. Read in either direction, the contingent becomes seen as the natural.

What has happened since the late 1980s, particularly following the war in the Gulf, has been the reimagining of all forms of military technology in terms of the "proliferation" image and the embedding of that image in a series of control practices. Alternatively, a series of control practices has been established around the range of military technologies, which has constituted the object of those practices as a "proliferation" problem.

Practices of Proliferation Control

The NPT established the basis for the practice of "proliferation" control. The primary commitments are those expressed in Articles I and II: that NNWSs will not acquire or seek to acquire nuclear weapons and that NWSs will not transfer nuclear weapons to NNWSs. At the same time, the treaty recognizes the importance of nuclear technology for purposes other than making nuclear weapons. In particular, Article IV recognizes the right of states party to develop and use nuclear technology for peaceful purposes and even to "participate in, the fullest possible exchange of equipment, materials and scientific and technological information for the peaceful uses of nuclear energy."[23] Thus the NPT promotes the movement of nuclear technology around the world for peaceful purposes, calling for the fullest possible dissemination of all elements needed to create a nuclear industry.

Nuclear energy for peaceful purposes is to be promoted by the NPT, but at the same time the dissemination of "equipment, materials and scientific and technological information" will inevitably also disseminate the wherewithal to produce nuclear weapons. For this reason, the NPT requires NNWSs party to place all of their nuclear facilities under safeguard. The test of a nuclear explosive by India in 1974 suggested that this system was inadequate, at least until all states became party to the NPT—

which India was not (and still is not). In response, the leading nuclear suppliers formed two supplier groups to oversee the dissemination of nuclear technology—the NSG and the Zangger Committee. The formation of supplier groups makes perfect sense in terms of a "proliferation" image. The technology that can give rise to nuclear weapons will inevitably do so without intervention. The IAEA safeguards provide one form of intervention—international supervision to ensure that the civilian technology does not spread so as to become dangerous. This control was not considered foolproof, however, and so earlier, preventative, intervention was considered useful. Controls could be placed on the technology *before* it began its outward movement, so an additional prophylactic is thereby added to the international controls of the IAEA. The result can be considered in terms of a two-tiered approach to proliferation control, illustrated in Table 4.1.

The particular practices of nuclear proliferation control were made possible by the understanding of the problem provided by the "proliferation" image. By imagining the problem in terms of a largely autonomous, technologically driven process that would inevitably result in the dissemination of nuclear weapons, "proliferation" privileged a set of practices that

Table 4.1   Two-Tiered Practices of Nuclear Proliferation Control

First Tier—Global Treaty Regime	
Nuclear nonproliferation treaty	• The five states that had tested a nuclear weapon before 1968 are the only states that can own nuclear weapons. • Any state other than these five must not acquire or seek to acquire nuclear weapons. • States will not provide nuclear weapons or associated technology and material except for peaceful purposes and under international safeguards.
Verification of treaty obligations	• International Atomic Energy Agency (IAEA) safeguards. • Parties to the treaty, other than the five nuclear weapon states, are to declare all of their nuclear facilities, which are subject to IAEA inspection for the purpose of maintaining an accounting of nuclear material.
Second Tier—Technology Controls	
Supplier groups	• Nuclear Suppliers Group (NSG) (London Club) • Zangger Committee
National implementation through export controls	• Members of the NSG and Zangger Committee operate individual systems of export control on the technology and material controlled by the two groups.

focused on the monitoring and control of the constituent technologies. As a doctor would monitor the growth of cells for signs of cancerous proliferation and would intervene to regulate healthy growth and, if possible, prevent the cancerous spread, so the IAEA and nuclear suppliers monitor and intervene to allow for the spread of nuclear energy for peaceful purposes while attempting to prevent harmful nuclear proliferation. The result is a set of practices that begins with an international nondissemination norm, together with permission for (even the promotion of) healthy trade in the constituent technology, underpinned by international monitoring and technology controls by suppliers. These practices, in turn, reproduce the underlying understandings of the "proliferation" image. This is important for my purposes, for as these practices are transported to other technologies of concern they tend to constitute their object in the same way nuclear proliferation practices constitute theirs. As questions of military technologies have come to be reimagined in terms of "proliferation," the practices used to control nuclear proliferation have been re-created in these other areas. In the process, the images by which the various military technologies had been or could be imagined have been downplayed.

With the interpretation of reported chemical weapons use by Iraq in its war with Iran as indicative of the weakening of the taboo against CW use, the issue of chemical weapons began to be imagined in terms of the "proliferation" image. By 1993 this had resulted in the conclusion of the Chemical Weapons Convention, but the immediate response was the 1987 creation of the Australia Group, formed as a supplier group for chemical weapons technology. The group sought to coordinate its members' export control policies on technology and material related to the creation of chemical weapons in exactly the same way the NSG and the Zangger Committee aim to control the movement of nuclear technology. The formation of the Australia Group depended on the prior reframing of chemical weapons in terms of "proliferation." The "taboo" frame in which CW had been imagined constituted a problem of use, not of technological spread. Considering that chemical weapons use extends at least to the nineteenth century, it might be supposed that the technology was already well spread. Efforts at international control had therefore involved codifying and strengthening the nonuse norm through legal restrictions on the preparation for and execution of chemical warfare. In such a context a supplier control group makes little sense. Only when the problem is reimagined as a "proliferation" problem, and hence a problem of the spread of constituent technologies, would states turn to forming a supplier group.

Also in 1987 the Group of Seven industrialized countries (G-7) created the beginnings of a supplier group for ballistic missiles. The Missile Technology Control Regime (MTCR) sought to coordinate members' export controls on ballistic missiles and their constituent technologies. Such a practice reproduces the technological object that is at the heart of the "proliferation" image. By acting on missile technology within the practices of a supplier group, the members of the MTCR constitute ballistic missile technology as the object of a "proliferation" discourse.

Thus in the late 1980s, the image of "proliferation," and the autonomous, technological object it constituted, began to encompass far more than the nuclear technology that had been its object up to that point. It was at this moment that the United States led the global coalition against Iraq in the Gulf War. The subsequent interpretation of the danger Iraq posed was as the end product of an unchecked process of proliferation. Thus it became possible to think about providing security in the new world order in terms of preventing proliferation.

Having extended the process of imagining military technologies other than nuclear in terms of proliferation, which had begun in the late 1980s, the leading states of the international system turned to devising practices by which to respond to this newly identified threat—taking "appropriate action," in the term used by the Security Council. As the threat was a "proliferation" threat, the practices adopted were those of proliferation control. Those actions can be seen as developing or extending tiered practices mirroring those of the nuclear nonproliferation regime across the range of technologies of "proliferation" concern. Table 4.2 outlines the raw materials with which states set about this task at the time of the Gulf War. The table reproduces the tiered structure from Table 4.1 but expands it to include chemical and biological weapons, missile technology, and conventional arms. The elements in each cell show whether there was something comparable to an element of the nuclear proliferation control regime that could later be used to develop a parallel to the NPT; the parentheses indicate recognized shortcomings, which mean the element in question was only potentially comparable.

Table 4.2   Elements of a Potential Proliferation Control Effort, 1991

	Nuclear	Chemical	Biological	Missile	Conventional
First Tier					
Global treaty	NPT	—	(BTWC)	—	—
Verification	IAEA safeguards	—	—	—	—
Second Tier					
Supplier group	NSG Zangger	(Australia Group)	(Australia Group)	(MTCR)	(COCOM)
Export controls	Yes	Yes	Yes	Yes	(Yes)

Note: Parentheses indicate element is only partially comparable.

The Biological and Toxin Weapons Convention, for example, lacked any enforcement or verification mechanism, and the Australia Group and the Missile Technology Control Regime did not have a sufficiently broad membership to capture the sort of supply covered by the NSG and the Zangger Committee. Finally, the Coordinating Committee on Multilateral Export Controls (COCOM) was a child of NATO, designed to prevent high-technology exports to the Soviet Union. Some of this technology was related to conventional weapons, but the group's focus was incompatible with the new proliferation control agenda, as COCOM's former targets were key suppliers of technologies now to be controlled.

The response to the newly enunciated international concern with proliferation has been to develop the various cells in Table 4.2 to resemble more closely those of the nuclear nonproliferation regime.[24] Along the top row of the table, international agreements with potentially global reach have been developed to enshrine norms for the control of particular technologies. These agreements included or have had added international systems of verification to ensure compliance with the agreements' norms. These actions have reproduced the first-tier practices of the nuclear proliferation control regime across the newly identified technologies of proliferation concern. At the second tier, supplier control groups have been developed or expanded to include most, if not all, of the relevant suppliers. As part of the expansion of these groups, the states of the industrialized West have provided training and assistance to new members to enable them to implement national export controls.[25] The expansion of supplier groups and the production of national export controls have reproduced the second-tier practices for each of these technologies. The development of a chemical weapons proliferation control regime has been the subject of much of this chapter. I can now demonstrate the development of a similar set of practices for the other technologies of concern: biological weapons, missiles, and conventional weapons.

Drawing on the close relationship commonly seen between chemical and biological weapons, the Australia Group added biological weapons technology to its mandate, providing a supplier group for biological, in addition to chemical, weapons. Biological weapons have been subject to the control of a global treaty since the 1971 adoption of the Biological and Toxin Weapons Convention. This agreement had been possible largely because it was generally felt at the time that biological weapons were unlikely to be made militarily useful. As a consequence, the BTWC has no process for verifying obligations not to produce or stockpile biological weapons. Developments in biochemistry have meant that usable biological weapons are now a real possibility, so biological weapons are one of the weapons technologies now identified as a "proliferation" concern.[26] The lack of verification measures in the BTWC represented the most serious deficiency in making biological proliferation control practices mirror those of nuclear proliferation control. Consequently, the states party to the BTWC created a committee to "consider appropriate measures, including possible verification measures, and draft proposals to strengthen the Convention, to be included, as appropriate, in a legally binding instrument."[27] The work of the committee, known as VEREX for verification experts, is not complete, but the 1996 review conference expressed the expectation that such measures would be in place by the next review in 2001.

The generalization of the dangers posed by Iraq, which has fueled the new proliferation agenda, has also included a reaction to the Iraqi Scud missiles—despite their comparative ineffectiveness.[28] In response, the MTCR, which began as a limited set of guidelines among the G-7 states, has been developed into a full-fledged supplier group, similar to those controlling the supplies of nuclear, chemical, and biological technology. The membership has increased to almost 30. No global treaty controls missile technology, but in keeping with attempts to model nonproliferation regimes on the nuclear regime, in 1993 MTCR members considered the way in which the group might be developed into a global convention governing the nonproliferation of missile technology.[29]

One of the most noteworthy features of the new proliferation control agenda is the inclusion of conventional weapons as a "proliferation" concern. States claim the right to defend themselves against armed attack, a right confirmed by the UN Charter. States also maintain that this right to self-defense entails the right to acquire the means to that defense—in other words, the right to produce and procure conventional weapons. The Gulf War, however, has been interpreted in such a way as to reveal a danger in this understanding; consequently, limits on the right to acquire the means to self-defense are being considered. Initially, the limit was phrased as "excessive and destabilizing accumulations of conventional weapons"—a formulation that enables practices of "proliferation" control, and increasingly, conventional weapons have come to be spoken of directly as proliferation problems. For example, U.S. Under-Secretary of State for International Security Affairs Lynn Davis told her confirmation hearing, "When Secretary Christopher discussed this position with me, he focused on nonproliferation and the priority which the Clinton Administration would be giving to counter *proliferation of very deadly weapons*—nuclear, chemical, biological, and *enhanced conventional weapons,* as well as their delivery systems."[30]

Because not all accumulations of conventional weapons are considered problematic, the proliferation control norms under consideration differ from those for other technologies of concern. Rather than impose a blanket ban on the production and stockpiling of weapons, in 1991 the General Assembly passed a resolution creating a Register of Conventional

Arms that aims to make the movement of arms internationally—and, ultimately, the production of arms domestically—transparent.[31] The goal is to allow states to judge whether an excessive and destabilizing accumulation of weapons is developing in time to take appropriate action. The Western states have also managed to create a supplier group for conventional weapons technology since the war with Iraq. During the Cold War, NATO members and a few others controlled the movement of high technology to the East through COCOM. It proved impossible simply to expand the membership of that body, largely because the old targets had to be the new members if reasonable coverage of potential suppliers were to be achieved. Therefore, COCOM was disbanded and, after several years of discussion, the Wassenaar Arrangement was established. The arrangement is "a multilateral control system for the export of conventional weapons and related dual-use goods and technology . . . [and obliged its members to] implement, for the purposes of the new arrangement, national export controls relating to items on lists to be agreed upon."[32]

Perhaps the most remarkable development in the reimagination of issues surrounding weapons in terms of "proliferation" has been the conclusion of a treaty to ban the production and transfer of antipersonnel land mines. Until recently, international control of these land mines consisted of the 1983 convention on certain conventional weapons (CCW). This convention restricted the use of a number of weapons "deemed to be excessively injurious or to have indiscriminate effects."[33] The CCW clearly framed antipersonnel land mines and the other weapons that were its subjects in terms of the laws of war. The goal of the convention was to identify particularly nasty weapons and to prohibit or at least restrict their use. The framing, in other words, was similar to that of chemical weapons prior to the chemical weapons convention—it focused exclusively on use, identifying practices in the conduct of war that were seen to be uncivilized.[34]

The transformation of the framing of land mines has been dramatic. Canada has taken a leading role in bringing about this transformation, and its minister of foreign affairs has noted the speed with which the change has come about:

> Support for a total ban on AP [antipersonnel] mines has grown at an astonishing rate. In early 1994, not a single country promoted the idea of a ban; by October 1995, 14 countries were in favour. One year later, at the Ottawa Conference, 50 countries pledged their support for a global ban. Most recently, in December 1996, 156 countries committed themselves to this goal at the United Nations General Assembly. We have seen the emergence of political will to act in a critical mass of states.[35]

The Canadian government convened the Ottawa Conference in October 1996 to discuss possibilities for a multilateral treaty banning land mines. The conference was followed by meetings in Vienna and Brussels through the first half of 1997 and by a three-week conference in Oslo in September 1997. The Oslo Conference produced a draft treaty, "Convention on the Prohibition of the Use, Stockpiling, Production and Transfer of Anti-personnel Mines and on Their Destruction" (generally referred to as the Ottawa Convention). The Ottawa Convention was opened for signature 3–4 December 1997 in Ottawa. Over a four-year period a ban on antipersonnel land mines went from having no state supporters to a treaty signed by 123 states.[36]

The general provisions of the Ottawa Convention are worth examining in detail, because they reproduce precisely those of the CWC:

Article 1. General Obligations
1. Each State Party undertakes never under any circumstances:
    a) To use anti-personnel mines;
    b) To develop, produce, otherwise acquire, stockpile, retain or transfer to anyone, directly or indirectly, anti-personnel mines;
    c) To assist, encourage or induce, in any way, anyone to engage in any activity prohibited to a State Party under this Convention.
2. Each State Party undertakes to destroy or ensure the destruction of all anti-personnel mines in accordance with the provisions of the Convention.[37]

If every instance of "anti-personnel mines" is replaced with "chemical weapons," the words of each subparagraph are identical to those of the CWC.[38] The treaty even establishes on-site inspection for monitoring compliance—a UN fact-finding mission is to have access to any potential violator within 72 hours of asking.[39]

In other words, the Ottawa Convention establishes a global regime of the kind "proliferation" practice requires, banning the production and transfer of a particular weapons technology. Suddenly—over the space of approximately four years—land mines have become a proliferation issue, along with nuclear, chemical, and biological weapons. The Ottawa Convention constitutes a problem defined in technological terms and thus bans the production and transfer of land mines, just as the NPT bans the production and transfer of nuclear weapons by or to NNWSs party and the CWC bans the production and transfer of chemical weapons. This development has two notable features. First, the Ottawa Convention is made possible by the "proliferation" image—and the speed with which it was achieved is indicative of the potency of that image. Second, treating antipersonnel land mines as a "proliferation" problem through the same forms of practice as nuclear or even chemical weapons is very odd.[40]

Antipersonnel land mines are not particularly high on the technological ladder. They rely on extremely simple technology both to master and to employ. The verification of the CWC requires practices that are extraordinarily complex and intrusive because of the widespread use of chemicals in industry. A similar verification regime for land mines would be impossible because the technology concerned does not even require the sort of industrial plant the most basic chemical industry needs. These are precisely the sort of weapons armed nonstate groups would be able to build—and, indeed, have built—such is their relative lack of technological sophistication. For all this, the convention that has been designed to respond to land mines has been modeled directly on the CWC, which, in turn, was closely based on the NPT.

The oddity of framing land mines in terms of "proliferation" is all the more clear if we consider some alternative responses. There is a new generation of antipersonnel land mines based on rather more sophisticated technology—so-called smart mines. "Smart mines are self-neutralizing or self-destroying; that is, they are designed to render themselves harmless at some point after being laid. The problem with antipersonnel land mines is generally considered to be their effect after the purpose for which they were laid. "Dumb mines" stay active for years, and long after the combatants leave the area the mines remain to kill and maim those—often children—who happen to wander through the minefields. This is the reason mines were included in the CCW. If minefields were to be laid with truly effective smart mines, this long-term danger would largely be removed. It could therefore be argued that one way to address the problem of mines as weapons of mass destruction in slow motion would be actively to spread smart-mine technology. Instead of banning the production and stockpiling of all mines, the international community could have worked to ensure that if a minefield is laid, it is laid with smart rather than dumb mines. The outright ban of the Ottawa Convention suggests that in the future, if minefields are laid they will tend to be laid with simple-to-produce dumb mines and also that those who lay them will be even less willing to accept responsibility for them after the fact than they are now.

I do not want to suggest that such an alternative strategy should be adopted or that it would necessarily be more effective than the Ottawa Convention in preventing civilian deaths and injuries; further, the mobilization of international political will to ban a weapon of this kind is to be applauded. What is of concern, in both senses of the term, is the way in which the "proliferation" frame shapes the options that can be considered. The idea of actively spreading weapons technology cannot be countenanced by a discourse that identifies that spread as the problem. Instead, the problem of any weapon identified as a concern is to be remedied by developing restrictions on its movement as a technological artifact. Spreading smart mines might not be the most productive solution, but, at the same time, restricting the solutions to limits or prohibitions on the manufacture and transfer of land mine technology is likely to have excluded solutions that would go further toward protecting civilians from the long-term effects of mines.

In the years since the war in the Gulf, considerable activity has been aimed at combating the problem of weapons proliferation. That activity has focused largely on developing measures—comparable to those used to prevent the proliferation of nuclear weapons—for the other weapons technologies now of proliferation concern. States have:

- Built or strengthened some form of international treaty or convention to enshrine the nonproliferation norms for the technology in question
- Included in that treaty, or added to an existing treaty, measures to verify the obligations created by those norms
- Created a supplier group that covers most major suppliers of that technology
- Implemented export controls at the national level that execute agreements reached within the supplier groups

This activity can be summarized by amending Table 4.2, as shown in Table 4.3.

Nonproliferation now refers to stopping the spread of all forms of weaponry and associated technology, not only nuclear weapons, and has moved from a relatively marginal security concern to a central concern of the post–Cold War world. The practices first devised to control nuclear

Table 4.3   Elements of the Proliferation Control Effort, 1998

	Nuclear	Chemical	Biological	Missile	Conventional
First Tier					
Global treaty	NPT	CWC	BTWC	—	UN Register of Conventional Arms
Verification	IAEA safeguards	OPCW	[VEREX]	—	Internal cross-checking
Second Tier					
Supplier group	NSG Zangger	Australia Group	Australia Group	MTCR	Wassenaar Arrangement
Export controls	Yes	Yes	Yes	Yes	Yes

Note: Square brackets indicate elements that are presently under negotiation but not yet in force. The parentheses from Table 4.2 have been removed because of the expansion of the Australia Group and the MTCR.

proliferation have been largely reproduced in each of the other areas of concern. Put another way, the security problems raised by the various military technologies have been reframed in terms of the "proliferation" image. This framing and the practices to which it gives rise constitute those problems, its objects, in the same way the problem of nuclear proliferation has been constituted: as an autonomous technological problem. As a consequence of this constitution of the problem, the "proliferation" framing subordinates other possible and actual framings of these problems and the very different objects they constitute.

Framing as Productive, Not Reactive

There is little doubt that the idea of interpretive images and state practices *constituting* the weapons technologies they confront is not the way in which these technologies are commonly considered. Debates over proliferation within the security studies literature assume that the objects are naturally so and that what is at issue is how to deal with them. Take as an example a passage from Brad Roberts, one of the most perceptive commentators on proliferation:

> Looking afresh at the proliferation problem, what are its essential features in the post–cold war era? Two stand out.
> First, nuclear weapons have been joined by other weapons as topics of concern. This is true of biological and to a lesser extent chemical weapons. In places like the Middle East and East Asia these weapons may be seen by decision makers to offer high political leverage or decisive military advantage in time of conflict. Today, the 5 or 8 or 9 nuclear states have been joined by another dozen or so states with programs aimed at waging war with biological weapons and 20 or so that have an offensive chemical warfare capability. Furthermore, some conventional weapons that upset stable balances or significantly increase the strategic reach of nations fall into this category of high-leverage weaponry, such as the Russian-built submarines now in Iran's navy or the ballistic and cruise missiles that are now found in many regions of the world.
> Second, the ability to produce weapons of all kinds has diffused even more widely than the weapons themselves. This is particularly true as regards conventional weapons. The defense industrial base associated with the production of military hardware is spreading.[41]

According to Roberts, there *is* a condition in the post–Cold War world that requires attention, and that condition is the spread of the full range of military technology. Notice, for example, that "nuclear weapons have been joined by other weapons" and that "the ability to produce weapons of all kinds has diffused." Autonomous processes confront decisionmakers with situations with which they are or are not capable of coping. Roberts's concern is that the policy responses of states are inappropriate: their "stance has been largely reactive" because they "tinker with policy instruments designed for the problems of a different time."[42]

I argue that this tinkering is more than purely reactive and that the broad sweep of the new proliferation agenda to which Roberts points is a construct of that tinkering. Consider Roberts's last point, that the defense industrial base necessary for the production of conventional weaponry is spreading and that this is a key feature of the contemporary problem of proliferation. Until recently, the ability to produce conventional weapons has been framed almost exclusively in commercial terms. As I noted in Chapter 3, even the new British government has announced that it "is committed to the maintenance of a strong defence industry, which is a strategic part of our industrial base as well as of our defence effort."[43] For the British government a strong defense industrial base is not part of a "proliferation" problem but rather is a pillar of the British economy. This is a view that for much of the Cold War found a parallel in approaches to Third World development. The "military as modernizer" school of thought argued that the defense industry could serve as a catalyst for wider economic development.[44]

Read in terms of a commercial frame or, in more extreme terms, the military as modernizer frame, what would seem by Roberts's account to be the *same* object is in fact produced as something quite different. Rather than the spread of a defense industrial base appearing as part of a broad security problem of proliferation, it is evidence of the strength and dynamism of global capitalism—the globalization of modern industrial development. This last object is highly prized in contemporary international life; it is seen as the force that won the Cold War, as the culmination of historical change, and—perhaps most ironically—as the key to world (liberal) peace. Liberal peace theory argues that liberal democratic states do not go to war with one another, so peace can be achieved by spreading the institutions of liberal democracy. Were the production of conventional weapons to be read exclusively through the commercial frame, in the context of wide acceptance of the tenets of liberal peace theory, the diffusion of a defense industrial base could be constructed as a sign of the coming of the liberal millennium.[45]

The practices a commercial framing enables would be radically different from those of proliferation control. Nevertheless, they are very much in accordance with other practices, which *are* being followed at present in what are understood to be other contexts. For instance, the tenets of liberal peace are invoked to support policies promoting the export of liberal-democratic forms of government. Perhaps more telling, they are also invoked in practices of engagement with the states of the former Eastern Europe. In these cases there is a concerted effort to promote liberal-democratic government, and economic transformation also. The argument is that the creation of modern capitalist economies within liberal-democratic polities creates the conditions for a liberal zone of peace. If we were to accept the argument of the military as modernizer school—much of which is implicit in the British foreign secretary's promotion of the British defense industrial base as a pillar of the British economy—then the security practice related to the defense industry would be to promote its development around the world as a pillar of the sort of economic transformation needed to construct the liberal peace.

What is important to recognize is that the *same so-called facts* are constituted in the two discourses in dramatically different fashion. It is simply not the case that there is a phenomenon out there—the spread of defense industrial capacity—that is to be seen unproblematically as a threat. Rather, the imagining of a "proliferation" problem constructs the global defense industry as a particular object—specifically, as a proliferation threat.

Conclusion

The end of the Cold War, together with the experience of the war in the Gulf, has led to a reexamination of the nature of international security by both those who make policy for states and those who write about it. The Cold War had defined security for most, if not all, states since the end of World War II. Coming as it did just as the realization that the Cold War was over was dawning on policymakers, the Gulf War served as a perfectly timed referent around which to begin to rethink issues of security. One of the most important elements of this reexamination of security in the contemporary world has been the identification of the problem of weapons proliferation as a pressing threat.

This chapter has shown how this seemingly passive examination, "largely reactive" in Brad Roberts's words, has, in fact, been an active constitution of a problem. The full range of military technology has come to be imagined in terms of a single frame, a frame founded on the image of "proliferation." This image constitutes a particular object at its focus: an autonomous technology that will spread if left unchecked, with potentially devastating consequences. In turn, this frame enables certain practices that aim to check this autonomous technological diffusion. The foundation of these practices is supplier groups, small groups of states that coordinate their own export controls on technologies now identified as proliferation concerns. This construction of the problems associated with weapons technology, however, is not universally welcomed—or accepted.

The possibility for opposing dominant framings is one of the most important reasons for developing alternatives. Unless the objects of both academic analysis and policy are first recognized as constructed in the images and practices to which they give rise, such opposition becomes much more difficult. Opposing the proliferation discourse, for example, comes to be seen as arguing in favor of proliferation and all of the ills that image ascribes to proliferation. The fact that military technology *has* been imagined in these various other ways, however, provides a powerful rhetorical tool for the critic to argue that it *can* now be imagined in other ways.

To see why someone might want to oppose this discourse, it is necessary to look at what else is constructed by particular frames. These frames and the practices they enable constitute not only the objects of those practices but also the subjects. The identities of those who act and those who are acted upon are no more given than the objects of practices. These identities are also constituted in and by practices, and the way in which they are constituted gives rise to subject positions that might object to the framing of issues of military technology in terms of "proliferation."

5

Entailing Self and Other

In autumn 1997 Iraq—or, as both the press and world leaders insist on saying, Saddam—provoked another in the seemingly endless series of crises with the United Nations and the United States. The Iraqi government objected to the presence of Americans on the team of international inspectors charged with disarming Iraq, claiming that the United States was "spying" on Iraq and that U.S. members of the UN Special Commission (UNSCOM) were therefore no longer welcome. The inspection team had a slightly different explanation for Iraq's actions, as a leading British Sunday newspaper reported on 2 November: "The United Nations team in Iraq told the *Observer* it was on the verge of uncovering the lethal VX liquid nerve agent when Saddam Hussein ordered US members of the team to leave last week. . . . 'I think we were getting hot, and maybe that's part of the reason why they took this decision in the last couple of days,' the UN's chief weapons inspector, Richard Butler, said."[1]

This episode raises at least two pertinent questions. First, how is it that more than six years after the UN Security Council authorized UNSCOM to oversee the disarming of Iraq in the cease-fire Resolution 687 that ended the Gulf War the inspectors were only on the verge of discovering a stockpile of an extremely dangerous chemical agent? The first director of UNSCOM reported on the scope of the resolution:

> Resolution 687 required Iraq to declare the location, amount and type of all items specified under paragraphs 8 and 12 *within 15 days* of adoption of the resolution. The items thus to be eliminated are all of Iraq's chemical weapons (CW), biological weapons (BW), stocks of agents, related subsystems and components, and all research, development, support and manufacturing facilities. . . . Disposal is to be carried out under international supervision through destruction, rendering harmless or removal of the proscribed items.[2]

Under the terms of a cease-fire resolution—not a permanent cessation of war—the defeated power was to declare all of its chemical and biological

77

weapons for destruction within 15 days of 6 April 1991. It was 2,401 days later when the head of the team charged with international supervision of this process was on the verge of discovering a stockpile of nerve agent "so powerful that a few grams could kill millions of people."[3] What happened in the interim? I return to this question later. This question, however, presupposes a prior one: Why is Iraq subject to Resolution 687 in the first place? Or more to the point, how did Iraq come to be identified as the primary "proliferation" problem of the post–Cold War world?

The common answer, of course, is the one I recounted in Chapter 1: that Iraq is the epitome of the weapon state, or rogue state, as we now call them. Iraq is considered to be the vanguard of the general problem of proliferation in the post–Cold War world. As Charles Krauthammer puts it, "The central truth of the coming era is that . . . relatively small, peripheral and backward states will be able to emerge rapidly as threats not only to regional, but to world, security."[4] But how does this happen? How do states emerge rapidly as threats to security? Indeed, how had Iraq emerged so rapidly as a proliferation threat, as the prototype rogue?

The answer, of course, is that it did not emerge rapidly as a threat to regional or even world security. Rather, throughout the 1980s, as it first fought and then recovered from a protracted war with Iran, Iraq was buying weapons at an unparalleled rate:

> In the period 1987–91, Iraq was the world's third largest importer of arms, acquiring major weapons valued at $10.3 billion. Iraq's war with Iran fuelled its demand for and increased its leverage to acquire weapons. During the war with Iran, Iraq took deliveries from some 30 supplier states, with the USSR and France being the most important suppliers. *One-third of the major weapons bought by Iraq in the period 1980–90 came from countries which ultimately joined the military alliance against Iraq.*[5]

SIPRI's assessment of the relationship between suppliers and the UN coalition is actually rather conservative, for it assumes that the USSR did not join the coalition. Although Soviet troops did not fight, the USSR did approve the various resolutions authorizing the coalition. When Soviet weapons are included, we can say that virtually all of Iraq's weapons came from countries contributing to the UN war effort in the Gulf. The supplying of Iraq's arsenal continued after the end of its war with Iran—continued, in fact, until the invasion of Kuwait in 1990 and the imposition of sanctions by the United Nations. Those sanctions were imposed by a Security Council resolution, as was the eventual cease-fire Resolution 687. This means that these resolutions were supported by the five permanent members of the Security Council, *all* of which were among those supplying arms to Iraq in the 1980s.

From the perspective of the United States, to take an important example, Iraq went—literally overnight—from an acceptable recipient of U.S.

arms to the epitome of the dangers of weapons proliferation. The irony is that the two are hardly unconnected, even if commentators like Krautham-mer engage in a little instant revisionism to speak of such states "emerging rapidly" as threats. From the perspective of traditional international rela-tions (IR) scholarship, the switch I have just recounted should be rather puzzling. Iraq had, of course, invaded a neighbor, and that neighbor was oil rich. It had done so 10 years earlier, however, and been rewarded with massive arms transfers. What is more, there is good reason to believe that the United States had signaled its acquiescence in Iraq's plans to invade Kuwait days before.[6] Even if it had not, Iraq did not transform itself overnight into the greatest threat of the contemporary period.

To account for the apparent transformation of Iraq and to think about its implications for understanding contemporary proliferation policy, it is necessary to consider more generally questions related to the nature of identity. As I argued earlier, images such as the "proliferation" image con-stitute the world, in part by rendering objects meaningful as objects of a particular sort. Chapter 4 detailed the objects created by the "proliferation" image. The worlds constituted by images not only contain objects; they are also peopled by actors of various kinds. That is, the image constitutes not only objects but also identities. The short story with which I began this chapter can be read as one of the transformation of the Iraqi identity in the process of reframing parts of international security in terms of the "prolif-eration" image. To provide the tools for such a reading, not only of Iraq but of the "proliferation" image more generally, I begin by interrogating the discipline of IR about questions of identity.

Identity in International Relations

Questions of identity have become of central concern to critical scholar-ship in IR, in large measure because the traditional approaches in the dis-cipline pay so little attention to them. These traditional approaches, by which I mean essentially realism and its neorealist and neoliberal off-shoots, contain a series of assumptions that render issues of identity un-problematic. IR theory proceeds from the assumption that the state is the sole important locus of collective identity in world politics. People are treated as citizens of states, both individually and collectively, and so can be collapsed into the state for purposes of thinking about international re-lations. What is more, the state itself is identified with the nation.[7] In other words, not only is the state seen as the sole locus of collective identity, but the *content* of that identity is also assumed—assumed to be a national identity.

This neat equation of state and nation, and the assumption that the na-tional state is the only relevant form of identity in world politics, is the focus of considerable sustained critique. R. B. J. Walker has captured the heart of this critique and its central paradox: "Whatever avenues are now being opened up in the exploration of contemporary political identities, whether in the name of nations, humanities, classes, races, cultures, genders or movements, they remain largely constrained by ontological and discursive options expressed most elegantly, and to the modern imagination most persuasively, by claims about the formal sovereignty of territorial states."[8] The first point made by the critical literature is that there is a wide range of ways in which individual and collective identity is constructed—Walker lists seven of those most commonly cited. What is more, in the contemporary world of global economies of production, communication, and travel, these alternative loci of identity are finding expression in collectivities that stretch beyond the borders of territorially based states—although, as Walker also notes, the power of the state as both an institution and an idea limits the possibility for both thought and action outside its confines.

A marked difference is present between the traditional and critical approaches that goes well beyond a disagreement over the status of the state or nation as a locus of identity. Critical thinkers point to a series of alternative, overlapping forms of individual and collective identity. More crucially, they will generally not claim that these forms of identity are necessary, exhaustive, or in any way essential. By contrast, traditional approaches to international relations assume the exclusivity and universality of the state and nation. For critical thinkers, identity is socially constructed. William Connolly has phrased it clearly:

> My identity is what I am and how I am recognized rather than what I choose, want or consent to. It is the dense self from which choosing, wanting, and consenting proceed. Without that density, these acts could not occur; with it, they are recognized to be mine. *Our* identity, in a similar way, is what we are and the basis from which we proceed.
>
> An identity is established in relation to a series of differences that have become socially recognised. These differences are essential to its being. If they did not coexist as differences, it would not exist in its distinctness and solidity.[9]

Individual or collective identity involves both being and, importantly, recognition. Identity is inseparable from that which is outside the individual or the collective being identified because it is not only "what I am [or we are]" but "how I am [or we are] recognized." Identity depends on the ways in which the I (or we) is named, and it depends furthermore on the demarcation of limits that separate identity from a series of differences.[10] Identity can be founded, as Walker suggests, in the name of a class, a gender, a race—or even a nation. To express identity in these terms, however, is also to indicate that which is outside that class, gender, race, or nation—the difference by which we know the same.

The lines of identity/difference are lines of tremendous political and ethical potential and significance.

> The definition of difference is a requirement built into the logic of identity, and the construction of otherness is a temptation that readily insinuates itself into that logic—and more than a temptation: a temptation because it is constantly at work and because there may be political ways to fend it off or to reduce its power; more than a temptation because it typically moves below the threshold of conscious reflection and because every attempt to come to terms with it encounters stubborn obstacles built into the logic of identity and the structural imperatives of social organization.[11]

The move from "difference" to "other," as Connolly puts it, is the moment of politics. Although difference is essential to the construction of identity, the creation of difference as other marks the constitution of hierarchy and exclusion. The temptation to which Connolly refers is the temptation to secure the self through the identification of difference as the other. It is a temptation we have seen constantly, and with devastating effects. Connolly speaks of the constitution of heretic and heathen in medieval Christianity as the internal and external others to the Catholic self. In both cases the confrontation with the other was violent, taking the form of conversions through individual and collective tortures or elimination through public executions and mass exterminations.[12] Closer to home, the Cold War saw the constitution of the Communist other, both internal and external, which gave rise to new forms of heretic hunting and the possibility of mass exterminations on an altogether new scale.[13] Crucially, Connolly notes that there are ways to counteract the temptation to "othering," but to do so one must first recognize the constructed and contingent nature of identity and difference.

This conception of identity and difference as constructed, contingent, and contestable has led to two principal forms of research in critical IR literature. The most common is the problematization of the state and nation as the locus of identity. By examining the various alternative forms of individual and collective identity, authors show how these forms intersect and transcend state practice and how they are subordinated and oppressed by the state and by the theoretical practice of statecentric IR theory.[14] The problematization of state and nation does not mean they are not real or meaningful, however. A second stream of critical IR research has explored the way in which states and nations—*particular* states and nations rather than the universalized state and nation of realist-inspired literature—are themselves constructed.[15] Nation and state are important forms of collective and even individual identity, as anyone confronted by a border guard can

attest. These forms of identity, however, are constructed through social practices of recognition and differentiation as are any others, and so they are
both as particular and as contingent as any others.

The particularity and the contingency of state identity are apparent in
the story of Iraq's transformation into the first rogue. The contingency of
identity is the heart of the story. From a bulwark against Islamic funda-
mentalism and a potential source of regional stability following the fall of
the shah in Iran, Iraq became the primary danger of the post–Cold War
world almost literally overnight. Here, it seems obvious, it is recognition
rather than being that is at issue.[16] Prior to August 1990 Iraq was governed
by a military-backed dictatorship bent on establishing the country as a regional power and willing to use military force against its neighbors to increase its access to oil—illustrated clearly by its invasion of Iran. After
August 1990 Iraq was governed by a military-backed dictatorship bent on
establishing the country as a regional power and willing to use military
force against its neighbors to increase its access to oil—illustrated clearly
by its invasion of Kuwait. What changed was the way in which Iraq was
recognized, named, and identified by the international community in general and the United States in particular.

The naming of Iraq in this case is especially significant, as it reveals
the particularity as well as the contingency of identity. Iraq was equated
with Saddam Hussein, who, in turn, was constructed through his insertion
into a discourse recalling Hitler's Nazi regime.[17] Both of these features of
the transformation I discussed earlier are fundamentally social. The nature,
even the behavior, of Iraq was insufficient by itself to forge its identity in
any particular way. Rather, it is the social act of recognition that gave Iraq
the identity it now "enjoys." The identification of Iraq with Saddam Hussein with Adolf Hitler illustrates another dimension of the sociality of
these acts of identification. Identifying Iraq through the use of the Hitler
metaphor requires a preexisting discourse of international evil built around
the iconic figure of Adolf Hitler. It is the story the name evokes, which
identifies Iraq in a particular fashion, and general recognition of that story
among the members of a society is the precondition for such a naming.
The use of the Hitler narrative, in other words, is a clear illustration of the
metaphorical constitution of, in this case, identity—the name links the understanding of the contemporary actions of Iraq with the commonly received discursive construction of the actions of Nazi Germany.

Following the events of August 1990, Iraq's identity was established by
more than the "purely linguistic" act of naming. At least equally important,
that identity was established through a practical engagement with Iraq in
those particular terms—in this instance, primarily practices of UN sanction
and military action. These two facets of the social constitution of identity
are inseparable. The naming of Iraq in a particular way, the interpretation

of its behavior as behavior of a certain kind, enables the practices of the United Nations and the coalition. At the same time, the engagement with Iraq as an enemy and a subject of sanctions produced and reproduced its identity. Finally, the identity that was forged in and around the Gulf War is not only an identity Iraq must still live with but also one against which it continues to struggle. The creation of identity may be a social act, but it is not one in which the subject, once constructed, is stripped of all contrary agency.

Identity is constructed in social engagement, so the discursive practices that forge the objects of international action also forge their subjects. Although the identities of states and other international actors may appear fixed, they are contingent upon the discourses that constitute them and on the practices through which they are expressed and reproduced. Therefore the creation of a new discursive construction of international security around "proliferation" has also meant the creation of new identities. One of these, of course, is the weapon state, a new identity for states but one that did not suddenly emerge like a species of insect science had never encountered. My objective in the rest of this chapter is to examine the other identities being forged in the proliferation agenda. The contingency of identity means these identities are contestable, so I shall also examine points of contestation—for identification is an intensely political act, particularly when the lines of difference become markers of othering.

Identities in the Proliferation Image

The central practice in the control of the spread of weapons and related technology is that of export control. It is worth remembering that in 1991 Canada proposed that "individual programmes of action on proliferation issues will be carried out so that by 1995, a subsequent conference might celebrate completion of the comprehensive network of specific non-proliferation regimes."[18] By 1995 what had clearly been achieved was the creation of a supplier group in each area of technological concern. Efforts have also been made to fill the first tier of controls with multilateral agreements setting out nonproliferation norms supported by a system to verify obligations—but by no means is a comprehensive network yet in place. At present, supplier groups agreeing to common export control strategies are at the heart of proliferation control efforts. Indeed, even in areas in which first-tier regimes are established, supplier groups continue to represent a central feature of control efforts. The NPT itself, despite its commitment to disseminate nuclear technology, has been supported by supplier groups from its inception. The Australia Group has declined to cease functioning as a chemical weapons supplier group, even in light of the conclusion of the chemical weapons convention.

Stated simply, supplier groups and their attendant export controls create two subject positions: supplier and recipient. To see just what this means, I examine the functioning of supplier groups and export controls in some detail. The nature of supplier and recipient as constructed in this practice is not self-evident; neither is the way in which these positions are constructed. I will focus on Canada's export control system because Canada is a member of all of the groups, has a clear and coherent structure in place for implementing the controls, and has taken it upon itself to instruct states in the former Eastern Europe on how to implement similar controls.

Export Controls: Suppliers and Recipients

The basic operation of the supplier group is relatively simple and uniform across the five major groups: the Nuclear Suppliers Group, the Zangger Committee, the Australia Group, the MTCR, and the Wassenaar Arrangement. The recent Wassenaar Arrangement exemplifies the form these agreements take. Within the arrangement the participating states meet as a group to exchange information concerning the transfer of conventional arms and dual-use technologies and to develop guidelines to ensure that such transfers are carried out responsibly. A key feature of those guidelines is a set of control lists that detail the items and technologies the supplier group aims to control. In the case of the Wassenaar Arrangement, this set includes the List of Dual-Use Goods and Technologies and the Munitions List, two of the control lists COCOM created during the Cold War to control sensitive exports to the Soviet bloc. The members also agree to exercise restraint when exporting any item that appears on the lists. In the Wassenaar Arrangement the participating states agree to prevent transfers to states that are "a serious concern" to members. Although the lists of items to be controlled are decided by the supplier group, the implementation of controls is left to the individual members. For this purpose, the members are expected to implement systems of national export control applied to the lists agreed by the group.[19]

To implement its controls, Canada publishes an annual compendium entitled *A Guide to Canada's Export Controls* that organizes the controls imposed by Canada into groups by the supplier group that has agreed to them.[20] Any Canadian company that wishes to export any of the goods on the lists must request an export permit stating the nature of the goods and their final destination. The Export Controls Division of the Canadian Department of Foreign Affairs determines whether the export contravenes the obligations Canada has undertaken as a member of one of the relevant supplier groups. Primarily, this determination means judging whether the recipient state's behavior causes serious concern or poses a threat to international peace and security. We can assume that being a member of the relevant supplier group largely excludes a state as posing a serious concern to other members—indeed, in Canada's case exports to the United States are explicitly exempted from most export controls. Therefore Canada and all other members of the group acting to implement export controls in a similar way are identifying states outside their number for sanction, which excludes them from receiving some items of Canadian technology. The Wassenaar Arrangement, however, claims that the controls will "not be directed against any state or group of states." They are, in fact, directed against a very large group of states—all but the 33 that are members of the arrangement.

The supplier groups therefore constitute a clear division between those inside, identified as suppliers, and those outside, identified as recipients. The arrogance of the suppliers on the inside—the authority that they arrogate to themselves, which translates into the common meaning of the term—is staggering. Consider that the states which signed the Wassenaar Arrangement determined that the new group would "prevent the acquisition of armaments and sensitive dual-use items for military end-uses, if the behavior of a state is, or becomes, a cause for serious concern of the participants."[21] Further, the states oblige themselves not to "interfere with the rights of states to acquire *legitimate means with which to defend themselves.*"[22] Now consider an instance in which a state outside the Wassenaar Arrangement has what it considers a legitimate grievance against some large group of those inside—NATO, for example. The Wassenaar Arrangement includes all of the members of the newly enlarged NATO except Iceland. The new NATO therefore accounts for 18 of the 33 Wassenaar states, and these 33 will determine if the behavior of recipients warrants their being denied access to the legitimate means with which to defend themselves. (Of course, no state needs to worry because NATO never poses a real threat to any other state, and so no state could possibly have legitimate need to defend itself from NATO!) In essence, the supplier groups are taking it upon themselves to police acceptable behavior of states not among the favored few.

Given this construction of inside and outside, it is worth asking who is included in the five supplier groups. Although the membership varies from group to group, it does not vary by much. As Table 5.1 shows, 36 states belong to one or more of the supplier groups—which range in membership from 29 to 34—and of those, 23 states belong to all five groups. This does not appear to be a large and varied series of functional aggregations of states but rather a repeated grouping of a select few, an impression greatly reinforced when we look at the states that are members. Of the 19 NATO members, only the Czech Republic, Iceland, Poland, and Turkey are not members of all five supplier groups. This means that 15 of the 23 states that belong to all five groups are members of NATO. The 8 states that are not NATO members—Argentina, Australia, Austria, Finland, Ireland, Japan, Sweden, and Switzerland—are not far removed. Perhaps an even more telling statistic is that 28 of the 36 states that belong to one or more of the supplier groups are members of the Organization for Economic Cooperation and Development (OECD)—generally recognized as comprising the world's leading industrialized states, that is "the North"—as are 22 of the 23 of those belonging to all five groups (Argentina is the exception). Finally, only Mexico is a member of the OECD and not a member of any of the five supplier groups.

It might be supposed that this set of memberships merely reflects who can produce and export the goods in question, but even a cursory examination undermines any such explanation. For instance, in 1997 26 states reported exporting weapons to the UN Register of Conventional Arms. These are necessarily major weapons systems and would fall under the terms of the Wassenaar Arrangement. Yet 4 of the 26 reporting states were not members of that group, and what is more, 10 of the 33 members of a so-called supplier group did not report supplying.[23] Furthermore, North Korea, Israel, and India, not to mention Iraq, are capable of exporting—and in some cases have exported—missile technology that falls within the guidelines of the MTCR, but they are not wooed to membership.[24] As for chemical and biological weapons technologies, they are so widespread that very few states could not export something covered by the Australia Group's lists if they chose to do so.

Supplying a military technology is, it would seem, insufficient grounds to cause a state to be constructed as supplier by the practices of proliferation control. On the other hand, recipients are far from being only those outside the supplier groups. Taking the 1997 UN Register declarations again, 21 of the 33 members of the Wassenaar Arrangement imported major weapons, including the United States—which is also far and away the market leader in military exports. The membership of these various groups suggests instead that the supplier-recipient construction of the practices of proliferation control is a reproduction of the division between the northern core and the southern periphery. Only 9 of the 36 states in Table 5.1 are not European—and those include Canada, the United States, Australia, and New Zealand. Perhaps the most telling way to characterize the "in" group is that of the 36 states, only Argentina, Brazil, and South Africa are not either members of the OECD or former Communist European states.

The acts of identification that enable the practice of supplier control and that the practice reproduces must be seen as active constructions rather than passive reflections. There are not suppliers out there that can then be gathered together for the purpose of cooperation; rather, there are states actively constructed as suppliers through their engagement in supplier

Table 5.1 Membership of Supplier Groups and OECD

	Supplier Groups					
	Zangger Committee	NSG	MTCR	Australia Group	Wassenaar	OECD
ARGENTINA	x	x	x	x	x	—
AUSTRALIA	x	x	x	x	x	x
AUSTRIA	x	x	x	x	x	x
BELGIUM	x	x	x	x	x	x
Bulgaria	x	x	—	—	x	—
Brazil	—	x	x	—	—	—
CANADA	x	x	x	x	x	x
Czech Republic	x	x	—	x	x	x
DENMARK	x	x	x	x	x	x
FINLAND	x	x	x	x	x	x
FRANCE	x	x	x	x	x	x
GERMANY	x	x	x	x	x	x
GREECE	x	x	x	x	x	x
HUNGARY	x	x	x	x	x	x
Iceland	—	—	x	x	—	x
IRELAND	x	x	x	x	x	x
ITALY	x	x	x	x	x	x
JAPAN	x	x	x	x	x	x
Korea (Republic of)	x	x	—	x	x	x
LUXEMBOURG	x	x	x	x	x	x
NETHERLANDS	x	x	x	x	x	x
New Zealand	—	x	x	x	x	x
NORWAY	x	x	x	x	x	x
Poland	x	x	—	x	x	x
PORTUGAL	x	x	x	x	x	x
Romania	x	x	—	x	x	—
Russia	x	x	x	—	x	—
Slovak Republic	x	x	—	x	x	—
South Africa	x	x	x	—	—	—
SPAIN	x	x	x	x	x	x
SWEDEN	x	x	x	x	x	x
SWITZERLAND	x	x	x	x	x	x
Turkey	—	—	x	—	x	x
Ukraine	—	x	—	—	x	—
UNITED KINGDOM	x	x	x	x	x	x
UNITED STATES	x	x	x	x	x	x
Total (36)	31	34	29	30	33	28[a]

Notes: The names of states that are members of all five supplier groups appear in capital letters.

a. Mexico is also a member of the OECD but not of any supplier group.

groups. The incorporation of the former Communist states of Eastern Europe into the groups, particularly the Wassenaar Arrangement, exemplifies this active construction.

Wassenaar grew from COCOM, a Western organization of the Cold War that served to deny Eastern bloc states access to Western technology.

The collapse of communism in Eastern Europe was followed by moves to incorporate the former Eastern bloc states into the Western capitalist economy and by the reconstitution of the security agenda within the "proliferation" frame. Eastern European states became both candidates for inclusion in the inside of the West and potential suppliers—despite having exported military technology throughout the Cold War. COCOM was recognized as both inadequate for the new task—its targets were precisely the states now to be redefined as insiders—and the only basis for a conventional proliferation supplier group. This contradictory origin of the new arrangement is reflected in the rather odd language in which the Wassenaar Arrangement was announced: "The Czech Republic, Hungary, Poland, the Russian Federation and the Slovak Republic *were welcomed as new participants and co-founders* by Australia, Austria, Belgium, Canada, Denmark, Finland, France, Germany, Greece, Ireland, Italy, Japan, Luxembourg, the Netherlands, New Zealand, Norway, Portugal, Spain, Sweden, Switzerland, Turkey, the United Kingdom and the United States."[25] One group of states *welcomed* another group as *new participants* while at the same time hailing them as *cofounders* of what was billed a "new export control arrangement." The group being welcomed consisted of the former Eastern bloc states, founding a new arrangement with what we can only surmise are old participants in a new group. The connection to COCOM was also very practical, as two of the three COCOM lists were adopted by the "new" arrangement as the basis for its controls.

The problem faced by the new participants and cofounders on joining the new arrangement was that they had no apparatus in place to carry out their obligations to implement national export controls. Canada, for example, responded to this problem in practical fashion—it invited customs officials from the former Eastern bloc countries to seminars in Canada to be trained by experienced Canadian officials in how to implement export controls. Applying export controls is one of the acts engaged in by those whose identity includes supplier. The former Eastern bloc states were now to be identified as suppliers and thus needed to be able to engage in the appropriate practices. Just as all societies educate their new members into the practices appropriate for the roles in which those members are identified— be they gender, class, or other identities—so, too, the extant members of the suppliers club educated their new members on the way to perform the tasks their new identity demanded.

States Behaving Badly

At its 1992 Summit, the UN Security Council determined that the proliferation of weapons was a threat to international peace and security. There are two indications in the council's communiqué of what makes proliferation a threat: first, that the accumulation of (conventional) arms should not be excessive and, second, that the spread of arms should not disrupt regional or global stability.[26] By characterizing the threatening effects of proliferation as those that disrupt stability, the proliferation image constitutes the space for the sort of state behavior that will cause serious concern for the guardians of international probity. It begins, in other words, to produce important subject positions within the "proliferation" image.

The work of Michel Foucault increasingly defines the way in which we think about the constitution of the subject in modern society. Throughout his work, Foucault examines ways in which discourses of normality establish the confines in which the subject may operate. Normal behavior is defined largely through identification of the forms of abnormality that constitute its limits, which, in turn, are rigidly policed. The proliferation discourse defines normality in terms of regional and global stability, and hence abnormality (or behavior that causes serious concern) in terms of threats to or disruptions of that stability. It is a constitution of the normal international subject policed by the UN Security Council and by the advanced industrial states through their export control regimes.

One notable feature of Foucault's accounts of the constitution of the modern subject is the complicity of various academic disciplines in defining the contours of the normal.[27] The idea of stability as the normal condition in international life also reveals academic complicity, having been produced and reproduced by the discipline of international relations. As I argue in Chapter 3, a particular characterization of balance has been defined in the practice of international relations scholarship largely with reference to the relationship among the Soviet Union, the United States, and the world order during the Cold War. This understanding of balance, particularly of balance of power, in turn, gives rise to stability as the normal condition of international life. Balances need to be maintained; instabilities upset these balances and produce disorder. By extension, those states that act to upset stable balances can be labeled in some way deviant.

I argue in Chapter 3 that the most important implication of framing security problems in terms of a balance that needs to remain stable is that it highlights dyadic relationships. During the Cold War the dyadic understandings of balance were reasonably appropriate to the superpower confrontation, as two roughly equivalent superpowers were anchoring two roughly equivalent alliances. Even then, however, the image downplays and hides those outside the central balance, rendering non-European states and regions either as invisible or as mere appendages to the superpower confrontation. To imagine third parties as autonomous would be to introduce problematic third- and higher-order masses into the metaphorical balance. The regional security systems that today are of greatest "proliferation" concern to those, mainly in the North and West, who use the image, however, simply do not resolve themselves into dyads. They are not dominated by the confrontation of two overpowering opponents; nor do they divide into two allied groupings. Nevertheless, the metaphor of balance leads to the characterization of these regions in dyadic terms.

In the Middle East, for example, the relationships among the various states are complex, yet even accounting for these varied relations misses the sub- and transnational dimensions of the politics of Middle Eastern security. For instance, the place of the Kurds in Iraq and their relationships to the Kurds in both Iran and Turkey are important elements of security relations in the eastern Middle East—and have been centrally involved in both Gulf wars since 1980.[28] Similarly, the Israeli relationship with the Palestinians involves complex relations among Palestinians living in Israel, Jews living in Palestine, Palestinians in neighboring countries, and those countries' states, not to mention the importance of the Jewish and Palestinian diaspora communities. Despite this complexity, the potency of the dyadic entailment is such that it shapes discussions of the region. The most prevalent dyadic construction is that which characterizes the region's complexities as "the Arab-Israeli conflict." Yet the two most recent wars in the region involved Iraq, an Arab state, fighting Iran, another Muslim (though not Arab) state, and a broad coalition destroying the Arabic Iraq—a coalition that included both Arabs and, to all intents and purposes, Israel.

The same problems arise in other regions of concern. In the North Pacific, although the relationship between North and South Korea is of central importance, the security dynamic cannot be understood outside the context of the relationships among those two states and the PRC, Japan, and the United States, at the least. These five countries do not break into two neat groupings, and yet the dyadic "North against South" representation of the problem is common. South Asia is, at its most simple, an intricate dance among India, Pakistan, and the PRC—a construction that hides the Kashmiris, Tamils, and Sri Lanka and downplays a complex mosaic of religious identity.[29] Despite the centrality of the triad of powers, there is a strong tendency to speak of the region in terms of the dyadic Indo-Pakistani relationship. Indeed, this tendency can be seen in part to have resulted in the growth of India's arsenal:

> The Indian military buildup may also be explained by the various decision-makers' political image of the state in international society. One of the problems with Indian leaders and policy-makers since the death of Prime Minister Jawaharal Nehru in 1964, is the feeling that India does not get enough respect, especially compared to China, with which it sees itself as essentially equal in size, population and economic development. Instead, India is constantly equated with Pakistan, a nation at one time one-fifth its size in population and capabilities, and only one-eighth its size since the creation of Bangladesh in December 1971.[30]

The problematic nature of the dyadic construction of South Asia was starkly revealed by the reaction to India's surprise nuclear tests in May 1998. The first point to notice is the remarkably widespread initial domestic support for the tests, largely, it would appear, because testing was seen to establish India as a major power and not comparable to its neighbor Pakistan. Internationally, the tests were considered to have potential ramifications well beyond Pakistan. Although the immediate concern was to prevent or perhaps limit Pakistani testing in response, fears about a much wider set of implications were rapidly articulated. The possible reactions of the PRC were at the forefront of this concern, but more interesting was the recognition that Pakistan bordered Iran—another potential nuclear proliferation problem. Iran, however, is generally imagined as part of the Middle East, not of South Asia. Only with the imminent possibility of a declared nuclear Pakistan did it "suddenly dawn" on the West that its neat packaging of the world into regions with an essentially dyadic structure might not accord with local imaginaries or practices.

By imagining the security context into which weapons flow as a result of proliferation in terms of stable balances, the "proliferation" image constructs recipients as members of regional dyads. The image produces the states as regional or local powers, analogous to the superpowers of the global Cold War balance. In doing so, it draws upon the bulk of the English-speaking canon of international relations scholarship, which has developed this conceptual language as used in the production of the Cold War. This image therefore produces a space for the "abnormal," for the state that seeks to alter the balance, to introduce instability. Normality is defined in the proliferation discourse in a profoundly conservative fashion—a conclusion that should not be surprising, given the makeup of the supplier groups policing this vision of the normal and the role of privileged scholars in producing it.[31] This account begs the question of who fills the position the image creates. How are subjects identified when they step beyond the bounds of the acceptable and exhibit behavior that causes serious concerns to the OECD?

Rogues, Outlaws, and Weapon States

In the early 1990s the United States faced a simple but profound policy problem: how to define a role for itself with the end of the Cold War and the collapse of the USSR. Indeed, it was this problem that led Charles Krauthammer to forecast a unipolar world and warn of the dangers of the weapon state.[32] Although this problem is far-reaching, it posed a very clear and particular challenge to the leaders of the U.S. military. The leaders recognized that the end of the Cold War put their funding under tremendous pressure, as it became increasingly difficult to justify continued military spending at the level to which they had become accustomed. In 1990 the military budget had been criticized by the chair of the Senate Armed Services Committee because of a "threat blank"—a lack of any credible argument as to what was threatening this expensively maintained military power.[33]

Michael Klare has examined the military's response to this threat blank, and his findings are fascinating. First, he reports that the Chairman of the Joint Chiefs of Staff, Colin Powell, ordered a new overarching military posture to guide the U.S. military without the lodestone of a Soviet enemy:

> General Powell's formal instructions to the Joint Staff have never been made public. One point, however, remains certain: his insistence that the United States remain a global superpower, whatever military posture was ultimately devised. . . . According to Powell, this would require the maintenance of a powerful, high-tech military establishment equipped with a full range of modern combat systems. Although this establishment might prove smaller than that fielded during the peak years of the Cold War era, it must, he insisted, be similar to it in its basic structure and capabilities.[34]

To maintain a military force essentially equivalent to that of the Cold War in the face of budgetary pressures, Powell needed to fill the threat blank. Essentially, the general's requirements were the same as Krauthammer's— find an enemy that will justify superpower military status, understood as it was in the Cold War, without the Cold War enemy. The solution he came to was the same as well. As Klare reports, "Out of this process came what might best be termed the Rogue Doctrine—the characterization of hostile (or seemingly hostile) Third World states with large military forces and nascent WMD capabilities as 'rogue states' or 'nuclear outlaws' bent on sabotaging the prevailing world order."[35] Conveniently, on the day U.S. President Bush announced the new posture based on the Rogue Doctrine, Iraq invaded Kuwait.[36]

Iraq was thus established as the paradigm rogue. It was a sizable Third World state with a substantial military. Iraq had long been on the short list of states thought to be seeking a nuclear capability, and it was also thought to be producing chemical weapons to go with the ballistic missiles it was known to have. To complete the picture, Iraq was clearly bent on regional destabilization, as it had enlarged itself militarily. The U.S. military could point to Iraq to show that the threat against which it wished to maintain a readiness was "real." As the U.S. secretary of defense told the House Armed Services Committee soon after the end of Desert Storm: "Iraq's forces were considerable, but not entirely unique. There are other regional powers with modern armed forces, sophisticated attack aircraft and integrated air defenses."[37] The watchword became preparation to defend against other Iraqs.

The U.S. military appears to have been central in the construction of a new category of threat, the rogue state governed by an outlaw regime. The timing of that construction was unfortunate for Iraq. As has been widely reported, U.S. Ambassador to Iraq April Glaspie met the Iraqi leadership a few days before the invasion of Kuwait. The message of that meeting seems to have been that the United States was not overly concerned with Iraq's border dispute with Kuwait. Even if the meeting could not be read as a tacit approval of the invasion (and it is not impossible to read it that way), it did not indicate the sort of response the United States mounted after 2 August.[38] The problem is that the Rogue Doctrine was a construction of the military and had not yet been formally announced. It is reasonable to assume that a diplomat in a relatively minor posting would not be aware of the reworking of U.S. military doctrine the president was about to announce. There is, of course, a much more cynical interpretation of these events, which would argue that the United States sought a convenient illustration of its newfound enemy. Either way, in July 1990 there were no rogue states because the category had not been articulated. In July 1990, as Glaspie met Hussein, Iraq was a regional power that had been employed by both superpowers during the Cold War and that had a not unreasonable grievance with one of its neighbors. On 2 August President Bush announced a new category, a new set of markers by which the identity of states could be interpreted. On 2 August Iraq acted in a fashion that fit this contemporaneously articulated set of markers.

Other Iraqs, rogues, and outlaws are now the currency of the international discourse of proliferation that grew out of the Western response to the Gulf War. These are the labels, drawn from the debate in the United States, applied to states whose behavior causes serious concern to the Western powers in their supplier groups. What sort of labels are they? What lines of difference do these labels establish? To answer these questions, we can look at rogues and outlaws as metaphors that link the proliferation image to other, more widespread discourses and discover the entailments they draw from these discourses. Rogues and outlaws are used similarly in everyday language. A rogue is defined by the *Oxford English Dictionary* as: "1. One belonging to a class of idle vagrants or vagabonds. . . . 2. A dishonest, unprincipled person; a rascal. . . . 5. An elephant driven away, or living apart from, the herd and of a savage or destructive disposition." Similarly, an outlaw is "one put outside the law and deprived of its benefits and protection. . . . More vaguely: One banished or proscribed; an exile, a fugitive."

Both *rogues* and *outlaws* are used in everyday language to identify criminals, although generally not the worst and most hardened criminals. Indeed, a certain romanticism is attached to both the rogue and the outlaw. The rogue is one who steps outside the limits of acceptable behavior but in a way that tends to be appealing to those who do not dare to commit such transgressions—thus, for example, the definition of rogue as rascal. Similarly, the outlaw is a common figure in U.S. romantic Western literature. Outlaws roamed the frontiers of the central United States, at once dangerous and admired for the rugged individualism they portrayed. Little of this romanticism seems to remain in the use of rogues in official discourse, however. U.S. Secretary of State Warren Christopher did not seem to admire the rugged individualism of potential rogues, for instance, when he told the Senate Foreign Relations Committee that "nuclear weapons give rogue states disproportionate power, destabilize entire regions, and threaten human and environmental disasters. They can turn local conflicts into serious threats to our security. In this era, weapons of mass destruction are more readily available—and there are fewer inhibitions on their use."[39]

Nevertheless, the use of rogue carries with it marked condescension. Rogues are, as often as not, young men, indeed even little boys, who are acting naughtily—in the former case often in a sexual manner. One of the many ironies that emerge in stories of proliferation is that at the same time the primary international rogue, Iraq, was under intense U.S. pressure because of its refusal to allow UNSCOM unfettered access to its presidential palaces, the U.S. president was being labeled a rogue for reports that he had perhaps allowed too much access to presidential parts. "Some of the President's intimates note his remarkable ability to compartmentalize his life: The policy wonk who genuinely admires his wife resides in one space; the rogue who risks political standing through personal indiscretion occupies another."[40] Put another way, the mature adult resides on the one side and the rather indiscreet little boy on the other.

The use of rogue to label states behaving in ways deemed unacceptable identifies those states as immature compared with the mature states doing the labeling—foremost among these the United States. Such an entailment fits well with the practices established for proliferation control. The mature elders gather together to determine which states are sufficiently responsible to be trusted with advanced technologies and military equipment—indeed, the practice smacks of Star Trek's Prime Directive. This notion of maturity is then reflected in academic commentary on contemporary security, as Charles Krauthammer's characterization of the weapon state threat illustrates: "relatively small, *peripheral and backward* states will be able to emerge rapidly as threats not only to regional, but to world, security."[41] Similarly, a repeated concern in the literature has been that new nuclear states would lack the maturity to control their weapons adequately, unlike the old nuclear states.[42]

Perhaps the most interesting definition of *rogue* and *outlaw* is the one they share: both terms are used to describe members of a community expelled from that community or no longer living within the constraints of communal life. In medieval Europe the outlaw was outcast, placed beyond the protection the law provided as punishment. Later, the outlaw in the mythology of the American West fled from life within the community to escape the (often rough) justice of the frontier. Similarly, the rogue animal is one that has been forced from the herd or that for some reason has left the herd. Evoking these terms in the proliferation discourse clearly marks the logic of identity and difference, of inside and outside, which were evident in the practices examined earlier. For there to be rogues and outlaws there must also be a larger, settled community whose rules the outlaws refuse to follow.

It would seem that the U.S. military's concern with defending its budget following the Cold War threw up a powerful new marker of identity/difference for the contemporary practice of international security. The idea of the rogue state has achieved wide currency in popular discussion of international affairs. Klare cites a U.S. Congress study to the effect that in major newspapers and journals, the use of *rogue nation, rogue state,* and *rogue regime* increased more than 1,500 percent between 1990 and 1993.[43] The label originally devised to categorize potential military opponents was quickly drawn into the construction of the new proliferation control agenda following the Gulf War, as Iraq was identified as the first of the rogues. The notion of the rogue state provides agency in an image of an international security problem largely devoid of agency. The term is used to label states whose behavior causes serious concern to the members of the supplier groups, identifying them as outsiders, immature states unable or unwilling to follow the rules of civilized state action—rules policed by that same core of supplier states.

Conclusion

Iraq is presently singled out as the preeminent villain of the proliferation discourse, identified as the paradigmatic rogue state. According to the conventional account, this rogue state sought the disproportionate power weapons of mass destruction provide to rogues. Iraq had built an excessive and destabilizing arsenal of conventional weapons throughout the 1980s and was bent on using its conventional and unconventional arsenal to establish itself as the preeminent power in its region. On 2 August 1990, this rogue showed its true colors by invading its southern neighbor. This attempt to augment further its power, by capturing both Kuwait's oil reserves and its access to the Gulf, was designed to upset the balance of power in the region in Iraq's favor. The response of the coalition forces marked the strength of the international community's commitment to respond to states that placed themselves outside that community in such a fashion—by acting as rogues.

Iraq, however, did not "suddenly emerge" as a heavily armed state; nor were its designs on regional hegemony any great secret. In 1980 it had invaded Iran and fought a long war that, in part, resulted in the arsenal it had accumulated by 1990. In this instance those states that have subsequently gathered themselves into supplier groups to sit in judgment of others, ever alert for behavior that causes them concern, without question acted as suppliers. These same states supplied Iraq with the military technology—and even nuclear technology—it needed to build the arsenal that caused such concern. The invasion of Iran did not seem to mark Iraq for particular condemnation in 1980, and it seems the U.S. ambassador suggested to the Iraqi leadership that neither would an invasion of Kuwait in 1990. The categories through which state action was interpreted, however, had changed by 2 August 1990. In the 1980s the Iraqi actions were interpreted within a Cold War frame that read regional conflicts as subordinate to the central confrontation and identified regional powers as clients of one or the other superpower (or, for the skillful few like Iraq, of both). On 2 August 1990 U.S. President Bush announced a new interpretive frame, one that defined what Iraq was in the process of doing as the action of a rogue—the new enemy of the post–Cold War world.

In a sense, then, Iraq did emerge suddenly as a rogue in August 1990. Suddenly there was a new way of categorizing certain states' actions, so Iraqi behavior suddenly became that of the rogue. To show how great a threat was rogue behavior, the United States mounted a massive response to the Iraqi invasion. Given the size of that response, the threat must have been supreme; thus by mounting such a large response the United States warranted the practices that followed—signaling the severity of the issue through the UN Security Council Summit in 1992. The "proliferation" image that was developed, and the practices that have instantiated that image, fill in the context in which rogues become the threat. Rogues and outlaws serve as markers of difference; they label the outsider against whom the insider is known. The insider is the state that follows the rules, that runs with the herd and is law-abiding. If we combine this labeling with the construction of identities in the practices of control and the identification of the security problems proliferation causes, we get a clear picture of the set of identities constituted by the "proliferation" discourse.

The central practices of supplier groups and their attendant export controls construct a core set of inside states, those sufficiently responsible and mature to take it upon themselves to judge the behavior of other states and sanction them for troubling activities. That set overlaps notably with the club of advanced industrial states of the North. There is also a clear move from within this privileged group to draw in the old East and to reconstruct (or rebuild, as efforts at transition are often called) those countries as part of that inside. Outside this privileged core states are gathered into regions, each of which is expected to remain stable through the balancing of power. Proliferation, that autonomous process the image constructs, can upset these balances—nuclear weapons give certain states disproportionate power and thus destabilize entire regions; even conventional arms can be acquired in sufficient quantities to be excessive and destabilizing. If states act in such a way that they upset or threaten to upset these balances, they are rogues, outlaws, immature or backward states unwilling to conform to the rules of civilized behavior.

The proliferation image creates two clear lines of difference. The first marks the distinction between those who can be trusted to make the rules—signaled by inclusion in the ranks of suppliers—and those who must follow the rules—the recipients. The second line marks those who do follow the rules from those who refuse—the rogues from the herd, the outlaws from the law-abiding. This second line marks the emergence of an enemy in this discourse of military security, for it is rogue behavior that poses a threat, that causes concern to those who make the rules. Thus the recipients are accepted as part of the community of the law-abiding and thus have access to prized technology the suppliers can provide. The recipients, however, are also potential rogues. Their behavior must be policed through export control and compliance monitoring to ensure that they conform to the rules and do not become rogues. This policing gives in to the temptation of othering difference Connolly discussed. Not only are those not included in the supplier groups to be marked as different, but they are to be labeled as potential enemies and sanctioned as such.

The proliferation image constructs states in the Third World as outsiders. Even if they do not become rogues, they are not permitted inside the privileged Northern club; if they do behave in ways that cause concern to the privileged, they are labeled *enemy* and heavily sanctioned. Not surprisingly, not all Third World states are entirely happy with the "proliferation" construction. Iran, for example, finds itself abiding by the rules of NPT membership, rules that are supposed to guarantee its access to nuclear technology for peaceful purposes. Nevertheless, its behavior—in this case, the domestic politics of government—causes concern among members of the supplier groups, and so it is sanctioned. India has established itself as the preeminent critic of the proliferation discourse in the Third World. India does not accept the problem as it has been constructed by the insiders, and it does not accept the practices to which the construction has given rise. In Chapter 6 I examine the alternative framings produced in this resistance and elsewhere to see the possible objects and identities hidden by the "proliferation" image that could serve as a basis for political opposition to that image.

6

Contesting Proliferation

The nuclear nonproliferation treaty is the linchpin of the new agenda to control proliferation. The NPT and the control regime that has grown around it have served as the bases for developing comparable regimes to control the proliferation of nonnuclear technologies. As this was happening, however, the NPT was threatened by a time bomb planted by its original authors. Article X.2 of the NPT set a time limit on the treaty: "Twenty-five years after the entry into force of the Treaty, a conference shall be convened to decide whether the Treaty shall continue in force indefinitely, or shall be extended for an additional fixed period or periods. This decision shall be taken by a majority of the Parties to the Treaty."[1] The NPT had entered into force in 1970, so a conference was called in New York for April 1995 to consider options for the future. One interesting feature of this article is that under its terms the treaty *had* to be extended; the only issues were the nature and duration of that extension.

The states driving the reformulation of international security around the "proliferation" image, led by the United States, began arguing for an indefinite extension of the NPT. Only indefinite extension, they argued, would provide the solid endorsement of the nonproliferation ideal necessary for building the broader regime of proliferation control efforts. As Brad Roberts, a leading proliferation commentator, put it:

> If the NPT is given only weak endorsement in April, the CWC languishes, and the BWC remains devoid of compliance mechanisms, the next decade may well witness a broad diffusion of these weapons, a redistribution of power away from the advanced industrial countries highly interested in stability, and outbreaks of the regional instabilities associated with conventional and unconventional arms races. . . . If the April 1995 conference is bungled, the CWC and BWC will also suffer.[2]

Anything less than the indefinite extension of the NPT would represent the weak endorsement Roberts feared. His defense of that option, however,

99

also indicates at least one reason some members of the NPT might be interested in indefinite extension than he had hoped. Weak endorsement might result, he argued, in "a redistribution of power away from the advanced industrial countries," and so, by extension, a strong endorsement would not result in such a redistribution of power. Given that the NPT has always been criticized for its unique inequality, to argue that it is required to maintain that inequality is, to say the least, an odd strategic choice in the context of an extension debate whose outcome was uncertain.

Opposition to the indefinite extension option coalesced around the question of inequality in general and the NWSs' commitment to eradicate it under the terms of the NPT in particular. Article VI of the NPT reads: "Each of the Parties to the Treaty undertakes to pursue negotiations in good faith on effective measures relating to cessation of the nuclear arms race at an early date and to nuclear disarmament, and on a Treaty on general and complete disarmament under strict and effective international control."[3] Complete fulfillment of the terms of Article VI is clearly difficult. General and complete disarmament is unlikely to happen quickly, and even twenty-five years is too short a time to expect its achievement. Twenty-five years is not too short a time, however, to expect "negotiations in good faith on effective measures relating to cessation of the nuclear arms race at an early date and to nuclear disarmament" and perhaps even complete nuclear disarmament under effective international control. Such a result would eliminate the fundamental inequality at the heart of the NPT and make it much more acceptable to the NNWSs.

The issue of Article VI had been raised repeatedly at the review conferences held every five years over the twenty-five years of the NPT. One measure in particular emerged as the talisman of the good faith promised by the NWSs: the completion of a comprehensive test ban treaty (CTBT).[4] The preamble to the NPT had specifically linked the achievement of a CTBT to the end of the arms race and nuclear disarmament, and the first review conference had reiterated the call for a CTBT. Ten years later, the third conference "recalled that in the Final Declaration of the First Review Conference, the parties expressed the view that the conclusion of a treaty banning all nuclear-weapon tests was one of the most important measures to halt the nuclear arms race and expressed the hope that the nuclear-weapon States party to the Treaty would take the lead in reaching an early solution of the technical and political difficulties of this issue."[5] Ten years later, in 1995, the Review and Extension Conference was called. It does not seem unreasonable to expect, as a minimum show of good faith, that a CTBT would have been achieved.

The CTBT was not achieved by the April 1995 Review and Extension Conference, although it was under negotiation in the Conference on Disarmament. On 25 January 1994 the CD passed a mandate establishing an ad hoc committee to negotiate a CTBT; this was the first time the CD had become involved in formal negotiations over the CTBT and was the first time since 1980 that any negotiations had been held on the issue.[6] The U.S. Congress imposed a moratorium on U.S. testing, and President Clinton endorsed the CTBT and called for a treaty to be completed for signing by September 1996 when the congressional moratorium expired. Although the United States resisted any formal linkage between the CTBT negotiations and the impending Review and Extension Conference, such linkage was hard to miss. Indeed, the director of the U.S. Arms Control and Disarmament Agency acknowledged that the CTBT would be an important demonstration of the commitment of NWSs to fulfill their Article VI obligations under the NPT.[7]

Let me recap. In 1968 the nuclear-armed states committed themselves to achieve a comprehensive test ban treaty in the preamble to the nuclear nonproliferation treaty. (This commitment was, in fact, a reiteration of an earlier commitment made in the 1963 limited test ban treaty.) Article VI of the NPT obliged the states party to stop the nuclear arms race at an early date and to work toward nuclear disarmament, a commitment that was the key to enabling the central inequality of the NPT. The CTBT, in turn, was an important part of the Article VI commitment. The importance of the CTBT was reiterated at the first and third review conferences of the NPT, but by January 1994—more than 30 years after the commitment in the limited test ban treaty—not only was there no CTBT but there had been no negotiations for almost 15 years. In January 1994, 15 months before a conference to determine the future of the NPT, the CD opened negotiations on a CTBT, and the U.S. president soon called for it to be completed by September 1996—which it was. Is it possible that the prospect for defeat of the indefinite extension of the NPT at the Review and Extension Conference spurred this rather dramatic change in the fortune of the CTBT?

It seems patently obvious that this was, in fact, the case, and it seemed equally obvious to a number of the leading members of the nonaligned movement who were less committed than the United States and its supporters to the idea of an indefinite extension of the treaty enshrining the North's monopoly on nuclear weapons. Not unreasonably, they argued that, if the prospect of losing the NPT was the only thing that had spurred the United States into action on a CTBT, then the only way to ensure continued progress on Article VI of the NPT was to institutionalize that pressure. An indefinite extension of the NPT, they reasoned, would remove the leverage that had so spectacularly produced real movement on the CTBT. This line of argument led to the proposal of a number of forms of extension other than the indefinite extension favored by the North. The details of these proposals were organized around the various interpretations of what might be meant by "extended for an additional fixed period or periods."[8] The principle of the proposals, however, was the same: deny the nuclear weapon states an indefinite extension so the possibility of the NPT's lapsing could be used as a lever for progress on disarmament.

Although the debate over the form of the extension and the relationship of the extension decision to progress on the CTBT obviously constituted a political disagreement, it also represents two different framings of the problem the NPT would address following the 1995 extension conference. For proponents of indefinite extension the NPT was a tool of nonproliferation and the linchpin, as Roberts put it, of the full range of control measures designed to stop weapons proliferation of all kinds. As such, indefinite extension was required to provide a permanent bulwark against the continuing threat of proliferation. The proponents of some alternatives saw the treaty in a rather different way. The nonaligned states, for example, put forward a series of proposals in September 1994. They argued that the NPT was ultimately a means to disarmament, but at the same time they valued its role in preventing nuclear nonproliferation *as part of* this broader project. The states proposed to use the 1995 conference as a means to promote the disarmament project.[9]

The key point I wish to draw from this discussion of the NPT extension debate is that even at the heart of the new proliferation agenda the "proliferation" image was neither automatic nor uncontested. In this chapter I examine the contestation of the "proliferation" image from two perspectives. The first is the rejection by some, particularly in the Third World, of the "proliferation" image and the alternative possibilities around which this rejection has been organized. The second perspective is that of alternatives to "proliferation" and the Rogue Doctrine in the North—the other ways security has been and could have been constituted to see how the problems gathered as "proliferation" could be framed. In both cases I concentrate on the way in which the alternative framings construct their objects and the identities of states and others in relation to these objects.

Contesting Proliferation

India has emerged as a leading critic of the "proliferation" image as articulated by the United States and its allies. As it is not a party to the NPT, India was not involved in the extension decision. Nevertheless, India made no secret of its opposition to indefinite extension:

> It would be futile to pretend that 1995 is 1970, that nothing has changed and nothing requires to be changed in the 1995 NPT. It would be a cruel joke on the coming generation to say that they will be safer with an

indefinite extension of the 1970 NPT. 1995 presents an opportunity; there is great scope for non-governmental agencies, intellectuals and academics, who believe in nuclear disarmament to work towards changing this mindset and spur governments in nuclear weapon countries to look at reality, to accept that there are shortcomings in the NPT and that nations, both within and outside the NPT, have genuine concerns which need to be addressed in order to make the NPT universal, non-discriminatory and a true instrument for nuclear disarmament.[10]

This formulation, delivered by a former Indian ambassador to the CD in 1993, prefigures the arguments of the nonaligned states in September 1994. Both note that there are shortcomings to the NPT, that the extension conference represents an exceptional opportunity to reverse those shortcomings, and that the NPT should become an instrument for disarmament.

What is particularly significant about the Indian ambassador's critique is the recognition that the problem rests in the *mind-set* of states. The ambassador recognizes, in other words, that the proliferation problem is not an objective problem but the product of a mind-set. The point of this book is to explore the way this mind-set has come about and to ask about its effects and the alternatives that were and are possible. One of the effects of this mind-set—or, more properly, the discursive construction of the "proliferation" problem and its instantiation in practices such as the indefinite extension of the NPT—has been to marginalize and alienate the second most populous country in the world. Ironically, in a time in which the promotion of liberal democracy has been argued as the road to global peace and prosperity, the effect has been to marginalize the most populous liberal democracy. In terms of the proliferation control agenda, the myopia of marginalizing India became glaringly apparent in 1998, when India chose to test a series of nuclear weapons. If this security agenda and its effects rest contingently on a discursive construction of a problem, however, then it is open to alternative framings. The nonaligned proposals accepted "the important role of the Treaty in the maintenance of international security" but argued, with the Indians, that the security problem should be framed as one of "disarmament."[11]

Through a Disarmament Frame

The argument that we should see problems of military technology through a "disarmament" frame rather than through the "proliferation" frame is potentially very creative. Such a framing of the problem would not necessarily deny the importance of tackling proliferation—the nonproliferation treaty initially emerged out of a "disarmament" practice, and the nonaligned states' submission to the NPT extension conference recognized the importance of proliferation control as part of a disarmament agenda.[12]

How would a "disarmament" image differ from the "proliferation" image were it to be the basis on which the control of military technology was enabled? What objects would a "disarmament" frame constitute, what identities would it constitute in relation to those objects, and how would they differ from those constituted by "proliferation"?

The first, most obvious, and most important difference is that a "disarmament" framing of the problem of military technology would highlight weapons themselves. The "proliferation" image has constituted as its problem the technologies that give rise to a military capability—up to and including their weaponization. "Proliferation" highlights the technological precursors and downplays, in many instances, the actual weapons. A "disarmament" image would reverse this emphasis, focusing in the first instance on existing rather than potential arsenals. By highlighting the weapons and therefore downplaying the technological precursors, a "disarmament" image would open possibilities for a different relationship between broad technologies and weapons from that warranted by the technologically determinant "proliferation" image.

The difference between the problematic object being constituted in terms of weapons rather than of the technological precursors to those weapons is seen even more clearly when the identities constituted by each frame are considered. The "proliferation" image constitutes states in the first instance, as suppliers or recipients, reflecting their position in the technological flow of concern to proliferation controls. "Disarmament," by contrast, constitutes states in the first instance as armed and would differentiate among states by the degree of arming. Whereas the "proliferation" discourse places the onus on recipients not to translate that technology into weaponry, a "disarmament" image places the onus on armed states to reduce and ultimately eliminate the weaponry they possess.

Suppliers and *recipients* are not the only terms by which states are identified in the "proliferation" image. It is not certain how the construction of regional balances or of rogues would change in a problematic framed in terms of "disarmament" rather than "proliferation," but certain tendencies are worth considering. The first is that a "disarmament" frame would not necessarily construct regions in terms of binary balances—although that is still a clear possibility. A primary identification in terms of relative level of armaments allows for defining regions in terms of that level and differentiating states by the sizes of their arsenals for disarmament practices. Given the way regions were constructed in the Cold War, however, with reference to the superpower balance and the role that "balance" played in superpower arms control and disarmament practices, the regions could be constructed in precisely the same way they are at present.

On the other hand, the rogue state construction would be difficult to establish or maintain within a "disarmament" image. By downplaying potential arsenals relative to existing arsenals, the sorts of exaggerated claims about future threats that sustain the notion of rogues and weapon states would be almost impossible to make. Only in the context of an image that constructs the security problematic in terms of *future* arsenals, of weapons falling into the wrong hands, can rogues or weapon states be elevated to the level of a primary threat. If the security problematic focused on the threat posed by existing arsenals, any possible future arsenal, although still a concern, would be greatly discounted in the present.

Here, then, is both the greatest potential and the greatest problem posed by a "disarmament" frame. With such a different object and set of identities, a "disarmament" image would enable a rather different series of practices. But on the other hand, the politics of instituting those practices would become somewhat more difficult because of the entailments of the "disarmament" image. Although considerable rhetorical support has been expressed for the goal of disarmament from the earliest days of the nuclear age and before, concrete disarmament practices have been difficult to achieve. Part of the problem has been a series of discursive and practical links enabled by the "disarmament" image. The first and perhaps most damaging has been the connection between the language of disarmament and the program of general and complete disarmament. Although many analysts and even policymakers might be willing to concede the value of eliminating some weapons—notice the ability to generate support for bans on land mines and both chemical and biological weapons—and possibly even all nuclear weapons, few are willing to express support for a goal they characterize as hopelessly utopian.[13]

The utopian features of general and complete disarmament gesture toward another politically difficult entailment of "disarmament"—the link between disarmament and weakness. Several unfortunate links are created by the language of "disarmament" that inculcate an entailment of weakness. The first is the characterization of those pressing for general and complete disarmament as pacifist, lefty, or even wimp by those entrusted with the arsenals of, certainly, the United States. The second problematic link is with the practices of the enforced disarmament that follows wars: losers are disarmed, so to disarm is to be a loser. This is not a promising way to generate political support. Finally, arms, in both senses of the word, are intimately tied to concepts of power and masculinity. To be disarmed is to be rendered powerless, to be emasculated. Even if the process of eliminating weapons produces enhanced security, the entailments of powerlessness and emasculation are difficult obstacles to overcome.

Despite the difficulties associated with the language of "disarmament," it is a framing worth exploring more deeply because of the alternate practices it enables. By producing very different objects and identities, "disarmament" warrants similarly different practices—even though some of the instruments would be the same. As the nonaligned states' letter makes clear, framing the problem of military technology in terms of "disarmament" would not, for example, eliminate the need for the NPT. Rather, it would change the balance of obligations within the framework established by that treaty, placing much more emphasis on the requirements of Article VI. The Chemical Weapons Convention provides another example of the difference such an altered framing would produce. The CWC can reasonably be described as a disarmament treaty. It calls on the states party to dismantle any chemical arsenals they may possess in addition to adopting the more obviously "proliferation" control measures, thus establishing controls on the future production of chemical arms. A "disarmament" framing of the problem of chemical weapons could have produced the CWC, just as the "proliferation" framing did—indeed, the CWC had been negotiated for years within a disarmament practice, albeit without success.

A marked difference, however, would exist between the surrounding practices of a CWC framed in terms of "disarmament" and the present practices. The Australia Group's controls on the movement of chemical technology would be unnecessary as a support to a CWC framed as a "disarmament" instrument. This argument was made by states that were not members of the Australia Group but that intended to become party to the CWC when the convention was under negotiation. Iran in particular argued that states party to the CWC should not be subject to Australia Group restrictions and that the supplier group should disband once the CWC was in force. Seen through a "disarmament" frame, this argument makes perfect sense. The problem such a frame constructs is the weapons themselves, a problem the CWC both confronts and subjects to extensive verification procedures. Seen through a "proliferation" frame, however, the Australia Group continues to be necessary, and proposals to disband it are treated with mistrust. The problem "proliferation" constructs is the *movement* of the underlying technology, an issue largely ignored in the CWC's text. Remembering that "proliferation" constructs the relationship between technology and weapons as one of inevitability, that movement always threatens to create future problems regardless of the disarming practices of the CWC. (Indeed, future chemical arming becomes a greater concern in the context of a general chemical disarmament.) What is more, because the focus of the "proliferation" image is on the movement of technology and the inevitability of its weaponization, suggestions to remove supplier controls are interpreted as indicating a desire to arm.

The variation in the relationship between the CWC and the Australia Group seen through the two frames returns us to the most important difference between a "disarmament" and a "proliferation" image: the relationship between weapons and the technology out of which they grow.

"Disarmament" allows for a less restrictive understanding of the relationship between weapons and their underlying technologies than does "proliferation." The nonaligned states' proposals to the NPT extension conference make the case clearly:

> 12. There continues to exist unjustified restrictions and constraints imposed on developing NNWSs regarding full access to nuclear technology for peaceful purposes. Unilaterally enforced restrictive measures, beyond safeguards required under the Treaty, must not be used to prevent peaceful development, especially in the nuclear area, and should be removed.
> 13. The inalienable right of all States Parties to develop the peaceful use of nuclear energy for economic and social development must be reaffirmed by all nuclear and non-nuclear States Parties. It is also essential that free and unimpeded access to technology be guaranteed, without exception, for all States Parties to the Treaty who have concluded relevant safeguards agreements with the IAEA.[14]

The passages make essentially the same case for nuclear technology that Iran made concerning chemical technology: unilaterally enforced restrictive measures—that is, export controls administered by supplier states in consultation with other members of supplier groups—should be removed. In both cases opponents of the export control component of proliferation control practices refer to the use of technology for development. This suggests a rather different framing of the technology underlying weaponry than that of the "proliferation" image, and it is a framing worth examining.

Development as an Alternative Framing

The idea of framing issues of military technology in terms of economic and social development would appear, initially at least, ridiculous. To begin with, military technology is an issue of international *security,* and as important a problem as development may be, it is a problem of a different kind.[15] Perhaps more to the point, military technology—or at least the spending on military technology—is generally considered to contradict economic and social development. This contradiction is most famously phrased as the trade-off between "guns and butter." Neither of these criticisms is telling, however, and the latter may actually prove to be a good reason for framing issues of military technology in terms of development.

One of the most important themes of this book is that there is no way to identify objectively what is and what is not international security. Security, as with proliferation, is a construction of those who speak it.[16] To say that security and development are two different problems is to restate a division that has been constituted in state practice and in international relations theory for the past half century at least, but it is not to make a definitive claim about the "real world." Indeed, the idea of a guns and butter trade-off belies the rigid division that says security and development are different things. If a trade-off exists between military security and economic development, then, to that degree at least, they must be part of the same political problematic.[17] Finally, the "proliferation" image refuses to distinguish absolutely between development and military technology. The whole point of the supplier groups is to control the movement of technology that *could* be used for military purposes, even though the expressed use is civilian.

The relationship of technologies to weaponry on one side and to civilian economic processes on the other is at the heart of much of the objection of those outside the privileged circle of supplier groups to the "proliferation" image. The Indian Department of External Affairs explains its government's position on nuclear energy as follows:

> The principal aim of India's nuclear energy programme is the development and utilisation of nuclear energy for peaceful purposes such as power generation, applications in agriculture, medicine, industry, research and other areas. India is, today, globally acknowledged as one of the countries most advanced in nuclear technology. *The country is self-reliant and excels in the expertise covering the complete nuclear cycle*—from exploration and mining to power generation and waste management.[18]

India has built a nuclear industry "covering the complete nuclear [fuel] cycle." Seen through a "proliferation" frame, this is troubling because it means India will inevitably accumulate the fissile material and expertise necessary for a nuclear weapons program.[19] The development of such a comprehensive program therefore identifies India as a potential threat, a possible rogue in the terms of the "proliferation" image. India's own justification for the policy, however, is rather different:

> The Department of Atomic Energy (DAE), while performing a key role in the scientific and technological scenario of the country, has also been vital to the overall nation-building exercise. The Department has fostered the nuclear technology in the country to a perfect state of self-reliance fulfilling the aims of the planners, marked by overall balanced developments and growth in all the spheres of its activities. The strategy adopted has placed India in an advantageous position to formulate its own energy policy with confidence, matching its energy needs with its natural resources, especially in the context of several restrictive technology control regimes that are being adopted by the developed nations.
>
> This strategy has accorded India the status of a "Developed Nation" amongst the "Developing Nations," a fact made clear by the election of India as the Chairman of the Board of Governors of the International Atomic Energy Agency (IAEA), in September 1994, where it occupies a position as permanent member since its inception.[20]

For India, the construction of a complete fuel cycle is an important element of a nation-building exercise and, as the second paragraph makes clear, a key to its development.

It could well be argued that the Indian case is the wrong one to use to make a point about framing nuclear technology in terms of development rather than proliferation; India tested a nuclear explosive in 1974, conducted a series of explosions it admitted were nuclear weapons tests in 1998, and has refused to sign the NPT or even the CTBT. India has consistently argued that the NPT is discriminatory in permitting some states and not others to hold nuclear weapons. India has declared its willingness to relinquish its nuclear weapons potential as part of a process in which the acknowledged nuclear weapon states do the same. I say more in Chapter 7 about the Indian interest in opposing the proliferation agenda. For the present, the important point is that India's framing of its nuclear energy program in terms of "development" is closely tied to its framing of the problem of (nuclear) weapons in terms of "disarmament."

Nuclear energy is increasingly being rejected as a basis for economic prosperity in the developed world—although on grounds of environmental danger rather than concerns about proliferation. The technologies at the heart of economic dynamism in the contemporary global economy, however, are also those of concern in the "proliferation" agenda. Information processing, communications, petrochemicals, and biotechnology are all leading civilian technology sectors and the bases for conventional and unconventional weapons. In fact, the category of *advanced* conventional weapons, which has been of particular concern in the proliferation agenda, is created by marrying sophisticated information processing technology to conventional arms. Therefore, even if nuclear energy were to be removed from a "development" frame because of its potential hazards, military technology could not be neatly isolated from the technologies that are central to economic and social development.

The importance of the attempted reframing of issues of "proliferation" in terms of "disarmament" is to allow for the dissociation of arms from their underlying technology. By constructing the problem as one of armament, "disarmament" enables technology to be imagined differently than in "proliferation's" notions of the inevitability of technological development giving rise to weaponization. The irony is that by constructing the problem in terms of the inevitability of the spread of technology and the weaponry derived from it, "proliferation" misses one of the key moments of weapons development on which effective controls could be placed. Weaponization is far from automatic. In the case of weapons of mass destruction, the most technically demanding part of the process is the creation of *usable weapons* from the underlying technologies of concern—Iraq may have enough VX nerve agent to kill millions, but this does not mean it has a reliable system of delivery. Similarly, it is not tremendously difficult for a state with reasonable access to resources to build a nuclear *explosive,* but it is much more difficult to build a militarily effective nuclear *weapon.* The practices of proliferation control, however, miss this crucial step entirely. Supplier groups and export controls target the movement of underlying technologies. IAEA safeguards monitor the movement of fissile material to ensure that none is diverted from power generation to explosives production. Even the chemical weapons convention targets the production of chemical agents rather than chemical weapons. A "disarmament" frame, by contrast, would construct the problem of military technology to highlight weapons and thereby enable practices directed at preventing weaponization of technologies. Such barriers could then allow a reframing of issues related to the movement of technology in terms of "development."

Resources for the Contest

The move to reframe the security problem of weapons in terms of a "disarmament" image and the movement of technology in terms of "development"—which appears to underlie the Indian position as well as the nonaligned proposals on NPT extension—has a number of resources on which to draw. These resources are interpretive frameworks that can be used to construct images of a security problematic. In Chapter 3 I examined the frameworks within which the military technologies of concern to the proliferation agenda had been imagined in the Cold War and argued that those framings provided resources for the construction of a security problematic after the Soviet-U.S. confrontation had ended. Some of these discursive resources, together with some additional ones, could be deployed by opponents of the proliferation agenda to struggle for an alternative framing of contemporary security, weapons, and technologies.

Nuclear Nonproliferation Regime

The most important of these resources is the nuclear nonproliferation regime. The statute of the IAEA establishes the purpose of the agency as to "accelerate and enlarge the contribution of atomic energy to health, peace and prosperity throughout the world."[21] To this end, the agency is authorized to assist research and development of peaceful nuclear technology and to serve as an intermediary in the transmission of services and technology. Furthermore, the IAEA is specifically authorized to ensure access to peaceful nuclear technology by the underdeveloped world.[22] These were the original functions of the IAEA. Only 10 years later did the NPT further authorize the IAEA to use its safeguards system to monitor compliance with its nonproliferation norms.

In addition to the IAEA's original mandate, the NPT was designed to *foster* peaceful uses of nuclear technology.[23] Taken together with Article VI, the commitment to foster the peaceful use of nuclear technology establishes the relationship between disarmament and development the nonaligned states sought to promote at the NPT extension conference. The bargain that is at the heart of the NPT is precisely this marriage of disarmament and development. Nonproliferation is a temporary expedient, preventing the problem of armament from becoming much worse before disarmament is achieved. The NNWSs party to the NPT renounced their right to develop nuclear weapons and accepted full-scope safeguards on their nuclear industry in the name of keeping the nuclear disarmament problem as manageable as possible. In addition, in Article IV they were guaranteed access to the technology needed to develop their nuclear industry.

As I have shown throughout this book, the later development of a comprehensive "proliferation" agenda has marginalized this central bargain, culminating with the indefinite extension of the NPT without the firm commitments on disarmament sought by the nonaligned states. Instead, the "proliferation" image has been constructed from this stopgap measure and the practices put in place to implement it, which have been extended to the full range of military technologies. In the face of this process, opposition to proliferation will require a greater set of resources than is provided by the IAEA and the NPT alone.

Conversion

The relationship between military and civilian technology is complex, even—perhaps particularly—in the most advanced industrialized states. In his study of the dynamics of the global arms transfer and production system, Keith Krause examines the relationship between military technology and civilian industrialization:

> An arms industry not only depends on a particular level of industrial development to succeed, but in turn can be regarded as a potential catalyst or leading sector for industrialisation, capable of stimulating economic development through its backward and forward linkages. . . . Advanced arms production has been variously associated with dominant sectors such as metal-working, naval engineering, iron- and steel-making, heavy industrial machinery manufacture, transportation and electronics, which has made it a clear adjunct to civilian technological advancement.[24]

Traditionally, arms production was seen to drive the leading edge of industrial development. Technological advances were made through the improvement of arms production and then found their way into the civilian economy. This spin-off relationship was reflected, for example, in research and development spending in the United States. In the 1950s defense R&D

accounted for over 50 percent of research and development spending. By 1990, however, this amount had fallen to under 20 percent.[25] This change reflects the relative shift from spin-off to spin-on, whereby advances in civilian industry are incorporated into the latest generation of armaments.

Whether the predominant relationship between civilian and military technological advances is one of spin-off or spin-on, there is no reasonable way to differentiate between military and civilian technology. Either military technology is a catalyst for civilian industrial development, or industrial development provides the resources for military advances. For example, to paraphrase Frank Barnaby's point on the relationship of nuclear technology to nuclear weapons, any state that develops a sophisticated information processing and communications industry will accumulate the resources necessary to develop advanced smart conventional weapons. The spin-off/spin-on relationship provides the developing world with potent arguments to oppose supplier groups. As David Mussington notes in an examination of placing controls and verification on dual-use technologies: "In the case of an industrial process, the inherent dual-use quality of such a system means that limits on its diffusion to developing countries carries very real economic and developmental costs. . . . Process technologies are of particular importance to industrialization in many developing countries. . . . In product technologies, such as personal computers and cellular telephones, restrictions on technology transfers are even more problematic."[26]

Little headway in opposing the proliferation agenda is likely to be made with an argument that suggests diffusing military technology as a means of economic development—although such arguments were current in the early period of decolonization, during which modernization theory emerged.[27] The links between civilian and military technology, however, have given rise to a new discourse that is potentially fruitful for an oppositional strategy founded on a development framing of technology. With the end of the Cold War and the consequent reduction in military budgets and arsenals in Europe and North America, the question was posed about what to do with the industrial resources that had been devoted to military production. The answer is broadly identified as conversion, which tends to encompass three rather different processes: the redirection of military budgets to other uses, the transformation of military assets into something else, and the conversion of military to civilian industry.

One of the most notable efforts at conversion has been made in the field of nuclear weapons. Part of this effort concerns coping with the quantities of high-quality fissile material freed from nuclear weapons under the START agreements. In particular, the United States has agreed to finance the conversion and storage of fissile material from the former Soviet Union for use in nuclear power facilities.[28] Such a use is the basis for nuclear weapons conversion: the fissile material can be downgraded and burned in nuclear generators. Somewhat broader conversion issues are raised by nuclear weapons production facilities. In the former Soviet Union these are the focus of considerable "proliferation" concern, as former nuclear scientists are seen as a potentially dangerous source of weapons expertise for rogue states. In the United States, by contrast, weapons makers are reinventing themselves as key contributors to future U.S. competitiveness. Los Alamos National Laboratory describes itself these days as "a national resource for solving complex problems where science makes a difference. The laboratory's core competencies include advanced computing, computer simulation and computer modeling, sensors and instrumentation for complex experimentation and measurements, nuclear weapons, earth and environmental science, bioscience and biotechnology, materials science, and nuclear science, plasmas, and beams."[29]

Hidden in the middle of this impressive list are nuclear weapons, until recently Los Alamos's raison d'être—the laboratory was founded as part of the Manhattan Project and was the location for most of the final research that developed the first atomic bomb. Since then, it has played a central role in developing each new generation of U.S. nuclear weapons and is still charged with the stewardship of the U.S. nuclear force. The laboratory acknowledges the continued importance of its national security role but places it in the context of this range of scientific expertise. In reality, all of the scientific and technological resources were a result of the laboratory's role in building and maintaining nuclear weapons; in other words, a nuclear weapons program can produce what the director of Los Alamos calls "one of the leading scientific institutions in the world."[30] With the reduced need for nuclear weapons development, Los Alamos has turned that resource toward industry. The laboratory created a new Commercialization of Technology Office, which seeks to develop links with private industry to use its scientific and technological expertise to improve U.S. competitiveness and to create jobs.[31] Military technologies, it would seem, can be usefully "converted" to provide new business, create job opportunities, and even improve the industrial competitiveness of the leading world economy.

Conversion is taking place not only in nuclear technology. Across the range of military technologies now considered to be problems of "proliferation," producers are engaged in sometimes desperate processes of conversion. Arms producers are turning to civilian production in an attempt to adjust to reduced arms sales in the post–Cold War world. The Bonn International Centre for Conversion publishes an annual *Conversion Survey,* which examines conversion across the full range of military technology in the past year. The 1997 report examined the conversion efforts of the 75 largest arms producers and concluded:

For 67 of the 75 firms, arms sales decreased in real terms between 1990
and 1994. . . . Adding the figures for the 67 companies with decreasing
defense sales, civilian sales increased by US $18.8 billion while military
sales decreased by US $55.3 billion. More than 1.1 million jobs were lost
in these 67 companies. Excluding the "failure" cases—those companies
losing more civilian than defense sales—the picture looks somewhat
brighter, with gains in civilian sales of US $102.5 billion, more than
making up for defense sale losses of US $42.9 billion.[32]

Clearly, arms producers have the capacity to satisfy more than military
demands. In fact, the United States has formally reworked its military
spending policy to make use of the overlap between military and civilian
technologies. As part of the 1996 national security strategy the U.S. administration wrote, "We are structuring our defense R&D effort to place
greater emphasis on dual-use technologies that allow the military to capi-
talize on commercial sector innovation for lower cost, higher quality and
increased performance."[33]

The move to conversion provides an important resource for those contesting the proliferation agenda. Conversion of all kinds of weapons—
conventional and weapons of mass destruction—makes problematic the
simple linear relationship between military technology and civilian industrial development. The practice of conversion also demonstrates that so-
called military technology does not inevitably lead to increased arsenals.
Indeed, conversion arguments *reverse* the relationship between weaponry
and its underlying technology by showing that military technology can
give rise to civilian industry. The conversion discourse allows the simple
inevitability of the relationship between civilian and military technology to
be made more complex—at least bidirectional. Such a framing of the relationship of technology to arms opens space for imagining that technology in a number of ways, particularly for locating industrial development
within a free market.

Competitiveness in Open Markets

By denying the inevitable and unidirectional link between arms and their
underlying technologies, such an oppositional strategy opens the possibility
for tying this alternative construction to one of the most potent international
political discourses of the 1990s: economic competitiveness in an expanding global market. For the purpose of contesting the "proliferation" image,
competitiveness has two important features. The first is that in the 1990s
competitiveness is articulated as an issue of security, and the second is the
centrality of free markets to economic competitiveness. These two features
are neatly captured in the U.S. administration's 1996 *National Security
Strategy of Engagement and Enlargement:* "The three central components

of our strategy of engagement and enlargement are: (1) our efforts to enhance our security by maintaining a strong defense capability and employing effective diplomacy to promote cooperative security measures; (2) our work to open foreign markets and spur global economic growth; and (3) our promotion of democracy abroad."[34]

In filling in the economic component of this three-pronged strategy, the document tightens the linkage between security and economic competitiveness: "A central goal of our national security strategy is to promote America's prosperity through efforts both at home and abroad. Our economic and security interests are increasingly inseparable. Our prosperity at home depends on engaging actively abroad. The strength of our diplomacy, our ability to maintain an unrivaled military, the attractiveness of our values abroad—all these depend in part on the strength of our economy."[35] This passage is immediately followed by the first element of the U.S. economic security strategy, "Enhancing American Competitiveness."

The United States has therefore explicitly linked security to *open* foreign markets and *global* economic growth. The need for global growth provides an entry point for contesting the "proliferation" image in the name of development. Global growth depends on economic development in the less developed world, and that development, in turn, requires access to technology. The U.S. national security strategy recognizes the "steps to improve American competitiveness: investing in science and technology; assisting integration of the commercial and military industrial sectors; improving information networks and other vital infrastructure; and improving education and training programs for America's workforce."[36] Science and technology are vital to improved competitiveness—as we already know from the shifting functions of Los Alamos. Similarly, integration of the military and civilian sectors of industry improves economic performance, as does improved access to information technology and to training. Such integration is precisely what proliferation control practices seek to restrain. Science, or at least its technological output, is the target of export controls—in particular, the highest end of technology, which can be used to create the sort of smart weaponry the United States deploys. Safeguards and similar practices aim explicitly to segregate military and civilian sectors of industry. Finally, although there are no formal controls on education and training, the United States monitors foreign nationals coming to the United States for training in sensitive areas and has contributed to efforts to keep Russian nuclear scientists "safely" in the former Soviet Union.

Perhaps the greatest irony of the focus of proliferation control on technology denial is the coincident drive to end other forms of state intervention in the global economy. The 1980s witnessed a dramatic opening of markets in the advanced industrialized world as a result of the victory of neoliberal economics in the politics of almost all Northern states. Indeed, the U.S. national security strategy emphasizes the need to maintain open economies: "To compete abroad, our firms need access to foreign markets, just as foreign industries have access to our open market. We vigorously pursue measures to increase access for our goods and services—through bilateral, regional and multilateral arrangements."[37] Competitiveness in a globally growing economy is central to U.S. security, and globally open markets are vital to promoting competitiveness. At the same time, technology controls are imposed in the name of proliferation control, effectively closing markets rather than opening them. Finally, it must be recalled that the technologies of civilian trade and weapons proliferation are increasingly indistinguishable.

The U.S. discourses of competitiveness and economic security provide potent resources for a strategy opposing "proliferation" in the name of "disarmament" and "development." The practices of proliferation control contradict the central features of the global economy the United States and its Northern allies are busy promoting in other areas. Importantly, these features of the global economy are increasingly discussed in terms of security, establishing the link between competitiveness and military technology without any effort. For the United States to achieve the sort of security it claims to be seeking in the open markets of a growing world economy, the restrictive practices at the heart of the proliferation control agenda must be discarded. Such an argument could prove politically potent, particularly if it is married to a plausible reframing of the "proliferation" problem. The goal of this chapter is to show that such a plausible reframing exists, that it is being articulated, and that it draws on discursive resources that are not foreign to those articulating the "proliferation" image.

Conclusion

The indefinite extension of the NPT has been seen as the heart of the new proliferation agenda. The United States and its Northern allies worked hard to ensure that the 1995 conference produced the result they wanted. The debate over the future of the NPT that necessarily surrounded the extension decision provided a locus for an alternative framing of the security problems surrounding military technology. This reframing, contesting the "proliferation" image, draws on other resources inherited from the Cold War framings of weapons and associated technologies. To date, it has not been articulated as a coherent alternative to "proliferation," but in this chapter I show how such an articulation is possible, drawing on some of the most powerful resources of contemporary international political discourse.

Despite drawing on many of the same resources as the "proliferation" image, the objects and identities constructed by an alternative image of "disarmament" paired with "development" are strikingly different. The "proliferation" image constructs an object that fundamentally connects the technology underlying weaponry to the weaponry itself and directs attention to that technology in the first instance. This technology, if left unchecked, will produce deleterious effects—the technological cells will proliferate outward from their source inevitably to produce the cancer of destabilizing weapons. This natural, autonomous process of spread must be controlled to prevent the cancerous outcome or be excised through "surgical" strikes.

The object of the "disarmament-development" image is in many ways the reverse of that constructed by "proliferation." Here weaponry is disconnected from its underlying technology, and it is the existence of the weapons themselves that is the problem rather than the movement of the technology on which they are based. That technology is then framed as instrumental to economic development, as well as potentially producing military capability. In this counterimage, the security focus is on the weapons, particularly their possession, and the emphasis is placed on the civilian side of the dual-use technology. If the discourse on conversion can be tied to this alternative image, the relationship between arms and their technological underpinnings can be reversed in a fruitful fashion—arms can now produce civilian technology as well as the reverse. Such a shift, which makes use of discursive resources articulated by defenders of the "proliferation" image in other contexts, allows the development discourse to be framed in terms of competitiveness and markets—language central to the political discourse of the global economy.

By framing the objects of the problem in different ways, these two images also construct a different range of identities in relation to that problem. As we saw in Chapter 5, the "proliferation" image constructs suppliers, recipients, and rogues or outlaws. This identity set can easily be read from the linear relationship between technology and weapons: the technology originates at a source (suppliers) and spreads outward (recipients); if left uncontrolled, it gives rise to problematic weaponry (rogues-outlaws). The "disarmament-development" image, by contrast, begins by constructing identities around axes of armed-unarmed and developed-undeveloped. In this framing the armed have an obligation to disarm, and the developed an obligation to aid in the development of the less developed—an obligation now phrased in terms of the need for an open and growing economy at the global scale. Suppliers and recipients are recast in the familiar terms of global capital, and the security problem is the armed state. Indeed, it would not be difficult to label the identity of the security problem as the weapon state, not in Krauthammer's terms but in the more intuitive formulation of the state with the largest number of weapons.

The practices that would be enabled by a "disarmament-development" image are also rather different from those of the "proliferation" image. Most important, supplier groups aimed at technological denial would have no place in a security environment framed in this fashion. Practices to manage global flows of technology, to the degree that they would be institutionalized, would aim at promoting technological flow for the purposes of global growth. Again, the resources exist within the range of practices inherited from the Cold War to facilitate this form of practical inscription of "disarmament-development." The IAEA was founded to facilitate the spread of nuclear technology for peaceful purposes—precisely the form of activity a "disarmament-development" frame would warrant.

I have worked hard to postpone an obvious objection: that India would clearly oppose the proliferation agenda. India has developed a nuclear capability, which it made public in a series of tests in 1998. Of course, the United States would promote a proliferation agenda that enables it to retain its privileged status as a nuclear weapon state and primary supplier, with the concomitant ability to determine the flow of technology. In general terms, the objection is that these positions are the result of the underlying interests of the parties involved. The objection is founded on the most fundamental assertion of traditional international relations: that states will act to promote and defend their national interest. To the degree that this is true, the outcome of the contest I have discussed in this chapter will be conditioned by the interests of those on each side of the proliferation divide. This concept is so important to conventional arguments about world politics, particularly about security in world politics, that I have postponed discussion until now. Where are the interests in this account of framing global security? It is to this question that I now turn.

7

Questions of Interest

On 10 September 1996 one of the longest-standing dreams of those opposed to nuclear weapons appeared to be realized when the UN General
Assembly voted 158-3-5 to adopt the comprehensive test ban treaty
(CTBT).[1] The CTBT had been a long time in the making. Following the
failure of attempts to develop international control of nuclear weapons following their use in World War II, the CTBT was the next in the line of disarmament measures to be discussed. Despite repeated negotiations over
the years, it proved impossible to reach agreement on a comprehensive test
ban throughout the Cold War. In 1994 the Conference on Disarmament
began negotiations on the CTBT, which the General Assembly adopted 3
years later. The dramatic shift from 40 years of stalemate to rapid completion saw a remarkable role reversal between the United States and India, a
reversal that raises important questions about the nature of interests in international relations in general and within practices of proliferation control
in particular. In this chapter I take up these questions, beginning with the
questions of how a CTBT was achieved at all and why India and the
United States took positions diametrically opposed to those they had held
throughout the Cold War negotiations.

India, the United States, and the CTBT

The impetus for the original CTBT negotiations came from the international fallout of the 1954 U.S. test of hydrogen weapons in the South Pacific—both literally and figuratively. A Japanese fishing boat was irradi-
ated by the fallout from the first U.S. test of a practical thermonuclear
weapon, which produced a yield almost double that expected. The graphic
illustration of the impact of the testing—all members of the crew of the
ship became ill by the time they reached port—led to political fallout and

international demands for an end to nuclear testing.[2] India was the first to propose a complete ban on nuclear testing a few months following the U.S. test at Bikini.[3] The first negotiations began in October 1958 among the United States, the Soviet Union, and the United Kingdom. The negotiations never achieved a CTBT, although they came close, stumbling most notably on the U-2 flown by Gary Powers and shot down over the Soviet Union. The Kennedy administration picked up the discussions, but final agreement on a CTBT proved impossible; in August 1961 the USSR resumed testing, which it had suspended during the negotiations. Nevertheless, this resumption of testing by no means marked the end of the CTBT.

The nuclear testing issue was picked up by the newly formed Eighteen Nation Disarmament Conference in March 1962—although it was never formally negotiated in that forum or in its successors until the CD discussions that produced the 1996 text.[4] Rather, the ENDC served as a focus for pushing the superpowers to discuss test bans, which, spurred by the dangers of October 1962, they did again in 1963. These negotiations produced the limited test ban treaty (LTBT), which outlawed nuclear tests other than underground tests. Two more partial bans were also negotiated over the next two decades. In 1974 the United States and the Soviet Union signed a threshold test ban treaty (TTBT), limiting their underground nuclear tests to a 150-kiloton yield. In 1976 the superpowers closed an important loophole in that treaty by setting rules for the use of peaceful nuclear explosions (PNEs).[5]

Both the LTBT and the TTBT looked forward to a CTBT in their preambles, but a CTBT was not forthcoming, although negotiations did continue. The most notable of these negotiations prior to 1994 were the trilateral negotiations (the United States, the Soviet Union, and the United Kingdom) that ran from 1977 until 1980. During these negotiations the CTBT came very close to being agreed. An article in the *Bulletin of the Atomic Scientists* in 1985 recalls:

> The Carter Administration, after obtaining Soviet agreement to a remarkable treaty draft during the trilateral discussions in Geneva, aborted future measures to complete an accord. Administration officials were afraid that under a test ban something might go wrong and give the Soviets an unspecifiable but critical advantage. Carter, according to Harold Agnew, then director of Los Alamos National Laboratory, had every intention of going ahead with a ban until Agnew and Roger Batzel, at that time head of Livermore National Laboratory, spent a mere two hours talking with him and "turned him around."[6]

When Ronald Reagan was elected president, the U.S. decided not to pursue the negotiations. Reagan declared in 1982 that a CTBT was not in the U.S. security interest at that time.[7]

> The Reagan administration argued that a CTBT would be dangerous to
> U.S. security interests for the following reasons: there is a pressing re-
> quirement to test more advanced "third-generation" weapons, such as the
> nuclear pumped X-ray laser, a possible kill mechanism for a "Star Wars"
> antimissile system; nuclear tests are necessary for the development of
> new warhead designs for strategic systems already planned for deploy-
> ment; tests are required to maintain the reliability of the existing stock-
> pile of nuclear weapons; and such an agreement could not be verified.[8]

Each reason was intimately tied to the deterrence relationship with the Soviet Union. Even the problem of verification was understood in terms of
the need to detect a violation by the USSR. The central verification measure proposed for the CTBT—and indeed enshrined in the 1996 CTBT—is
a system of seismic monitoring stations. The problem is that a state with a
sophisticated nuclear weapons program might be able to circumvent seismic monitoring by either testing weapons of very low yields (under 1 kil-
ton) or decoupling a larger explosion by detonating it within a large underground cavern. The verification problem had been cited by the United
States from the earliest CTBT negotiations as the principal obstacle to
agreeing on a treaty, with the United States insisting on on-site verification
to overcome problems of deception and the Soviet Union unwilling to permit the sort of access the United States demanded.[9]

In 1986 the governments of six states offered to help overcome the
impasse over verification—Argentina, Greece, Mexico, Sweden, Tanzania,
and, most important for my purposes, India joined in what came to be
called the Six Nations Initiative. The six states offered their services as
monitors, volunteering to establish seismic monitoring stations at the test
sites of the two superpowers and to make other monitoring arrangements
in areas in which decoupling was possible. They also offered to establish
on-site procedures to distinguish between large chemical explosions and
nuclear tests.[10] Despite the offer, in 1987 the United States again refused
to agree to a negotiating committee within the CD. Its explanation for this
refusal was noteworthy: "the United States reiterated its view that a comprehensive ban on nuclear testing is a long-term objective which must be
seen 'in the context of a time when it and its allies did not need to depend
on nuclear deterrence to ensure international security and stability.'"[11]

Five years later the U.S. president determined that the CTBT was now
in the security interests of the United States and gave U.S. backing to the
negotiations that produced the 1996 text. Indeed, it was the U.S. president
who set autumn 1996 as the deadline toward which the negotiations were
to work. One might suspect from this that the United States had renounced
its reliance on nuclear deterrence—that with the end of the Cold War the
time had come when it and its allies did not need to depend on nuclear deterrence for their security. This is, however, simply not the case. At the

same time as it was pressing the CTBT negotiations, the U.S. administration was undertaking a nuclear posture review to determine the nuclear strategy required by the United States after the Cold War. In the administration's own words, "A key conclusion of this review is that the United States will retain a triad of strategic nuclear forces sufficient to deter any future hostile foreign leadership with access to nuclear weapons."[12] The U.S. position on the CTBT in 1996 must therefore be seen to constitute a significant change of policy, for the context was still one in which the United States relied on nuclear deterrence to ensure international security and stability. This context was supposed to rule out U.S. acceptance of a CTBT, but now it did not.

As the 1996 work of the CD began, substantial progress had been made toward agreeing on a CTBT text. The conclusion of the CTBT, however, was less smooth than might have been expected. One delegation adopted a "blatantly obstructive role" and in the end denied consensus for adoption of the treaty. Since the CD operates by consensus, this meant the CTBT could not be adopted by the CD. Because of this refusal of consensus in the CD, the CTBT was adopted by the UN General Assembly rather than the CD, as is common practice. What is notable about this obstructive role is that it was played by India in what seemed a reversal of its previous position on the CTBT and even in these negotiations.[13]

More than just a reversal in Indian policy occurred in 1996; the year also saw a remarkable exchange of roles in relation to the CTBT. The United States, which had refused to agree to a CTBT for most of the past 40 years, led the charge to complete the agreement in short order. On the other hand, India, which had first proposed a test ban in the early 1950s and had led calls for a CTBT during those same 40 years, refused to agree to the treaty or even to abstain to allow for consensus among the rest of the CD. This reversal was produced by the reframing of the CTBT from a central element of the "disarmament" frame to the new "proliferation" frame. A brief return to the issue of verification will allow us to see how reframing produced the CTBT and the effect of that reframing on the interests of the United States and India.

For the United States, the problem of verification of a CTBT was whether the United States could reliably detect and identify a nuclear explosion of arbitrarily low yield. The issue was phrased in technical terms, of whether remote sensing could detect all nuclear explosions and, even if it could, whether it could discriminate between nuclear explosions and other events. This is a problem, however, only if the concern is with a technologically capable nuclear state—the Soviet Union, for example—developing new forms of nuclear warheads. If the concern, by contrast, is with preventing nonnuclear states from becoming nuclear by banning the testing of their weapons and threatening to detect them if they try, the verification problem becomes very different. This was clearly recognized in a report prepared by the IRIS Consortium for the U.S. Congress as part of its consideration of the CTBT at the time of the recent negotiations. The report concluded that "monitoring a global CTBT in the context of proliferation is fundamentally different from monitoring nuclear weapon states in the context of bilateral threshold restrictions." The report spelled out those differences in tabular form (Table 7.1).[14]

The IRIS Consortium's use of *situation* to describe the differences between the two contexts is a bit disingenuous; it suggests that a change has occurred in the objective condition in which states generally, or at least the United States in particular, now find themselves. Table 7.1, however, provides no evidence of such an objective change in condition. The only change that might be described in this fashion is the one labeled *structure*, pointing to a shift from an essentially bilateral treaty, or at least one restricted to the nuclear weapon states, to a global treaty that aims to include all the states in the international system. This change, however, is one of U.S. making, for until 1992 it was the United States that routinely refused to allow the leading multilateral disarmament forum, the CD, to negotiate a CTBT. Nevertheless, the context in which the CTBT was considered in 1992 had changed, largely because of a shift in the discursive context in which nuclear testing had been located and a change in the way in which issues of nuclear security more generally were understood. There had been a change, in other words, in the frame rather than in the situation.

Table 7.1   IRIS Consortium's Comparison of the CTBT Before and After "Proliferation"

Old Situation	New Situation
Intent	
Manage vertical proliferation	Prevent vertical and horizontal proliferation
Parties	
Nuclear states	Nuclear states and first-timers
(known weapons and tests)	(unknown devices and procedures)
Structure	
Basically bilateral	Global
(NATO/Warsaw pacts)	(100+ countries)
Task	
Police a threshold	Detect an occurrence
(degree of violation)	(yes or no)
Approach	
Monitor down to a specific level with high confidence	Monitor all seismic events and increase confidence
Emphasis for Monitoring	
Police threshold	Increase confidence

Source: IRIS Consortium's report to the U.S. Congress, p. II-18.

In the final session of the CD debate over the CTBT, India restated the objections that had led it to deny consensus to the text that had been negotiated. The Indian representative began by saying, "I would like to reiterate our position that India cannot and does not accept CD/NTB/WP.330/ Rev.1 and now CD/NTB/WP.330/Rev.2 as the CTBT we were mandated to negotiate."[15] The remarkable feature of the Indian argument was the claim that the CTBT, as it was finally negotiated in 1996, was *not the same treaty* that had been under discussion from 1958 onward. What makes this remarkable is that the operative elements of the treaty are precisely the ones under discussion throughout this period. The 1996 CTBT bans nuclear explosions in all environments for all time, establishes an international body to monitor for suspected tests, and empowers that body to investigate on-site. The Indians cited several objections to the text, but the primary one was as follows:

> It may be recalled here that during the negotiations since January 1996 India put forward a number of proposals consistent with the mandate adopted by the CD. These proposals were aimed at ensuring that the CTBT be a truly comprehensive treaty which banned all nuclear testing and did not leave any loopholes for qualitative refinement and development of nuclear weapons. We also underscored the importance of *placing the treaty in the disarmament context* as a part of a step by step process aimed at achieving complete elimination of all nuclear weapons within a time-bound framework.[16]

The Indians' objection, then, was that the CTBT, as it was finally negotiated, was not the one for which they had been working—not because it was substantively different but because it was framed as a tool to control "proliferation" rather than as an instrument of "disarmament."

The most obvious evidence of the reframing of the CTBT is the entry-into-force provisions of the treaty contained in Annex 2. A "disarmament" CTBT would require no more than that the five nuclear weapons states sign before entry into force—as the IRIS Consortium report I cited earlier notes, only known nuclear states need to be party to such a test ban. The 1996 CTBT takes a very different tack in creating the necessary conditions for entry into force, requiring ratification by those states that were members of the CD and were recorded by the IAEA as having nuclear power or research reactors.[17] That is, potential first timers, those with precursor technologies to nuclear weapons, rather than those who are armed with nuclear weaponry, are identified by the treaty as the crucial targets of its restrictions. The entry-into-force requirements of the CTBT are a clear product of its "proliferation" framing.[18]

The CTBT approved by the UN General Assembly in September 1996 was articulated to a very different problem from that of the earlier versions proposed from 1958 onward. The 1996 CTBT is an instrument of proliferation control, conceived and achieved within a discursive context, which frames the problems of military technology—including, indeed especially, nuclear technology—in terms of its acquisition by states that do not already have it. Taken out of the context of an arms control practice, which assumed that it was the testing of established nuclear powers that was at issue, and placed into this new context of a proliferation control agenda, the nature of the CTBT changed radically. Suddenly the United States, which had stalled a CTBT for so long, was able to accept that which had not been in its security interest a few years previously.[19] Suddenly India was unable to accept that which it had urged for so long.

It is important to recognize that in strictly technical terms nothing about the CTBT has changed. The ban on testing still makes development of new nuclear weapons by the United States difficult, if not impossible.[20] Even more important than warhead development, the test ban poses the same problems for safety and reliability that it did in the late 1980s. Indeed, a number of officials within the Pentagon and U.S. nuclear laboratories opposed the test ban on these grounds.[21] What is more, the United States restated its commitment to nuclear deterrence as central to its security strategy. On the Indian side, the effects of the test ban are similarly unchanged. India had conducted a single explosion before the ban, and signing the CTBT would have posed no greater threat to its nuclear program than doing so would have done in 1986 at the time of the Six Nations Initiative. Nevertheless, despite the unchanged effects of the test ban on the nuclear capabilities of both states, the interests each demonstrated in relation to the ban were reversed as its framing was changed. For the United States, a CTBT that was part of a "proliferation" frame *was* now in its security interest, despite its continued reliance on nuclear deterrence; for India, so long a proponent of a CTBT as part of a "disarmament" frame, it now was not.

The CTBT experience raises important questions about interests: What are they? How are they formed, and what part do they play in the constitution of a security problematic? Indeed, what part do they play in the formation of the security problem of proliferation, which is the focus of this work?

Interests and International Relations

The notion of *interest*, or more precisely, *the national interest,* is central to the discipline of international relations. Disciplinary lore tells of the founding of international relations in the debate between realists and idealists. The first figure in this debate, at least on the victorious realist side, is E. H. Carr, whose realist critique of idealism focused on idealism's assumption of a harmony of interest, particularly the assumption that all states have a common interest in peace that could be relied on to found an institutionalized international peace.[22] In place of the harmony of interests, the early realists placed the national interest at the heart of their theory of world politics. As Arnold Wolfers wrote in 1952, "Statesmen, publicists and scholars who wish to be considered realists, as many do today, are inclined to insist that the foreign policy they advocate is dictated by the national interest."[23] What, then, is this concept of *interest* to which realists appeal?

Ironically, despite the importance of interest to realism, the concept is poorly theorized in realist writings; nevertheless, it is possible to read from their usage of the term the understandings that inform it. The place to begin such an investigation is with Hans Morgenthau's *Politics Among Nations,* in which Morgenthau argues that the "main signpost that helps political realism find its way through the landscape of international politics is the concept of interest defined in terms of power. This concept provides the link between reason trying to understand international politics and the facts to be understood."[24] Furthermore, the "concept of interest defined as power imposes intellectual discipline upon the observer, infuses rational order into the subject matter of politics and thus makes the *theoretical understanding* of politics possible."[25] Interests, then, play a crucial role in the realist understanding of international relations, as they provide the possibility for a theoretical understanding of international politics, tying together the analyst and the empirical universe she is trying to comprehend. This is a crucial concept indeed.

Morgenthau defines interest simply in terms of power, so to gain further insight into his use of the term we must see what he means by *power*—notoriously, a concept perhaps even more ill defined than is interest in realist writing. To begin, Morgenthau argues that the notion of "interest defined as power" is universally valid but that the content of that power varies historically.[26] When he sets out that content, however, the space for variation is limited indeed, with the most fundamental elements of national power—geography, national resources, and industrial capacity—variable only over a tremendous time span. Interest, defined in terms of this understanding of power, is very stable—necessarily so given the analytic weight the realist puts on it. Furthermore, despite the fact that Morgenthau defines power as "man's control over the minds and actions of other men," the elements of national power are notably nonrelational. They are conceived as attributes of particular nations rather than as characteristics of relationships between them.

If interests are defined as power and power is a set of attributes, how does the national interest dictate policy? The answer must be that policy should seek to protect or augment those elements of power—that, in other words, national interests and national security are one and the same to realists. This is the position Wolfers adopts, and it is reinforced by Kenneth Waltz's conception of national interests in *Theory of International Politics,* the defining neorealist text: "To say that a country acts according to its national interest means that, having examined its security requirements, it tries to meet them. That is simple; it is also important."[27] Waltz may be right that his equation of interest and security is simple, but he is less convincing about "important." Wolfers drew very different conclusions from the equation almost 30 years before Waltz.

> In a very vague and general way "national interest" does suggest a policy which can be distinguished from several others which may present themselves as alternatives. It indicates that the policy is designed to promote demands which are ascribed to the nation rather than to individuals, subnational groups or mankind as a whole. It emphasizes that the policy subordinates other interests to those of the nation. *But beyond this it has very little meaning.*[28]

Simple and banal might have been a better conclusion for Waltz.

Following the publication of Waltz's book, the neorealist position was the focus of a number of sustained critiques. The critique that shared the most with the neorealists was initially organized around the concept of the regime. How did this neoliberal alternative to neorealism conceive of interests, and did it advance the concept beyond the realist simplicity? The standard reference work for regime analysis is Stephen Krasner's edited collection, *International Regimes,* in particular the introductory chapter by the editor. Krasner locates interests in the regimes research program: "This project began with a simple causal schematic. It assumed that regimes could be conceived as intervening variables standing between basic causal variables (most prominently, power and interests) and outcome and behavior."[29] For regime theorists, interests are basic causal variables—autonomously discovered factors that give rise to the outcomes of concern to analysts. The question that remains for both neorealists and neoliberals is, where do these interests come from? Robert Keohane, the leading neoliberal theorist, confronted this problem, at least as far as it affects neorealist thinking:

> Sophisticated contemporary thinkers in the Realist tradition, such as Gilpin, Krasner, and Waltz, understand that interests cannot be derived simply on the basis of rational calculation, from the external positions of states, and that this is particularly true of great powers, on which, ironically, Structural Realism focuses its principal attentions. Realist analysis has to retreat to a "fall-back position": that, *given state interests,* whose origins are not predicted by the theory, patterns of outcomes in world politics will be determined by the overall distribution of power among states.[30]

The best the realist tradition can produce, then, is to take state interests as given. As Jutta Weldes notes in her critique of the realist conception of interests, "The realist 'national interest' rests upon the assumption that an independent reality is directly accessible both to statesmen and to analysts."[31] Regime theorists advanced a little on realists, for although they began by treating interests as basic causal variables that entirely preceded theory, one of the conclusions of their work—which has informed later neoliberal thinking—was that "once principles, norms, rules, and decision-making procedures [i.e., regimes] were entrenched they may alter the egoist interests and power configurations [the basic causal variables] which led to their creation in the first place."[32]

The implication of this conclusion in neoliberal thinking is that interests do not exist prior to practice but emerge out of practice—in the same way I argue throughout this book that objects and identities emerge out of practice. Despite its being the implication of their own work, neoliberals are not comfortable with this conclusion because, ultimately, it requires embracing the epistemological break between the empirical universe and our knowledge of that universe that is at the heart of postpositivist conceptions of social life. Keohane argues, for instance, that "under different systemic conditions states will *define their self-interests differently.*"[33] Self-interests, according to this formulation, are not inherent or objective but rather are the products of self-definition. Put into slightly different language, this means interests are a product of *interpretation* rather than a feature of the real world. The act of the self-definition of self-interest is *precisely* the sort of inescapable recourse to interpretation that leads to David Campbell's conclusion that there is "nothing outside discourse." For neoliberals such as Keohane, that way madness lies, and so they are unwilling to accept the implications of their own arguments.

Both neorealists and neoliberals trace their conception of interests to Morgenthau's early realist notion of interest defined as power and refuse to break with his epistemological claims about the possibility of an objective science of international relations.[34] These positions still form the mainstream of security studies, but other scholars have been less reticent than neoliberals to follow the logic of interests as a product of interpretation rather than objective conditions. In one of the most widely noted articles of the 1990s, Alexander Wendt explicitly picked up neoliberal implications that interests are defined within institutional settings.[35] Wendt argues that identities are formed by interaction within intersubjectively constituted institutional settings—of which the traditional features of international anarchy, self-help and power politics, are two. Furthermore, "identities are the basis of interests. Actors do not have a 'portfolio' of interests that they carry around independent of social context; instead they define their interests in the process of defining situations."[36] This is essentially the same point Keohane makes from a neoliberal position. The difference is that Wendt is willing to accept some of the implications of that argument, although not the radical epistemological implications.[37]

Weldes has advanced Wendt's argument that interests are a function of identity and that both are products rather than exogenous variables without following Wendt's further project of reclaiming neoliberal, and even neorealist arguments.[38]

> In contrast to the realist conception of "national interests" as objects that have merely to be observed or discovered, then, my argument is that national interests are social constructions created as meaningful objects out of the intersubjective and culturally established meanings with which the world, particularly the international system and the place of the state in it, is understood. More specifically, national interests emerge out of the representations . . . through which state officials and others make sense of the world around them.[39]

These representations—in both their linguistic and practical moments— constitute the world around them. Weldes argues that these representations also produce the interests actors have:

> In providing a vision of the world of international relations—in populating that world with objects and in supplying quasi-causal or warranting arguments—these representations have *already* defined the national interests. Because "identities are the basis of interests," the interests of the state are already entailed within the representations in which the identities of and relations among the relevant actors or objects are established. . . . Once a situation has been described, that is, the national interest has already been determined—it *emerges* out of the representations of identities and relationships constructed by state officials.[40]

There are two important points concerning Weldes's argument. First, the analysis of interests as emerging out of representations goes a long way to explaining the apparent objectivity of those interests. Weldes suggests that interests do not need to be constructed separately from objects and identities but flow from the way the latter are represented. In other words, the policymaker or scholar reading an authoritative representation of international life or an international problem would see interests embedded in that representation. If the reader assumes the possibility of unmediated access to the empirical world, it would be reasonable to assume that the interests that appear come not from the representation but from that real world.

The second point is that Weldes's argument allows the account I am developing of the proliferation problem to consider the place of interests without conceding theoretical ground to realism, which has seemingly claimed interests as its exclusive domain. Weldes suggests that the interests states and others have in proliferation practices emerge from the representations that constitute those practices in the first place. I can now return to the "proliferation" image to ask what interests it constitutes. Before I do, however, it is important to remember that the interests constituted in and by a particular discourse are not the sum total of an actor's interests. States may not have objective interests, but they do participate in more than one discourse constitutive of interests. Thus the "proliferation" image can be seen to highlight, downplay, and hide the other interests by drawing links to some but not all of these other discourses or by constituting interests consonant with those produced in other sites of state practice.

Interests in the Proliferation Image

Kenneth Waltz argues that it is both simple and important to recognize that a state acts in its national interest if it examines its security requirements and tries to meet them. Having listened to Weldes, we might now be prepared to agree with Waltz's formulation, although its meaning would be changed beyond recognition. Both the state which acts and the security requirements to which it responds do not exist prior to their discursive formulation—to that very act of examination to which Waltz refers. The examination of security requirements takes place in the form of a series of the sort of representations Weldes discusses, populating a world with objects and actors. Thus the act of examination constitutes the state that acts and the security requirements that are the subject of examination. Also entailed in that constitutive representation are the interests the state seeks to pursue. Read in this fashion, we can agree with Waltz about importance, although we might quibble with his assertion of simplicity.

The "proliferation" image has emerged from just such a process of state examination of its security requirements. In particular, the United States and its allies have established proliferation as a threat to their security and have tried to meet that threat through the practices I discuss throughout this book. In Waltz's terms these states are acting in their interests, but the particular interests they are pursuing are a product of the identities produced by the image on which they are acting. States gain identities as suppliers, recipients, rogues, and weapon states only in the context of the practices of proliferation control. It is in this capacity that they can then exercise interests, as only within this image do those interests have meaning. What, then, are the interests attached to these identities in the "proliferation" image?

Perhaps the most important but, ultimately, the most problematic interest constituted by the "proliferation" image is the interest in *preventing* the spread of military technology. The way in which the image frames the movement of technology—as inevitably producing military capability which, in turn, affects the regional and global balances of power—naturalizes a universal interest in preventing that movement in the first place. The preambles to the major treaties that form the global level of the proliferation control regime reflect the claims to universality of the interests represented by the "proliferation" image (Table 7.2). In each case the preamble makes at least one reference to the threat its object poses to the universal, in some form. The NPT, CWC, and BTWC refer to the interest of "all mankind" in achieving the target of the agreement. The CTBT and the UN Resolution establishing the Register of Conventional Arms claim to be contribute to "international peace and security." Even the Ottawa Convention prohibiting the production, stockpiling, and transfer of antipersonnel mines notes the "desirability of attracting the adherence of all states."[41]

The universality of the interest in preventing proliferation is an important warrant for practices of supplier control. The Wassenaar Arrangement,

Table 7.2 Universal Claims in the Preambles to Major Proliferation Agreements

NPT
Considering the devastation that would be visited upon all mankind by a nuclear war and the consequent need to make every effort to avert the danger of such a war and to take measures to safeguard the security of peoples . . .

CWC
Determined for the sake of all mankind, to exclude completely the possibility of the use of chemical weapons, through the implementation of the provisions of this Convention, thereby complementing the obligations assumed under the Geneva Protocol of 1925 . . .

BTWC
Determined, for the sake of all mankind, to exclude completely the possibility of bacteriological (biological) agents and toxins being used as weapons . . .

CTBT
Affirming the purpose of attracting the adherence of all States to this Treaty and its objective to contribute effectively to the prevention of the proliferation of nuclear weapons in all its aspects, to the process of nuclear disarmament and therefore to the enhancement of international peace and security . . .

UN General Assembly Resolution 46/36L
Realizing that excessive and destabilizing arms build-ups pose a threat to national, regional and international peace and security . . .

Ottawa Convention (Anti-Personnel Mine Convention)
Emphasizing the desirability of attracting the adherence of all states to this Convention, and determined to work strenuously toward the promotion of its universalization in all relevant fora . . .

for example, "has been established in order to contribute to regional and international security and stability."[42] Even NATO, in turning its attention to proliferation, bases its claim to a right of action on the threat posed to *international* security, not just to the security of the alliance itself.[43] The presumption that suppliers act as arbiters of the consequences of the flow of military and related technology is therefore predicated on this universal interest in preventing proliferation. Only because it constructs this interest as universal, for example, can the Australia Group, made up of only 30 states, decide unilaterally to continue its activities even after the entry into force of the CWC.

Such a universal construction of interest in preventing the spread of military technology is not necessarily found in the other frames through which this technology has been imagined. The "arms control" frame, for example, which was so important during the Cold War, acknowledges a universal interest in preventing nuclear war but does not translate that interest into a restriction on the spread of nuclear technology. The SALT agreements involved placing qualitative and quantitative limits on the superpowers' arsenals to maintain international stability. In some cases these limits were substantially above the levels of the extant deployed arsenals of the two sides. The interest in maintaining stability required not that nuclear technology be prevented from being turned into nuclear weaponry but rather that the levels of weaponry be maintained in some form of numerical and qualitative equivalence. In some circumstances seen through an "arms control" frame, the universal interest in avoiding nuclear war translated into an interest in the (vertical) proliferation of nuclear weapons.

I do not intend to evaluate here these rival claims to the route to a secure and peaceful world, but they have given rise to extensive debate in U.S. scholarly and policy circles between so-called nuclear optimists and nuclear pessimists.[44] Nuclear optimists point to the role of nuclear balance in maintaining a stable peace during the Cold War and counsel more of the same for the post–Cold War world. In its most extreme versions, the optimistic argument calls for deliberate provision of nuclear weapons to a number of new nuclear states.[45] The very fact of this debate, which involves some of the leading names in U.S. strategic analysis and is carried out in the principal policy-relevant journals, reveals the ways in which interests are contingent upon the framing of a security problem. The universal interest in preventing the spread of military and related technology is not universal in the sense that it transcends all limitations of space and history; it is very much a contingent interest resulting from the framing of issues relating peace, war, and military technology in terms of the image of "proliferation."

Always carrying the caveat that these interests are constrained by the universal interest in proliferation control, the various subject positions constructed by the frame constitute a number of varied interests for states in those positions to pursue. The first of these distinct subject positions is that of supplier. The interest we would expect would adhere to suppliers is that in supplying the technology in question. Although this interest is recognized by the supplier groups, it is downplayed. The recognition is found in the practice, common to each of the supplier groups, of leaving the final decision on particular exports to the members independently. When suppliers engage in the practice of supplier controls—that is, when the members act qua suppliers within the "proliferation" frame—they act on a rather different interest. As the Wassenaar Arrangement puts it, "This arrangement is also intended to enhance co-operation to *prevent* the acquisition of armaments and sensitive dual-use items for military end-uses."[46] In fact, throughout the document the actions of the *group,* as opposed to those of the individual members acting outside the group, are directed at the denial of technology transfer.

An interest to supply on behalf of suppliers is therefore masked by the practices of proliferation control. I return to this problem later, inquiring into the origin of this interest and into the implications of its being downplayed by the "proliferation" image. But what of the interests of recipients, as opposed to suppliers, in the practices of control over technology transfers? Again, an interest in acquiring military and dual-use technology is implicitly recognized by the practices of supplier control; it finds expression in the Wassenaar Arrangement, for example, in two ways. The first is in the group's fundamental purpose of "promoting transparency and greater responsibility in transfers of conventional arms and dual-use goods and technologies, thus preventing destabilising accumulations." The second comes in the limitation the group places on itself not to "impede bona fide civil transactions."[47] Recipients therefore have an interest in engaging in bona fide commercial transactions and also in acquiring military capabilities, providing they are responsible and thus do not lead to destabilizing accumulations.

The interests recipients pursue within the "proliferation" image are thus constrained. Recipients have an interest in acquiring dual-use technology for civilian purposes and even in acquiring military technology, within reason. The reason in question is determined in two related ways. First, recipients have a right to "acquire legitimate means with which to defend themselves pursuant to Article 51 of the Charter of the United Nations,"[48] and, second, those means become illegitimate when they lead to destabilizing accumulations. The limits are very important to the "proliferation" image, because once a state steps beyond them it can be identified not as a legitimate recipient but rather as a rogue or an outlaw state. The only states to pursue an interest in acquiring military or military-related technology beyond these limits, in other words, are those identified as enemies by the "proliferation" image; these limits, however, are by no means natural, and they are impossible to determine in advance. Again, the Wassenaar Arrangement is illuminating in this regard. The conditions in which states act on illegitimate, rather than legitimate, interests are determined by the members of the arrangement. They seek to deny military equipment "if the situation in a region or the behavior of a state is, or becomes, *a cause for serious concern to the Participating States*."[49]

The nature of the constraint placed on recipients, the line that divides the interests of recipients from those of rogues or outlaws, is determined by the serious concern of the members of the Wassenaar Arrangement. If we return for a moment to Waltz's characterization of the national interest, a glaring problem emerges. For Waltz, "To say that a country acts according to its national interest means that, having examined its security requirements, it tries to meet them."[50] The way in which the "proliferation" image constructs the security environment in which states make such examinations, however, precludes most states from the ability to do this. A state may examine its security requirements and try to meet them, only to be told by the members of Wassenaar or any other supplier group that, unfortunately, the state was mistaken about its security requirements and that such action goes beyond the security requirements of the state, leading instead to destabilizing accumulations. It is important to recognize that the state in question is incapable of determining its security requirements in advance of the authoritative determination by supplier groups and so, on Waltz's terms, is unable to act in its national interest.

Different framings of these same problems would construct the interests of the actors in rather different ways. If we return to the images I outlined in Chapter 3, for example, we can find the possibility of somewhat different interests. The right of states to self-defense and the concomitant right to acquire the means to that defense were recognized in the Cold War period—indeed, evocations of that right routinely cite Article 51 of the UN Charter as authority. At the same time, the arms trade was framed largely by a commercial image. Such a framing makes the distinction between legitimate and illegitimate purchases much more difficult to sustain—markets tend to generate norms of consumer sovereignty. Let us then assume that controls were to be applied to regional arms accumulations in terms of an "arms control" frame. Such a framing was possible at the end of the Gulf War, as U.S. President Bush's May 1991 speech to the U.S. Air Force Academy proposed a Middle East arms control process.[51] What followed from the speech was the production of the "proliferation" frame, but regional arms control was also clearly possible. Such a frame allows for a negotiation of legitimate interests among those most directly affected by the accumulations. Interestingly, the overall goal of an arms control process is similar to that espoused by proliferation control: to maintain stable regional balances. The difference is that those in the region determine the nature of that stability and the limits that constrain legitimate interests. None of this is to say that such negotiated limits will necessarily be agreed in all or, indeed, any instances but that the *interests* in each case are very different because the descriptive frame within which the all-important examination of a given state's security requirements takes place is also different.

The possibility that a framing in which the limits on interest are to be negotiated might not succeed in generating agreement on those limits creates an important problem. If interests are determined *entirely* within the discourse in which they are pursued, such negotiation should not be possible. States, however, participate in a series of overlapping discourses that constitute interests in ways not necessarily compatible. The recognition of multiple discourses is important to allow discourses to highlight, downplay, and hide objects, identities, and interests. Without recognizing the multiple discourses within which states both act and are constituted, the only way I could speak of highlighting, downplaying, and hiding would be to speak of a grounding in an extradiscursive reality.[52]

Intersecting Interests

In autumn 1993, newly installed U.S. president Clinton told the UN General Assembly, "I have made non-proliferation one of our nation's highest priorities."[53] Read from the perspective of Waltz's understanding of interests, it would seem that the United States examined its security requirements, found proliferation to be a threat to its interests, and acted to counter that threat. Thus, for example, the new under-secretary of state for international security affairs was assigned to counter the threat: "When Secretary Christopher discussed this position with me, he focused on non-proliferation and the priority which the Clinton Administration would be giving to counter proliferation of very deadly weapons."[54] We have seen, however, that more—or less—was going on than the United States determining a threat to its security interests. The identification of weapons proliferation as a threat was driven in large part by the search within the U.S. military for a justification of its continued institutional prominence.

In Chapter 4 I discussed Michael Klare's findings concerning the role of the U.S. military in constructing the threat of rogue states: "Having filled the "threat blank" identified by Senator Nunn in early 1990 [with "the general model of a 'rogue state' ruled by an 'outlaw regime'"], senior Pentagon officials began to develop a strategic blueprint to guide the development of military policy and justify the preservation of near–Cold War military apparatus."[55] The process had been driven by the requirement of

Colin Powell, Chairman of the Joint Chiefs of Staff, that "the U.S. remain a global superpower . . . [which] would require the maintenance of a powerful, high-tech military establishment equipped with a full range of modern combat systems."[56] There are two important points concerning this story and its relationship to the interests of a "proliferation" image.

The first implication of the role played by the U.S. military in constructing the "proliferation" frame is that it problematizes the simple reading of the United States examining its security requirements and seeking to act on that examination. This Waltzian reading—the same reading I illustrated earlier from Charles Krauthammer, who saw the threat of weapons proliferation slowly dawning on the West—equates the interests embedded in the examination process with the national interest. Because the United States is acting against weapons proliferation, the United States must have identified an interest in preventing proliferation—a claim warranted by Morgenthau's argument that interest is what connects analysis to the object of that analysis. Klare's story suggests that the institutionalized military in the United States had an interest in maintaining a particular form of organization and level of material resources. That interest propelled the creation of the "proliferation" frame, and it was the sort of bureaucratic policy process—so well described by Graham Allison— that produced proliferation control as one of the highest U.S. priorities.[57]

From where did this interest in preserving a particular form of military establishment emerge in the first place? I have suggested that actors—states primarily but by no means exclusively—enter into discursive practices, such as proliferation control, with interests already partially constituted by their engagement in other practices. Which discourse created such a strong interest within the U.S. military in "a powerful, high-tech military establishment equipped with a full range of modern combat systems"?[58] The answer is suggested in part by Klare's account of General Powell's argument: Powell saw this form of military establishment as required of a global superpower. In more general terms, General Powell assumed a relationship exists between a particular form of military organization and equipment and a particular location in the international system. This assumption draws on a rich set of resources concerning the nature of the state, sovereignty, and the military in international life. It is a discursive relationship that is important if one is to understand the movement of military technology, but it is also one that is downplayed or even hidden by the "proliferation" image.

Military power is not merely a requirement of global superpowers, it is intimately tied to the nature of the modern state. Keith Krause has noted the relationship between arms and statehood: "The primary driving force behind the large-scale production of arms is the existence of states in potentially conflictive relationships operating under the security dilemma in a self-help system. . . . The first consequence is that large-scale arms production should emerge wherever a state system exists, and more specifically as a simultaneous accompaniment to the birth of the modern state system out of the European feudal order."[59]

Unfortunately, Krause seems here to take the nature and operation of states systems as natural and given, as arms production emerges necessarily wherever a state system exists. The end of the quotation is more promising, however, relating large-scale arms production to the birth of the modern European states system. A considerable body of literature has emerged in international relations in the 1990s exploring the nature of the discursive underpinning of the modern states system. R. B. J. Walker's work, for example, shows how states, the security dilemma, and the self-help system are products of theoretical practices of interpretation and action.[60] Sovereignty is particularly important in the construction of the modern state as a 1996 collection of essays on sovereignty found: "Sovereignty provides textual and/or contextual prescriptions for what a state must do to be recognized as sovereign."[61] One of the most important things a state must do to be recognized as sovereign is to construct a modern military.

Mark Suchman and Dana Eyre have studied the role the construction of sovereignty plays in driving the building of arms and military organizations. They argue that "countries procure arms simply because such actions are an inherent part of the role of the 'independent,' 'modern' nation-state."[62] This drive to arm to demonstrate a state's independence or sovereignty means the symbolic value of the weaponry rather than its military utility is what matters. Suchman and Eyre further suggest that the same argument applies to individual weapons as well as to a military as such. Thus particular weapons—they cite supersonic aircraft as an example—will be procured because of the meanings ascribed to those weapons rather than because they fill a particular strategic need.[63] At the entry level of the international system, possession of some form of modern military and its attendant contemporary technology is a badge of membership. Possession of a military is a potent symbol of statehood, and the potency is derived from its importance in gaining and sustaining the international recognition that is constitutive of sovereignty. At the other end of the scale, a global superpower needs a powerful, high-tech military establishment equipped with a full range of modern combat systems. In between these two positions, differential locations in the hierarchy of states are marked off in part by specific weapons, so the possession of certain weapons is considered the sine qua non for claiming places higher up the international ladder. Perhaps of central importance in this regard are nuclear arms.

When elected in May 1997, the first Labour government in the United Kingdom for almost two decades promised it would conduct a comprehensive defense review. Remarkably, such a review had not been undertaken since the end of the Cold War, despite the global desire to realize a peace dividend in a context of government fiscal restraint. Despite the end of the Cold War and the election of a Labour government for the first time since the 1970s, the review was not all-encompassing. As an official Ministry of Defense explanatory document put it, the "Review did not start with a blank piece of paper, but operated within parameters set out in the Government's General Election manifesto, including strong defense, security based on NATO, *and retention of Trident* combined with multinational arms control. . . . Within these guidelines, the Review took a fresh look at all aspects of defense policy and programmes."[64] Trident is the British nuclear submarine fleet, its sole nuclear weapons capacity. Thus the parameters of the defense review, which were otherwise extremely broad, explicitly excluded this one weapons program from a review of "all aspects of defense policy."

Several points are noteworthy about the British government decision to exclude Trident from the defense review. Throughout the 1980s the Labour Party had been fiercely antinuclear in general and anti-Trident in particular. Although the party had dropped much of its antinuclear policy during the modernization process designed to make it electable, the possession of nuclear weapons was still hardly the cornerstone of party policy. More to the point, the end of the Cold War had made continued reliance on nuclear deterrence increasingly questionable. During the Cold War the United Kingdom and France could at least argue that their independent deterrent was necessary to guard against decoupling. Without these nuclear capabilities, Western deterrence rested on the U.S. threat to risk the continental United States for the protection of continental Europe—a threat many in Western Europe found hard to believe. The decoupling problem, however, required enmity with the Soviet Union as a precondition. Once the USSR was dissolved and the East came to join the West—particularly now that the former Warsaw Treaty Organization states are lining up to join the Atlantic Alliance—the arguments for Trident, rooted in the "deterrence" image of the Cold War, became unsustainable. Finally, the Labour Party came to power promising to maintain the previous Conservative government's overall spending targets. In other words, if the party were to spend more on areas both traditionally associated with Labour and on which it had campaigned—notably education and welfare—it had to find savings somewhere else. Trident is the most expensive program in the British military.

On the face of it, then, there was every reason to expect the Trident program would be downgraded if not eliminated in a Labour defense review. Instead, and rather remarkably, we find it is not even to be considered in that review. It would seem that just as the Labour government discovered upon taking power that a defense industry was an important part of the British industrial base and so entered into defense contracts with Indonesia, it also found that a robust nuclear deterrent was something the United Kingdom could not do without. The policy framework within which the defense review proceeded outlined the interests the United Kingdom sought to promote through its defense policy, which were summarized in five paragraphs of a supporting essay. The only interest that can easily be read in a way that requires a nuclear submarine force is the first, that "Britain's place in the world is determined by our interests as a nation and as *a leading member of the international community.*"[65]

At a time when Britain's place in the world has been under threat not only because of its century-long decline—powerfully symbolized by the withdrawal from Hong Kong so soon after the election—but also from potential transfers of sovereignty to the European Union, particularly in the form of a single European currency, nuclear weapons remain a potent symbol of Britain's claim to be a leading member of the international community. Colin Powell was determined that the United States would remain a global superpower, which meant maintaining a military force similar to that held by the superpowers when superpower really meant something. Similarly, Tony Blair seems determined that the United Kingdom will remain a global power, as symbolized by its permanent seat on the UN Security Council along with the other nuclear powers. The continued recognition of the UK's place as a great power, it seems, requires maintaining an arms industry and particularly a nuclear capability.

The production of arms and the possession of weapons of mass destruction and advanced conventional weapons are intimately tied to the core discourses of the modern world system: sovereignty and statehood. Part of what it means to be a state in the modern states system is to possess a military that is "modern" by whatever markers of modernity are in play at any given time. Part of what it means to be a global superpower in the modern world system is to possess a comprehensive high-technology arsenal. Part of what it means to be a power in the modern world system is to possess a credible arms industry; to be able to put *great* in front of *power,* it seems sufficient, if not necessary, to possess a nuclear arsenal. The constitutive discourses of the contemporary international system, as a moment of the modern states system, constitute interests in the production and possession of precisely the technologies of primary concern to the proliferation agenda.

It is important to recognize that these discursive constructions also play a crucial part in establishing the dynamics of the proliferation process. Krause's study of the dynamics of the global system of arms production and trade has determined that for most states export is a crucial component of maintaining an arms industry. In the Cold War, only the United States and the Soviet Union were capable of maintaining their defense-industrial base from supplying domestic demand.[66] Now, only the United States might be able to make such a claim, and even that is not certain—since the late 1970s the United States has been far more concerned with selling arms abroad than it was previously, and it has clearly become the world's leading supplier of weapons. The potency of this dynamic is also seen in the British volte-face on Indonesia. Thus on the so-called supply side of the transfer of arms and technology, the discursive construction of sovereignty and its relation to an arms industry contain an interest in supplying.

On the so-called demand side, this discursive construction is no less potent. As Eyre and Suchman put it in a 1996 study of the dynamics of conventional arms proliferation, "Weapons spread not because of a match between their technical capabilities and national security needs but because of the highly symbolic, normative nature of militaries and their weaponry."[67] High-technology conventional weapons symbolize modernity and sovereignty in the contemporary world. Weapons of mass destruction, particularly nuclear weapons, symbolize great-power status, as evidenced recently by the British decision on Trident but as also reflected in the French decision to acquire and maintain a nuclear arsenal. This symbolism is seen most powerfully, of course, in the permanent membership of the UN Security Council. In the face of these symbolic meanings attached to particular technologies, states that seek statehood or to establish themselves as powers within the international system have little choice but to seek the appropriate forms of military technology.

This connection between sovereignty-statehood and weaponry raises the greatest irony of the proliferation agenda. The spread of military technology, which is of such concern to states of the West, is driven largely by interests found in the representations of state and sovereignty that circulate throughout the contemporary international system. That circulation takes place through the practices of states that reproduce the discourses out of which those representations flow. In other words, when the United Kingdom "ring-fences" the Trident program in its defense review, it is reproducing the nuclear arsenal as a marker of status in the international system. Similarly, when the United States revises its military posture in the aftermath of the Cold War on the basis of a need to maintain a fully functional, high-technology military capable of fighting two or more wars simultaneously, it strongly reinforces the relationship among statehood, status, and that particular form of military organization and equipment. To produce that military posture in the post–Cold War world, the United States played a central role in building proliferation as a primary international security threat and the rogue state as its central villain. In other words, the very process of developing and responding to a "proliferation" agenda in the past few years has reproduced and reinforced the discursive construction of what it means to be a sovereign state in the contemporary world, which, in turn, is central to the spread of advanced weaponry and related military technologies.

These interests, so important to the global production and transfer of arms, are at best downplayed and more commonly hidden by the "proliferation" image. By gathering states together as suppliers, "proliferation" recognizes the interest these states have in supplying but masks that interest behind the overarching interest in preventing proliferation. Because of the way state sovereignty is understood in the contemporary international system, the more general interests that states necessarily have in the acquisition of military technology are almost entirely hidden by the "proliferation" image. The spread is conceived and acted on as an autonomous, technologically driven process, not as one motivated by the requirements of *being* in the state system. What is more, the miscreants in the "proliferation" image are seen as acting in an excessive or aggressive manner and are constructed as outlaws—those who step beyond the established rules of the international game. There is absolutely no recognition that rather than the behavior of outlaws, the acquisition of the trappings of modern state power is central to admission to the game in the first place, that states behave this way precisely because that is what it means to be a state.

Conclusion

It has been a truism of international relations theory that states act in their own interests. The provenance of those interests, however, has been largely ignored. I demonstrate in this chapter that those interests are produced in the same fashion as the states and their actions are produced— through discursive representations and engagement in practice. The discourses that produce interests—and objects and identities—are not discrete and entirely self-contained. Rather, the discourses intersect, producing both reinforcements of and contradictions among the interests constituted in different discursive fields. Only in this way, in fact, can we examine discourse and practice to discover what is highlighted, downplayed, and hidden without retreating to an appeal to the extradiscursive.

The role of discourse in producing interests allows us also to understand the seeming puzzle of the history of the CTBT. From the time the idea was first proposed, the CTBT had been framed within a "disarmament" image, as a crucial instrument in slowing and ultimately reversing the growth of the superpower nuclear arsenals. As such and in conditions of a cold war, the United States found the CTBT not to be in its interests; India, however, a leading proponent of disarmament, was a leading supporter of the CTBT. By the time the CTBT was negotiated, the treaty had been

reframed as an instrument of proliferation control. That reframing constituted a different series of interests in relation to the treaty's conclusion
and, most dramatically, saw the United States and India reverse positions.

As interesting and dramatic as the reversal of positions on the CTBT
might be, however, the more important interests produced outside the "proliferation" image and then intersecting with it are those connected with the
nature of sovereignty itself. Those interests were instrumental in giving rise
to the "proliferation" image, which, in turn, downplayed and hid them. This
intersection of the "proliferation" image and the state sovereignty discourse
suggests an important contradiction at the heart of the proliferation agenda.
It begs for questions of the efficacy and the future of proliferation control
practices to be addressed and therefore leads me to consider the two most
important sites of proliferation activity: the UN weapons inspection system
in Iraq and the nuclear tests conducted in South Asia in May 1998.

8

Appropriate Actions?

In the history of "proliferation" 1998 may prove to be a watershed year. The year began and ended with crises over the UN weapons inspection system in Iraq. The crisis late in the year included extensive air strikes against Iraq, which seem likely to mark the end of UNSCOM, at least as it has operated since 1991—if not entirely. Sandwiched between these two crises, in May 1998 India became the first state since the NPT was signed to test nuclear weapons openly, and it was followed immediately by Pakistan. These events should be profoundly troubling to the promoters of proliferation control. For 25 years the NPT seemed to have worked to prevent any expansion of the nuclear club. Now, just as the NPT was extended indefinitely to serve as the linchpin of a broad set of proliferation control practices, its record was blemished for the first time in its history. On the other hand, Iraq was the prototype rogue and had been subjected to the most intense control practices imaginable. The Indian test and the apparent demise of UNSCOM lead us to question how appropriate the practices of proliferation control have been, even in their own terms. In this chapter I explore that question through a brief consideration of the UNSCOM experience and the Indian nuclear test.

The UNSCOM Experience

In the crisis over Iraq in autumn 1998, three of the permanent members of the UN Security Council were not convinced that military force was the appropriate response to Iraq's intransigence. Although the United States, supported by Britain, seemed willing to use force, the other three countries sent UN Secretary-General Khofi Annan to Baghdad to see if he could work something out. It turned out that he could. Once more, as had happened so often over the previous six years, at the last possible moment

Iraq backed off just far enough to avoid a fight with the United States and its diminished band of allies. The Iraqi letter signaling a willingness to back down arrived at the Secretary-General's office within hours, reportedly, of a massive U.S. assault; even then, the United States and Great Britain initially refused to accept the Iraqi retreat. Frantic diplomatic maneuvering was needed to earn the Iraqis another chance.

In response to the Iraqi retreat, the United States led the UN Security Council in reminding Iraq that it faced the "severest consequences" if it failed again to comply. This was a reminder to Iraq of the threat included in UN Security Council Resolution 1154, which had been passed on 2 March 1998—the last time Iraq and the UN–United States had all but come to blows over compliance with UNSCOM inspections.[1] By the terms of that resolution Iraq should have faced the consequences with its latest act of defiance, but it appeared that Iraq had won another reprieve. The pattern of the crisis earlier that same year had been repeated almost exactly.[2] This time, however, the next crisis came extremely quickly. Thus in December 1998 the United States and its British allies showed what they had meant by "severest consequences," launching a series of air strikes over a four-day period. The strikes were more extensive than any since the Gulf War, and they rivaled even those.[3] Following this series of raids Iraq was defiant and, at the time of this writing, was refusing to allow UNSCOM to return. In February 1999 the Security Council established advisory boards in an attempt to restart the inspection process, but at the time of writing it seemed clear that UN inspection practices in Iraq would be fundamentally reconstituted, if not stopped entirely.

The United Nations, victorious in the Gulf War, set out the terms of its cease-fire in Security Council Resolution 687 of 8 April 1991. This resolution established the Special Commission that was to oversee the destruction of Iraq's weapons of mass destruction and their production facilities. It is worth remembering that Resolution 687, which Iraq accepted (if under duress), called for Iraq "to submit to the Secretary-General, within fifteen days of the adoption of the present resolution, a declaration of the locations, amounts and types of all items specified in paragraph 8 and agree to urgent, on-site inspection as specified below."[4] This means that by 23 April 1991 Iraq should have provided a full declaration to the United Nations of all of its weapons of mass destruction. It is fair to say that the time line was too short, given the scope of the task. What is of particular interest at this point in the discussion, however, is the nature of the on-site inspections established by Resolution 687. What had the UN Special Commission been doing for the previous seven years, and why did Iraq still have *any* chemical, biological, or nuclear weapons capability?

At the beginning of October 1997, the chair of the UN Special Commission submitted to the Security Council his regular report on the recent activities of the commission in Iraq—the twenty-ninth such report since the end of the Gulf War.[5] This report covered UNSCOM's activities in Iraq for the preceding six months; the other twenty-eight had reported on activities from the time of the first substantive inspection in May 1991, less than three months after the end of the Gulf War. The report summarized the state of UNSCOM's knowledge concerning Iraq's missile program, as well as its chemical and biological weapons program (the IAEA is concerned with inspection of the nuclear program). This summary makes for quite remarkable reading:

> Significant progress has been achieved in the missile area. The Commission is now in a position to be able to account for practically all, except two, imported combat missiles that were once the core of Iraq's proscribed missile force. The Commission has also accounted for all declared operational missile launchers, both imported and indigenously produced. To achieve the ultimate objective of full disposal of Iraq's proscribed operational missile assets, the next important step is to account for proscribed missile warheads. . . . More work is still required to achieve the same results in the area of Iraq's indigenous production of proscribed missile systems.[6]

Somewhat less had been achieved in terms of Iraq's chemical weapons program: "Important progress has been made in this area, of which the recently completed destruction of chemical weapons–related equipment and materials is an example. However, the ability of the Commission to report positively on disarmament of this category of weapons of mass destruction will require the provision by Iraq of much more and accurate material and related access by the Commission relevant to the warheads and VX questions."[7] Finally, on the issue of biological weapons, "This is an area that is unredeemed by progress or *any approximation of the known facts* of Iraq's programme."[8] UNSCOM was unable to report that Iraq had been disarmed in any of these three areas, although it was close to revealing the full extent of the Iraqi ballistic missile capability and had made clear moves toward chemical disarmament. Most remarkably, UNSCOM had no "approximation of the known facts" concerning Iraq's biological weapons.

This conclusion after six years of UNSCOM's operation is astonishing, but the degree to which this should concern us can be made apparent only by considering what UNSCOM had attempted in an effort to gain an approximation of the known facts. By the time of the October 1997 report there had been 56 UNSCOM inspection visits specifically concerning biological weapons, each of which spent roughly one working week in Iraq for a total of more than a year of full-time inspection work. What is more, by April 1995 UNSCOM had established a permanent system of biological monitoring in Iraq. Here is a description of the activities of the monitors over a six-month period (April–October 1997):

As with chemical monitoring, the number of sites and items of equipment subject to biological monitoring has continued to grow. Full implementation of the biological annexes has shown that the items contained therein amount, in Iraq, to many thousands of pieces of dual-capable equipment and materials. There are some 90 sites subject to regular monitoring and 893 items of tagged equipment. The biological monitoring group has undertaken some 240 inspections in the reporting period.[9]

UNSCOM's attempts to determine Iraq's biological weapons capabilities comprise a full working year of directed and dedicated inspections over a six-year period plus three years of full-time monitoring of up to 90 sites by monitors who averaged more than one inspection visit a day every day. Given such an intensive effort, backed by the weight of the UN Security Council and repeated U.S. demonstrations of willingness to support the efforts militarily, the conclusion that the commission could not approximate the state of Iraq's biological weapons appears beyond belief.

UNSCOM's conclusions about Iraq's biological weapons are only the most remarkable of a set of generally consistent conclusions. UNSCOM has expended tremendous effort to carry out the mandate of UN Security Council Resolution 687. By October 1997 there had been over 200 UNSCOM inspection visits to Iraq, as well as almost 100 "special visits" by UNSCOM officials.[10] In addition, UNSCOM has established ongoing monitoring systems in Iraq not only for biological weapons but also for chemical weapons, missiles, and exports-imports. These monitoring systems essentially replicate those already in place for nuclear weapons under IAEA full-scope safeguards. With all of this effort, after more than six years we might expect more definitive and substantive conclusions from the UNSCOM chair, and we might also expect that reassembling the missile boats would be unnecessary.

For my purposes, the crucial feature of the UNSCOM experience is that it is an instantiation of the "proliferation" image. What is more, given the attention and resources lavished on UNSCOM compared to any other element of proliferation control practices, if these practices are to work anywhere it should be here. It is barely conceivable that a more extensive and thorough effort to combat proliferation *could* be mounted, let alone that it *would* be. The degree of access granted to UNSCOM in Iraq resulted from Iraq's defeat in the Gulf War. No state except one that had experienced a similar defeat would accept the kinds of intrusive monitoring practiced on Iraq, and it is unlikely that the members of the United Nations would be willing to pay for an operation on the scale of UNSCOM in any but the most extreme circumstances. UNSCOM therefore has pushed the practices of proliferation control as far as they can be pushed.

"Proliferation" imagines the security problems of military technology as produced by "the spread of technology related to the research for or production of [weapons of mass destruction]."[11] It therefore divides control strategies by the particular technology and applies controls to those uses identified as legitimate, as well as tracking the global movement of the relevant technologies. The "proliferation" image is precisely reproduced in the practices of UNSCOM. From the beginning, inspections were organized first on the basis of technologies. The initial UNSCOM inspections were conducted by the IAEA to "develop an over-all picture of the nature, direction and capabilities of the Iraqi nuclear programme."[12] The majority of the remainder of UNSCOM's work was organized according to a plan finally submitted to the Security Council on 2 October 1991. The plan outlined the means of "ongoing monitoring and verification of Iraq's compliance with its obligations" under Resolution 687.[13]

The organization of the plan clearly reflects its reliance on the understandings constitutive of the "proliferation" image. Having set out the scope of the plan with reference to Resolution 687 in Section A, the document lists general provisions relating to the rights of the commission and the duties of Iraq in Section B. Section C details provisions related to chemical items, Section D lists provisions related to biological items, and Section E includes provisions related to missiles. The structure is repeated in the annexes, with detailed descriptions of the rights of UNSCOM inspectors followed by three annexes detailing the technologies that might be related, in turn, to chemical, biological, and missile production. The beginning of annex 2, on chemical weapons, is particularly revealing: "The following list contains chemicals that could be used for the development, production or acquisition of chemical weapons, but which also have significant uses for purposes not prohibited by Resolution 687 (1991)."[14] Here we see a focus on precursor technologies rather than on weapons and a recognition of the need to police the border between legitimate and illegitimate applications of these technologies.

Given this initial plan, it is not surprising to find that the practical work of the commission fits neatly with the "proliferation" image. UNSCOM inspections are numbered according to a dual system. Here, for example, are the designations of the first five UNSCOM missions in the 200 range, which took place in August and September 1997: BW 56/UNSCOM 200, CIM 7/UNSCOM 201, CW 41/UNSCOM 202, CW 42/UNSCOM 203, BM 58/UNSCOM 204. The inspections are numbered sequentially as UNSCOM missions and also sequentially according to their technological focus: BW for biological weapons, CW for chemical weapons, BM for ballistic missiles, and CIM for concealment investigation missions.

The UNSCOM numbers are given to inspection visits by UNSCOM inspectors. In addition to this form of inspection, UNSCOM has established permanent monitoring facilities in Iraq, which continuously survey Iraqi activities. Again, these monitoring regimes are established by technology, with one each for chemical weapons, biological weapons, and ballistic missiles, as well as IAEA monitoring for nuclear weapons. As with the safeguards system, these monitoring regimes watch the application of technologies that could be used for the production of prohibited weapons to verify that they have not been so used. A fifth ongoing monitoring system has been established jointly by the IAEA and UNSCOM, which is particularly interesting from the point of view of this argument; it is an export-import monitoring mechanism for Iraq. Such a system to monitor the flow of materials into Iraq (resulting in "some 130 inspections at sites inside Iraq, including points of entry" in the period from April to October 1997)[15] is the logical extension of a practice founded on supplier controls and committed to the control of the movement of technology.

The use of export-import monitoring in Iraq marks UNSCOM as the ultimate "proliferation" practice. The sovereignty discourse generally prevents suppliers from systematically monitoring imports of controlled technologies and the uses to which they are put. The best they can achieve is control over exports with the addition of end-use certification, a declaration from the recipient of the uses to which the technology will be put. Iraq's unique position as the vanquished allows the Security Council to impose something that would otherwise be impossible—the intrusive monitoring of imports to verify the uses to which technology is put. UNSCOM's export-import monitoring is the practice implied by the use of supplier groups and export controls, a practice prevented only by intervention of the norms of sovereignty.[16]

UNSCOM needs to be seen as the creation of the "proliferation" image, as an instantiation of the meanings constitutive of the proliferation control agenda that is the focus of this book. What is more, UNSCOM is the most refined form of the practices made possible by that image. The kind of access UNSCOM has to Iraq is predicated on Iraq's status as the paradigm rogue state and particularly by its defeat in the Gulf War. The 1991 plan, for example, establishes for UNSCOM "the right (a) to designate for inspection *any* site, facility, activity, material or other item in Iraq" and "(c) to conduct *unannounced* inspections and inspections at short notice."[17] The connections to the more general practices of proliferation control are clear, with both nuclear and chemical inspection regimes claiming as wide and as short-notice access as possible. Nevertheless, such universal and immediate access is unimaginable except in the special conditions in which Iraq finds itself. This means that the general proliferation control practices are attempting to do what UNSCOM is doing without the means UNSCOM has at its disposal. UNSCOM, on the other hand, with the facilities to make hundreds of inspections a year and with the right of unfettered access backed by U.S. warships, cannot approximate the true facts of Iraq's biological weapons program.

I want to make it clear that I am not faulting UNSCOM or its inspectors for this remarkable conclusion. As we are routinely reminded whenever the question of biological weapons is raised, making useful quantities of biological agent is a simple process, requiring only the kind of equipment necessary to run a microbrewery. Therefore we should not be surprised that verifying compliance with the biological weapons provisions of Resolution 687 is proving next to impossible, because anyone can run a microbrewery in their basement. Nevertheless, what *is* astonishing is that supposedly hardheaded strategic analysts and policymakers continue to put faith in a broad plan of action that requires something as patently implausible as verifying the state of the biological weapons program in a country the size of Iraq—or a country the size of Andorra, for that matter. What is truly remarkable about the UNSCOM finding is that the "proliferation" image seems so robust in the face of such strong evidence of its impotence.

The difficulties UNSCOM has faced in Iraq stem from the contradiction between the "proliferation" image and state sovereignty. For UNSCOM to implement the most extensive version possible of proliferation control, Iraq's sovereignty must be radically denied. Iraq is unable to declare any of its territory (presidential palaces, for instance), possessions (papers or laboratory equipment), or activities off-limits to international inspection. "Normal" sovereign states can do just that—implicitly declare *all* of their territory, possessions, and even activities to be off-limits. Nevertheless, the potency of sovereignty is such that despite formally denying Iraq those sovereign rights, UNSCOM is still limited by them. The Special Commission mounted concealment investigation missions separate from the general missions of monitoring and verification. If Iraq ordered members of the UNSCOM inspection teams to leave, as it did several times, they had to leave. When Iraq declared presidential palaces off-limits to the UNSCOM inspectorate, UNSCOM did not enter those facilities.

The UNSCOM experience suggests that the practices of proliferation control might not be appropriate, if by that we mean they can achieve their technical goals. In May 1998 we had a startling demonstration of how inappropriate these practices are in terms of the broader political goal of preventing the emergence of new weapon states. For the first time since the completion of the NPT, a state declared itself to be a nuclear weapon state by openly testing such weapons. In 1974 India had conducted a test explosion it insisted was of a peaceful nuclear device. In 1998 there was no such pretense; India tested a series of nuclear weapons, tests that were followed two weeks later by Pakistani tests.

Indian Nuclear Tests and Proliferation

The NPT has generally been hailed as a tremendous success. The treaty was negotiated at a time when it was commonly expected that there would be roughly 20 nuclear weapon states by 1980, with France and the PRC having just joined the three initial nuclear powers. India's 1974 peaceful nuclear explosion (PNE) test was the only open blemish on the NPT record after it was signed—although a number of states were trying to achieve nuclear status, of which several had actually developed some form of nuclear weaponry. By 1980 there were still only the five nuclear powers declared by the NPT's conclusion in 1968, and that figure still stood at the time of the UN Security Council Summit in 1992. As we have seen, Iraq was discovered to have been close to building a nuclear weapon, and South Africa had both built and dismantled six nuclear bombs.[18] Thanks to Mordecai Vannunu, Israel's secret arsenal was made less secret, although it was still not officially acknowledged.[19] Indeed, the apparent success of the NPT explains in part its importance in the construction of the "proliferation" image in the post–Cold War world. The fact that India and then Pakistan have *now* openly tested nuclear weapons should be of tremendous concern to those who have championed the "proliferation" image. It is no coincidence that the move to declare nuclear status came when it did; rather, the events on the subcontinent in May 1998 can be seen as a product of the practices I have examined.

India's opposition to the "proliferation" image is rooted in its long-standing opposition to the NPT. That opposition is founded on the legislated inequality of the NPT, which legitimates nuclear possession for some while denying it to others. The inequality, however, was conceived as a contingent inequality to be overcome by the nuclear weapon states' commitment to end the arms race and move to nuclear disarmament. For more than 20 years the promise of that commitment proved sufficient to keep India from openly declaring itself a nuclear state, but it was not enough to bring the state into the NPT fold. For that, India wanted a definite process leading to nuclear disarmament among the recognized nuclear weapon states. The end of the Cold War brought an end to the arms race, but instead of continuing on the path of nuclear disarmament *proliferation* was identified as the greatest threat. The inequality of the NPT was not being overcome by fulfillment of the pledge for nuclear disarmament, and further that inequality was being reproduced across the full range of military technologies and, what was worse, their civilian counterparts.

In this context, the CTBT's achievement in the way it was achieved must be seen as something of a disaster. The CTBT had taken on considerable symbolic meaning in discussions of the NPT commitment to nuclear disarmament. The CTBT was seen as the vital first step in demonstrating a real dedication on the part of the nuclear weapon states to abide by that commitment. As I demonstrated in Chapter 7, however, the CTBT as it was concluded in 1996 is a "proliferation" rather than a "disarmament" instrument. This means it can be seen, and is seen by India, as further institutionalization of the inequality of the NPT. As a consequence, India refused consensus within the negotiating forum and then voiced strenuous objections when the same text was adopted by the UN General Assembly and opened for signature—objections that centered on its inclusion in the list of states that had to ratify for the CTBT to enter into force. This provision, India argued, marked the first time a state had an obligation imposed on it by a treaty to which it had not agreed.

India has long promised to accept a test ban that is part of a process of nuclear disarmament, pledging its willingness to forgo proceeding along the path to nuclear weapons if those who had traveled that path before would lead the way back. Instead, a CTBT has been signed that India sees—quite reasonably—as requiring that it forgo its nuclear option without the declared nuclear states giving up theirs, which is what the Indians have objected to within the nuclear nonproliferation regime all along. The leading states in the international system have made it clear that their weapons are sacrosanct. The United States has reversed its long-standing objection to the CTBT now that it believes it can maintain its stockpile (and even possibly improve on it) through simulated testing. France and China rushed to complete a last series of tests before the CTBT to bolster their nuclear positions. The United Kingdom launched a defense policy review that excluded the place of its Trident nuclear submarine fleet in Britain's military posture. The three nuclear states in NATO have resisted calls from some of their nonnuclear allies to rethink NATO strategy and remove its nuclear component.[20] Taken together, these practices reproduce and reinforce the NPT's fundamental inequality and rearticulate the connection between military power and international position that has as its pinnacle nuclear possession.

By the end of 1996 India was thus faced with an international practice that not only foreclosed the possibility of meeting its objections to the NPT but also reproduced and reinforced those objections in a variety of ways. Such a circumstance would not automatically produce an open nuclear test by India, but it created conditions of possibility for such an action. The constraints on India's openly declaring its nuclear status were removed with the conclusion of the CTBT. Put simply, the production of the "proliferation" image in the years following the Security Council's pledge to take appropriate action to prevent proliferation enabled India's nuclear tests. Furthermore, having consistently imagined South Asia in terms of the India-Pakistan dyad, the "proliferation" image almost demanded the subsequent Pakistani response.

The process that has been started since the tests occurred also reveals the connections I am making and strengthens the case that the "proliferation" framing of the CTBT was an important condition of possibility for the Indian tests. The heart of that process has been a series of bilateral negotiations among the United States, India, and Pakistan. At the same time, there have been discussions involving a range of other states, both bilaterally and at the United Nations. By autumn 1998 these various processes had produced a commitment by Pakistan to sign the CTBT by the end of 1999, as well as indications from India that it might be willing to sign under certain conditions.[21] The UN General Assembly had passed two resolutions, one calling on India and Pakistan to refrain from testing and to sign the CTBT, and another—sponsored by India—calling on the nuclear powers to change their nuclear doctrines and move toward nuclear disarmament.[22] A number of themes directly relevant to my argument have emerged from these processes: the connection to disarmament, access to high technology, and issues of status.

The Indian objection to practices of proliferation control rather than disarmament has been repeated strongly since the tests. The objection found its most public expression in the resolution on nuclear doctrine India sponsored in the First Committee of the General Assembly, which the committee adopted in November 1998. Furthermore, Indian officials repeatedly linked India's willingness to sign the CTBT and possibly even the NPT to a broader process of nuclear disarmament. For example, the Indian defense minister put two conditions on India signing the CTBT, one of which "centered around the question of disarmament, including nuclear disarmament which defines the CTBT."[23] If attempts are made to link India's acceptance of the CTBT—which is required for the treaty to enter into force—to a program of disarmament, the Indian tests may be seen as an important act in a drama of reframing. That is, the political pressure exerted by the Indian test may prove sufficient to rearticulate the CTBT to the "disarmament" image from which it was taken by the "proliferation" framing.

The second key Indian objection to "proliferation" has also been aired increasingly since the tests—restrictions on access to high technology. The problem was thrown into high relief by the immediate U.S. response to the May 1998 tests, which was to impose sanctions, including limits on high-technology exports to India (and Pakistan). India objected both to the general principle of denying access to technology and to the specific sanctions leveled against it. On the former, Indian "Prime Minister Atal Behari Vajpayee . . . regretted that the international nuclear regime today was highly distorted. 'On the one hand, the traditional nuclear weapons states want to keep the destructive power of nuclear technology in their own hands and resist nuclear disarmament. On the other hand, they restrict the enormous benefits of peaceful nuclear energy from reaching humanity at large that needs it most.'"[24] At the same time, Prime Minister Vajpayee set access to high technology as one of the conditions India would seek before signing the CTBT.[25] The linkage of high-technology access to the CTBT by both the United States and India is indicative of the reframing of the CTBT in terms of "proliferation."

The final important element of the posttest process is the connection between nuclear weapons and international status. A central problem with the "proliferation" framing and the practices that have emerged around it is the way in which they reinforce the link between status and nuclear possession. This link has been reaffirmed by the response to India's tests. The Indians have tentatively drawn attention to this linkage in statements on their conditions for joining the CTBT. The other condition enunciated by the defense minister in October 1988 was that India "would first like to have a clear view [of] how the US and other P-5 [five permanent members of the UN Security Council] states which are unwilling to accept its claim as a nuclear weapon state look at the issue and recognise it."[26]

The importance of status claims generally and of the recognition of India as a nuclear weapon state in particular can be seen from the U.S. response to the tests. Speaking at the Brookings Institution in November 1998, Deputy U.S. Secretary of State Strobe Talbott stated, "I would agree . . . that India and Pakistan deserve more attention than they have traditionally received from the United States government."[27] Nevertheless, Talbott also made it clear that the United States refuses to acknowledge India as an NWS, a refusal he tries to clothe in the mantle of multilateral consensus: "First, we remain committed to the common position of the P-5, G-8 [Group of Eight], the South Asian Task Force, notably including the desirability, the importance of the long-range goal of universal adherence to the Nuclear Non-Proliferation Treaty. That is to say we do not, will not concede even by implication that India and Pakistan have established themselves as nuclear weapons states under the NPT."[28]

At least one member of both the P-5 and the G-8, however, seems less absolute. France's response to the tests was more muted than that of the United States, and the French worked to moderate the Security Council response. In addition, France's direct discussions with India were interpreted, at least by the Indian press, as providing tacit acceptance of India's nuclear status—directly contradicting Talbott's position.[29] In fact, some suggest that the United States will concede, at least by implication, India's status as an NWS. This suggestion comes in the form of reports that the United States is willing to provide India with test simulation technology, as it has to other nuclear weapon states to win their acceptance of the CTBT.[30] If this report proves to be true, it would amount to the sort of tacit acceptance of India's nuclear status the United States publicly denies it is willing to give.

The reframing of the CTBT in terms of "proliferation" enabled the 1996 text by altering the U.S. interest in the CTBT in such a way that the United States led the drive for its completion. At the same time, however, it created the conditions of possibility for the most serious breach of the nuclear nonproliferation regime—the Indian tests and the subsequent tests by Pakistan. The linkages that have emerged between India's accession to the CTBT and issues of disarmament, technological access, and international status provide evidence of the importance of this reframing. Each of these issues is central to the contestation of the "proliferation" image, and none had previously been raised by India with reference to the CTBT. Indeed, the CTBT had been pursued by India as an alternative to the NPT, which it criticized precisely in these terms. The conclusion seems obvious: once again the practices of proliferation control seem far from appropriate, producing outcomes that are perverse.

Conclusion

UNSCOM and the NPT are central to the "proliferation" image. Because of the circumstances of its birth, UNSCOM represents the acme of proliferation control practices. It is impossible to imagine a more intrusive regime with more wide-ranging powers and with a greater commitment— by the United States at least—to support it. What is more, UNSCOM is clearly constituted by the "proliferation" image, instantiating the understandings that compose that image. On the other hand, the NPT is generally acknowledged as the linchpin of the broad proliferation control regime. The nuclear nonproliferation regime and its apparent success in stemming the growth of the nuclear club both spurred the creation of the "proliferation" image and served as the model for its practices. The events of 1998 around these two central sites reveal the dangerous flaws at the heart of "proliferation." UNSCOM has proven incapable of containing the prototype rogue, despite the resources it was able to mobilize and the skill and dedication of its members. The NPT's success was shattered at almost the very moment of its crowning achievement: indefinite extension as the centerpiece of the broad efforts of proliferation control. What is more, it was the conclusion of the CTBT as an integral element of the new proliferation control agenda that in large part produced the test that ended the NPT's success.

The conclusions to be drawn from this brief examination of UNSCOM and the Indian tests are damning. Both the repeated crises in Iraq and the shocking nuclear tests in South Asia must be seen as products of the practices of proliferation control, practices the states of the Western world have developed in answer to the UN Security Council's 1992 pledge to take appropriate action to combat the evils of proliferation. It is difficult to see any way to claim that actions which produced the events in Iraq in 1998, as well as the first two instances of open nuclear proliferation since the NPT was signed, are at all appropriate.

9

Conclusion

In January 1992 the UN Security Council pledged to take appropriate action to combat the proliferation of weapons of mass destruction, their means of delivery, and of advanced conventional weapons. This proliferation was identified as a threat to international peace and security, a determination of particular significance in the context of the UN Charter. As a consequence, a considerable and largely concerted effort has been made across states and institutions, at least of the North and West, to combat proliferation. Supplier control groups have been established or expanded in scope and membership. A series of multilateral agreements has been negotiated and signed. The president of the United States identified the fight against proliferation as one of the country's highest priorities; at the same time, the world's leading military alliance pledged to fight proliferation. Yet as the 1990s come to a close, the claim that this action was appropriate seems difficult to maintain. Despite the years of dedicated action, the global weapons state took a decided turn for the worse in 1998.

Conventional accounts of this fight against proliferation tend to include several elements. The end of the Cold War removed the central focus of attention for international security, allowing lesser threats to be more clearly seen and recognized. Thus in Charles Krauthammer's terms, the threat posed by the proliferation of weapons of mass destruction "suddenly dawned" on the West. The catalyst for this sudden recognition of the problem of proliferation was the war against Iraq. Fortunately, the war also served to unite most of the rest of the world in opposition to Iraq and, furthermore, indicated the possibility of effective multilateral action now that the obstacles produced by the Cold War had been removed. All of the world's states and people could be expected to support a renewed drive to control proliferation because the dangers of the spread of deadly weapons were manifest. If any state did not support this program, it could only be because it harbored ambitions to acquire some or all of these weapons for the purpose of upsetting international peace and security.

These common features create a narrowly constrained universe within which to debate the politics and policy of proliferation control. New responses at the global, regional, or national level can be proposed, and the relative merits of various suggested agreements can be debated. The scope and efficiency of the many supplier regimes are investigated, and amendments are proposed and debated. Put another way, the practices I discussed earlier, most prominently in Chapter 4, constitute the universe of possible responses to the problem of proliferation, and the debate centers on how best to manage and amend those practices. The object of this book has been to question the boundaries of this problem, to reveal them as products of acts of interpretation rather than as features of the world. These common features inform the "proliferation" image, an image shared by policy-makers and scholars who contribute to policy debates. It is an image that frames the world in a particular way and in doing so produces a world that appears natural and within which only certain actions become possible. Once it is recognized as a product, however, the "proliferation" image can be contested in a much broader fashion.

I have shown that the "proliferation" image is rooted in a technological rendering of the security problem of weapons. By generalizing to all forms of weaponry the view that nuclear technology of any kind produces the capacity for nuclear weapons, "proliferation" constructs as its object of security concern the movement of that underlying technology. This framing highlights the connections between technological development and military capacity while downplaying or hiding other crucial features of the practices of arms production and transfer. These masked features include the reasons for which states produce, transfer, and acquire arms—including, crucially, links between the possession of arms in general and certain categories of arms in particular and claims to statehood and status within the international hierarchy of states. "Proliferation" hides the fact that to be a state in the contemporary world means having certain military assets; moreover, to be a leading state means, among other things, having access to a wide range of highly advanced military technologies. Indeed, and ironically, the "proliferation" image tends to hide weapons themselves in its focus on the technological underpinnings of those weapons.

The central technological character of the "proliferation" image produces a particular range of practices in response. Those practices are centered on a set of supplier controls that restrict and monitor the movement of technologies for producing arms. It is here that ignorance of the weapons is at its most blatant and its most damaging. Technologies have increasingly wide applications; the term *dual use* misses—often by several orders of magnitude—the uses to which technologies relevant to arms can be put. The point in the process of arms acquisition that is the most difficult and in some ways the most visible is the point at which certain technologies are assembled into arms—the point of weaponization. Yet this point of possible intervention is largely ignored by a "proliferation" image that produces a problem of technology movement rather than of arms production and possession.

An image that frames a problem produces more than the objects of that problem, it also peoples its world in particular ways. "Proliferation" is no different, as it produces three classes of subjects in its discourse. Again, because of the construction of the problem in terms of underlying technologies, the first of these subjects is suppliers. These suppliers gather in groups to impose restrictions on the movement of technologies to the second set of subjects, the recipients. I have shown that the creation of these groupings is not a mere reflection of some pregiven capacity but rather is an active process of identification, with clear political consequences. Suppliers are not those states with the capacity to supply; rather, they are the states of the advanced industrialized world and those of the former Eastern bloc that the West has been aiding in their conversion to market economies and liberal democracies. Recipients, by contrast, are those outside the privileged few identified as suppliers, even if they are capable of supplying technology to others. Indeed, if recipients *do* supply technology to others, they may then be identified in the third class of subject: the rogue state, the villain of the "proliferation" frame. Importantly, the image includes no account of this move from recipient to rogue. The "proliferation" image provides no explanation for why states might build arsenals; weapons are simply the inevitable outcome of unchecked technological spread.

Objects are constructed through framings and in practice, as are the identities of the subjects that framing produces. Once we have subjects and objects, it takes very little more to produce interests—they are embedded within the representations that produce objects and identities. The ready appearance of interests, once objects and identities are in place, has meant that interests have been less extensively retheorized by those concerned with the contingencies of international life than have, for example, identities. This feature of interests has also provided the bulwark for the defense of traditional approaches to questions of security, as it makes interests appear natural. I have shown how the interests pursued within the proliferation agenda, to the contrary, are the product of the image that gives rise to that agenda in the first place. There is no universal interest in preventing the spread of technologies related to the production of weapons; such an interest emerges only once there is a "proliferation" problem, with its attendant suppliers, recipients, and rogues.

In the main, my object in this book is to make this case for the contingent and produced, against the objective and natural. It is an exercise in critical practice, following Foucault's characterization of that practice as "making facile gestures difficult."[1] As such it will, I hope, find its place within the increasingly vigorous defense of critical practice in international relations against the charge that it is engaged in nothing more than a prolix self-indulgence. What is more, I have confronted the most recalcitrant of the defenders of a largely realist discipline on their own terrain: matters of weapons, war, and arms control. Here the stakes are considered to be so high that possibilities which might be apparent in other areas are foreclosed. I trust I have made clear that there are only ever possibilities.

By itself, such an exercise in critique is unlikely to find purchase among the community of scholars and policymakers concerned with questions of proliferation. I hope to begin to reach out to them by having ended the book with a review of the UNSCOM experience and the Indian nuclear test. The events of 1998 are deeply troubling to the world of proliferation control. The apparent end of UNSCOM in a series of disputes with Iraq removes a crucial control on the paradigmatic rogue; the testing of nuclear weapons in South Asia is the frightening realization of the danger "proliferation" struggles so hard to prevent. It might appear that Krauthammer was prescient in calling this the era of weapons of mass destruction. I have shown, however, that these events can be seen as outcomes produced in large part *precisely by* those efforts to control proliferation.

The analysis presented in this book therefore has policy implications that are not far removed from the traditional writing on weapons in general and on nuclear weapons in particular. I am extremely wary of pronouncing policy advice, however, for a number of reasons. Hugh Gusterson expressed a similar unease in his marvelous study of a U.S. nuclear weapons laboratory:

> The analysis of this historical moment offered here departs from most recent writing on nuclear weapons issues in that it does not adopt a stance of what one might call "policy positivism." In fact it seeks to problematize such a stance. Policy positivism is the doctrine that there is a single best, or most "realistic," set of policies in regard to nuclear weapons and that it is the purpose of public policy debate and expert discourse on nuclear weapons, through the power of reason, to finally determine what those policies are.[2]

Such policy positivism underpins the debates over proliferation. At its most abstract, the question is whether proliferation is beneficial or harmful. More commonly, the questions are, which area is ripe for a global agreement, how can supplier controls be strengthened, and what place does military force have in countering proliferation. For a positivist debate of this kind to occur, a great number of things need to be taken for granted, and it is those taken-for-granted assumptions that I have aimed to expose in this book. The danger of policy prescription lies in the possibility of reifying another set of contingencies, proposing the wholesale replacing of one image by another for no reason other than that I prefer it. Nevertheless, it is difficult to write on a question as central to contemporary policy as weapons proliferation is without falling into some form of policy prescription. Indeed, it might be thought in some ways irresponsible not to state my case on weapons, having spent so much time decrying the weapon state produced by "proliferation."

The heart of any move away from "proliferation" must consist of two related processes. The first is breaking the linkage between weapons and technology in the framing of security problems; the second is to redirect the security gaze to weapons themselves. These processes confront the most problematic feature of the "proliferation" frame: the way in which technology, rather than the possession of arms, is demonized. The question is how to move in that direction from the starting point of where we are today, and it is a difficult question. The story of the CTBT is salutary in this regard, revealing the way in which meanings are transformed in practice. A 40-year history of the CTBT framed in terms of "disarmament" was overturned in favor of a "proliferation" framing—with disastrous consequences. Nevertheless, there are immanent possibilities for change.

The most likely sites of change emerge from the apparent disasters of 1998. The issues of both Iraq and India will need to be reconsidered as a result of the UNSCOM crises and the South Asian nuclear tests. The latter in particular raise the possibility of a fundamental rethinking of "proliferation" because of India's explicit contestation of its central features. The Indians have repeatedly decried the inequities of the "proliferation" image that permit some and not others to be armed and that restrict access to technologies that are crucial not only for arms but also for civilian economic processes. Their argument, which has been largely consistent throughout the nuclear era, has been that they would forgo any nuclear option as part of a general process of nuclear disarmament.

Now that India has tested nuclear weapons, the possibility exists for reinvigorating nuclear arms reduction and for again reframing the CTBT as an instrument of "disarmament" rather than "proliferation"—indeed, of beginning the process of dismantling the proliferation agenda of the 1990s. Much will depend on the way the aftermath of the Indian tests is managed, just as the production of the "proliferation" frame depended on the way in which the aftermath of the Gulf War was managed. If a way can be found to reverse the Indian nuclear program, as part of a wider process of nuclear arms reduction leading to the virtual elimination of nuclear weapons from the arsenals of the five accepted nuclear weapon states, it will constitute an important move toward reframing the security problems associated with weaponry.

Clearly, such a move will conflict with some entrenched interests. What is important to recognize is that these interests are not the universal interests of the "proliferation" image but rather parochial interests within the nuclear states. Labeling these interests parochial, however, is not to suggest that they are unimportant or that overcoming them will in any sense be easy. However, the experience of the nuclear weapons laboratories in the United States—one of the entrenched institutional interests in favor of maintaining robust nuclear arsenals—suggests that those interests can be overcome or at least redirected.

Ironically, the second of the two features necessary for any alternative to "proliferation" provides a way in which those interests can be confronted. I have argued that the discourses of liberalism and economic growth, in many ways politically problematic discourses, provide an important oppositional opening in this case. Commercial interests in the West, particularly in the United States, oppose the imposition of export controls. If the security problems attendant on weapons are constituted in terms of the weapons themselves, the movement of technology can be freed from its proliferation-imposed limits. This is not to advocate a laissez-faire arms trade—indeed, precisely the opposite, as arms rather than their precursors would be seen as the problematic technology. By contrast, it is to recognize the multiple uses of most technologies and the importance in the contemporary economy of allowing those technologies to circulate. Such a move could mobilize powerful interests, at least within the United States, that might prove sufficient to counter those who would oppose a move away from "proliferation."

What would the implications be of such a reconstituted agenda for UNSCOM and Iraq? A body such as UNSCOM could still operate in such an environment, although its scope would be reduced. Its goal would be to disarm the Iraqi state—a goal well in keeping with the history of the treatment of defeated states. The difference between such a goal and the one UNSCOM has pursued is that it would lack the ancillary task of ensuring not only that Iraq had no weapons but that it did not have the capacity to produce weapons. This latter objective, a clear product of the technological object of "proliferation," demands the unprecedented level of intrusion by UNSCOM. This objective also renders UNSCOM's task impossible and has led to the inability even to approximate Iraq's biological weapons capability.

As it presently stands, the "proliferation" image is remarkably effective, although not in the instrumental sense of achieving the goals it has been set. The events of 1998 have demonstrated in no uncertain terms that in the sense of its stated goals, proliferation control has been a failure. "Proliferation" has been effective in the somewhat different sense of having produced effects. What "proliferation" is effecting is a world in which a rift is produced between rich and poor, North and South, masquerading as a collective effort to produce universal security. Iraq's recalcitrance in complying with

UNSCOM is central to that masque; it plays the part of villain with consummate skill, enabling the repeated display of force so central to a security play. Yet the impressive displays of high-technology destructive power cannot entirely hide the fact that such displays are needed. The more mundane practices of monitoring the movement of technologies have consistently failed to achieve their aims, so the oceanic displays of missiled might are necessary. By producing a world of inside and outside, which is a world of haves and have nots, the proliferation discourse also effects the one thing so clearly lacking in its image of the relationship between technology and arms: a reason for those with the technology to turn it to a military use, as India did in May 1998.

We have seen this before. We have lived in a world of insides and outsides that produced nothing so well as reasons for those on either side to amass military might. We have lived in a world of a rift constantly formed and reformed, policed by arms and by export controls. We were sure we had left that world behind, that as the most potent symbol of the rift was dismantled, so too was the need for divisions. But old habits die hard. We knew how to make security when we lived with the rift. Why should we be surprised to find that when we try to make security again, we make another of those rifts? On the other hand, why should we be willing to accept it?

Glossary

ABM	antiballistic missile (treaty): ABMs are systems designed to destroy ballistic missiles in flight; they were restricted and then eliminated by the United States and the USSR in the ABM treaty.
ACDA	Arms Control and Disarmament Agency (U.S.): Agency within the U.S. State Department responsible for arms control.
Australia Group	supplier control group that controls technology related to chemical and biological weapons.
BTWC	Biological and Toxin Weapons Convention: Agreement banning the production, stockpiling, and use of biological weapons. Sometimes referred to as BWC.
BW	biological weapons
CCW	Convention on Certain Conventional Weapons: Also known as the Inhumane Weapons Convention; governs the use of a number of weapons judged to be excessively injurious.
CD	Conference on Disarmament: Multilateral arms control and disarmament conference, which meets three times a year in Geneva; negotiated the CWC and the CTBT.
CFE	conventional forces in Europe: Talks following from MBFR concerning conventional arms control in Europe; produced a treaty of the same name limiting those forces in 1990.
COCOM	Coordinating Committee on Multilateral Export Controls: Supplier control group composed mainly of NATO members controlling the export of high technology to the Eastern bloc during the Cold War.
CSCE	Conference on Security and Cooperation in Europe, a periodic conference that ran from 1973 until 1990,

163

	bringing together all the states of Europe to discuss matters of security, economic cooperation, and human rights. It was replaced in 1990 by the OSCE.
CTBT	comprehensive test ban treaty: Agreement banning all forms of nuclear testing for all time in all environments.
CW	chemical weapons
CWC	chemical weapons convention: Agreement banning the production, stockpiling, and use of chemical weapons.
ENDC	Eighteen Nation Disarmament Conference: Precursor to the CD.
G-7	Group of Seven
G-8	Group of Eight
IAEA	International Atomic Energy Agency: International governmental organization mandated by the NPT to put safeguards on the nuclear energy programs of all states party to the NPT.
INF	Intermediate-Range Nuclear Forces Treaty: A treaty between the United States and USSR, signed in 1997, which eliminated all intermediate-range nuclear missiles from Europe. It is hailed as the first treaty to have eliminated an entire class of weapons.
IR	international relations
LTBT	Limited Test Ban Treaty (also known as the Partial Test Ban Treaty [PTBT]): Bans nuclear tests in any environment other than underground.
MAD	mutual assured destruction: The condition in which both sides of a possible nuclear conflict could retain sufficient weapons to destroy the other side even after an all-out nuclear attack.
MBFR	mutual and balanced force reduction: Cold War–era negotiations on conventional arms control in Europe; replaced by the CFE.
MIRV	multiple independently targetable re-entry vehicle: System that allowed a single ballistic missile to deliver warheads to a number of discrete designated targets; first developed by the United States in the 1960s.
MTCR	Missile Technology Control Regime: Supplier control group that controls technology related to ballistic missiles.
NATO	North Atlantic Treaty Organization
NNWS	nonnuclear weapon state: A party to the NPT other than the five accepted nuclear weapon states.
NPT	nuclear nonproliferation treaty: Opened for signature in 1968, entered into force in 1970, extended indefinitely in 1995.

NSG	Nuclear Suppliers Group: Nuclear supplier control group whose members are not necessarily party to the NPT.
NWS	nuclear weapon state: One of the five states accepted by the NPT as possessing nuclear weapons because they tested those weapons before the NPT was signed.
OECD	Organization for Economic Cooperation and Development: An organization of 29 of the world's richest states, which discusses and develops social and economic policy.
OPCW	Organization for the Prohibition of Chemical Weapons: Executive body of the Chemical Weapons Convention; includes the Technical Secretariat, whose function is to verify the CWC.
OSCE	Organization for Security and Cooperation in Europe: Formal organization created out of the CSCE in 1990 by the Treaty of Paris.
P-5	The five permanent members of the UN Security Council.
PNE	peaceful nuclear explosion: Nuclear explosion used for civilian purposes rather than as a weapon or a weapon test; India claims its 1974 test was of a PNE.
PRC	People's Republic of China
R&D	research and development
SALT	strategic arms limitation treaty (talks): Nuclear arms control discussions and agreements between the United States and the USSR in the 1970s; produced two sets of agreements—the interim agreement (SALT I) and SALT II.
SDI	Strategic Defense Initiative (or Star Wars): U.S. program to develop a comprehensive ballistic missile defense system, which would be largely space based.
SIPRI	Stockholm International Peace Research Institute: Leading independent research body concerned with issues of weapons production, transfer, and control.
START	strategic arms reduction treaty (talks): Nuclear arms control discussions and agreements between the United States and the USSR and its successors beginning in the 1980s; has produced agreements on the reduction rather than the limitation of nuclear arsenals.
TTBT	threshold test ban treaty: Places a maximum limit of 150 kilotons on underground nuclear tests.
UNGA	United Nations General Assembly
UNSCOM	United Nations Special Commission: Body created by the UN Security Council to implement the provisions of the cease-fire resolution with Iraq (Resolution 687 [1991]) concerning the destruction of Iraqi weapons capabilities.

VEREX   Verification Experts Committee: Special committee es-
                        tablished by the states party to the BTWC to create
                        legally binding obligations and verification procedures.

Wassenaar   supplier control group controlling conventional weapons
    Arrangement   technology.

WMD   weapons of mass destruction: Nuclear, chemical, and
                        biological weapons; sometimes called ABC or NBC
                        weapons for atomic or nuclear and biological and chem-
                        ical weapons.

Zangger   nuclear supplier control group whose members are all
    Committee   party to the NPT.

Notes

Prologue

1. Charles Krauthammer, "The Unipolar Moment," *Foreign Affairs* 70 (1) 1991, 30–31.
2. External Affairs and International Trade Canada, "Post-Hostilities Activities," *Backgrounder,* 8 February 1991. The proposal was announced in two speeches that day, one by Prime Minister Mulroney and one by External Affairs Minister Joe Clark.
3. "Bush Proposes Arms Control Initiative for the Middle East," *Text of a Speech by President George Bush to the Air Force Academy,* EUR304, 29 May 1991, 3.
4. U.S. Department of States, "Fact Sheet: Middle East Arms Control Initiative," *Department of State Dispatch,* 3 June 1991.

Chapter 1

1. UN Security Council Summit "Final Declaration," reported in "Summit at the UN: Security Council Summit Declaration: 'New Risks for Stability and Security,'" *New York Times,* 1 February 1992, A1.
2. Treaty on the Nonproliferation of Nuclear Weapons, Article II.
3. See Frank Barnaby, *How Nuclear Weapons Spread: Nuclear Proliferation in the 1990s* (London: Routledge, 1994), 1–11, for a brief explanation of the link between civilian nuclear programs and nuclear weapons.
4. The IAEA also provides safeguards on individual nuclear sites in states that are not NNWSs party to the NPT and that do not wish to sign a full-scope safeguard agreement. NWSs party to the NPT may place any of their nuclear facilities under IAEA safeguard, and states not party to the NPT may also sign partial or full-scope safeguards agreements.
5. Adolf von Baekmann, "The Treaty on the Non-Proliferation of Nuclear Weapons (NPT) (1968)," in Serge Sur, ed., *Verification of Current Disarmament and Arms Limitation Agreements: Ways, Means and Practices* (Aldershot: Dartmouth for UNIDIR, 1991), 176–177.

6. "Report on the Seventh IAEA On-Site Inspection in Iraq Under Security Council Resolution 687 (1991), 11–22 October 1991," 12 November 1991, *S/23215,* 3.

7. The IAEA's findings suggested that the Iraqis had not yet managed to develop a functioning implosion weapon, although the program was moving in that direction.

8. As the IAEA and its supporters point out, safeguards did not fail in Iraq; they were circumvented by a state that understood that the safeguards system was not sufficient to prevent or even to detect the development of a parallel nuclear program for the production of nuclear weapons.

Chapter 2

1. Krauthammer, "The Unipolar Moment," 32–33. Although Krauthammer was among the most prominent commentators to warn of the dangers of proliferation, he was far from alone. I surveyed five leading U.S. foreign policy journals in the 10 years from 1985 to 1994 (the journals were *International Security, Foreign Affairs, Foreign Policy, Orbis,* and the *Washington Quarterly*). Only 7 articles on the problem of proliferation appeared between 1985 and 1989, of which 5 were concerned solely with nuclear proliferation. Nine articles were published in the year between 1989 and the start of the Gulf War. In the 3 years following the Gulf War, 56 articles on various aspects of proliferation appeared in these journals, including Krauthammer's.

2. Ibid., 30.

3. Hans Morgenthau, *Politics Among Nations,* 5th ed. (New York: Knopf, 1978), 12.

4. Ibid., 4.

5. Michel Foucault, "Practicing Criticism," in Lawrence Kritzman, ed., *Michel Foucault, Politics, Philosophy, Culture: Interviews and Other Writings 1977–1984* (London: Routledge, 1988), 155.

6. Ken Booth, "Security and Emancipation," *Review of International Studies* 17 (4) 1991, 315–316.

7. For a clear account of the assumptions on which the study of strategy was based, see John Garnett, "Strategic Studies and Its Assumptions," in John Baylis, Ken Booth, John Garnett, and Phil Williams, eds., *Contemporary Strategy I: Theories and Concepts* (London: Holmes and Meier, 1987), 3–29. For the leading account of challenges to those assumptions in terms of a critical security study, see Keith Krause and Michael Williams, "From Strategy to Security: Foundations of Critical Security Studies," in Krause and Williams, eds., *Critical Security Studies: Concepts and Cases* (Minneapolis: University of Minnesota Press, 1997), 33–59. For an attempt to rework the assumptions of strategic studies while maintaining distance from critical security studies, see Barry Buzan, Ole Wœver, and Jaap de Wilde, *Security: A New Framework for Analysis* (Boulder: Lynne Rienner, 1998), particularly 21–47.

8. The language is from Stephen Walt's definition of security studies as "the study of the threat, use and control of military force." Stephen M. Walt, "The Renaissance of Security Studies," *International Studies Quarterly* 35 (2) 1991, 212.

9. See Krause and Williams, "From Strategy to Security," 35–36, for a discussion of the attempt to dismiss alternative concerns as problems. As they write:

"It is important to be clear about what is at stake here. The issue of the distinction between threats [the traditional category of security studies] and problems is a conceptual one. It determines their status not according to their significance for human welfare and survival, but by their relationship to prevailing conceptual structures and analytic categories of security studies" (35).

10. Booth, "Security and Emancipation."

11. In a contributors' guide the criteria for selection are given as follows: "The editors and reviewers evaluate manuscripts on the basis of four primary criteria: subject, *policy relevance,* observance of scholarly standards or evidence and argumentation, and readability." In case this was not clear enough, the subjects are defined as "examinations of *current policy choices;* analyses of theoretical issues and of technical issues of importance *to current policy questions;* and historical arguments and discoveries of relevance *to current policy questions*" (emphases added). Teresa Pelton Johnson, "Writing for *International Security:* A Contributors' Guide," *International Security* 16 (2) 1991, 172.

12. David Campbell, *Writing Security: United States Foreign Policy and the Politics of Identity* (Manchester: Manchester University Press), 1992, 1.

13. Jutta Weldes, "Constructing National Interests," *European Journal of International Relations* 2 (3) 1996, 280 (emphasis added).

14. Terry Nardin, *Law, Morality and the Relations of States* (Princeton: Princeton University Press, 1983), 6.

15. Anthony Giddens has phrased this relationship in the elliptical language typical of discussions of this nonlinear conception of practices: "In analysing social relations we have to acknowledge both . . . the patterning of social relations in time-space involving the reproduction of situated practices, and . . . a virtual order or 'modes of structuring' recursively implicated in such reproduction." Giddens, *The Constitution of Society: Outline of the Theory of Structuration* (Berkeley: University of California Press, 1984), 17.

16. Kenneth E. Boulding, *The Image* (Ann Arbor: University of Michigan Press, 1956), 64.

17. Mark Neufeld has stated the relationship between these intersubjective meanings and practices: "the relationship between 'intersubjective meanings' which make up the 'web of meaning' and human practices is not one of correlation, where 'intersubjective meanings' serve as an 'intervening variable' in a causal sequence. Rather, 'intersubjective meanings' are constitutive of those practices." Neufeld, "Interpretation and the 'Science' of International Relations," *Review of International Studies* 19 (3) 1993, 45.

18. Charles Taylor, "Social Theory as Practice," in Taylor, *Philosophy and the Human Sciences* (Cambridge: Cambridge University Press, 1985), 93.

19. Ibid.

20. On the centrality of the study of war to the discipline of international relations as traditionally practiced, see K. J. Holsti, *The Dividing Discipline: Hegemony and Diversity in International Theory* (Winchester, Mass.: Allen and Unwin, 1985), 16–22.

21. Roxanne Doty, "Foreign Policy as Social Construction: A Post-Positivist Analysis of U.S. Counterinsurgency Policy in the Philippines," *International Studies Quarterly* 37 (3) 1993, 303.

22. Chris Hables Gray, *Postmodern War: The New Politics of Conflict* (London: Routledge, 1997), 266.

23. For a discussion of metaphorical entailment, see Paul Chilton, *Security Metaphors: Cold War Discourse from Containment to Common House* (New York:

Peter Lang, 1996), 55–57, and George Lakoff and Mark Johnson, *Metaphors We Live By* (Chicago: University of Chicago Press, 1980), 91–94.

24. Chilton, *Security Metaphors*, 413.

25. Ibid., 48.

26. Lakoff and Johnson's work is an important starting point for Paul Chilton's. See ibid., 48–57. For my own, more extended treatment of Lakoff and Johnson, see Mutimer, "Reimagining Security: The Metaphors of Proliferation," in Krause and Williams, eds., *Critical Security Studies*, 193–200.

27. Lakoff and Johnson, *Metaphors We Live By*, 163.

28. Ibid., 56–60.

29. Ibid., 118. Deborah Cameron accuses Lakoff and Johnson of biologism in her "Naming of Parts: Gender, Culture, and Terms for the Penis Among American College Students," *American Speech* 67 (4) 1992, 377–378. Cameron does recognize, however, that Lakoff becomes more sensitive to this concern in his later work on the subject, George Lakoff, *Women, Fire and Dangerous Things: What Categories Reveal About the Mind* (Chicago: University of Chicago Press, 1987).

30. Chilton, *Security Metaphors*, 413 (emphasis added).

31. David Campbell, *Politics Without Principle: Sovereignty, Ethics and the Narratives of the Gulf War* (Boulder: Lynne Rienner, 1993), 8.

32. I have drawn the terms from Andrew Goatly, *The Language of Metaphors* (London: Routledge, 1997). I should be clear that he invokes the terms to refer to the common understanding of metaphor in order to dismiss it in favor of an understanding consonant with my use here: "The only real difference between literal language and metaphorical language is that, in literal use, we adhere to conventional criteria for classification, whereas in metaphorical use . . . the criteria for interpretation are relatively unconventional" (3).

33. Walt, "The Renaissance of Security Studies," 223.

34. Judith Butler, *Bodies That Matter: On the Discursive Limits of Sex* (London: Routledge, 1993), 10. The entire passage from which this excerpt was taken reads as follows: "To claim that discourse is formative is not to claim that it originates, causes, or exhaustively composes that which it concedes; rather, it is to claim that there is no reference to a pure body which is not at the same time a further formation of that body. In this sense, the linguistic capacity to refer to sexed bodies is not denied, but the very meaning of 'referentiality' is altered. In philosophical terms, the constative claim is always to some degree performative" (10–11).

35. Ibid., 11.

36. Lakoff, *Women, Fire and Dangerous Things*, 5–6. On the importance of categorization to understanding and of metaphor to categorization, see also Goatly, *The Language of Metaphors*.

37. For a useful discussion of the role of counterfactual argument, see James Fearon, "Counterfactuals and Hypothesis Testing in Political Science," *World Politics* 43 (2) 1991, 169–195.

38. Chilton, *Security Metaphors*, 73–74.

Chapter 3

1. *A Report on the International Control of Atomic Energy.* Prepared for the Secretary of State's Committee on Atomic Energy, Washington, D.C., U.S.

Government Printing Office, 16 March 1946. Department of State Publication 2498 (http://www.learnworld.com/ZNW/LWText.Acheson-Lilienthal.html) [hereafter *Acheson-Lilienthal Report*]. This report, prepared by a committee chaired by Dean Acheson and David Lilienthal, set out the framework for international control that was proposed by the United States, represented by its chief negotiator, Bernard Baruch. For a useful discussion of the proposal and the failure of the Baruch Plan, see McGeorge Bundy, *Danger and Survival* (New York: Random House, 1988), 130–196. Bundy points to one key feature of the final plan as a primary reason for its failure: the addition of sanctions and the removal of the Security Council veto for consideration of those sanctions, which had not been included in the Acheson-Lilienthal proposals.

2. The classic treatment of the development of the strategy of nuclear weapons is provided by Lawrence Freedman in his *The Evolution of Nuclear Strategy* (London: Macmillan, 1981). Freedman notes that atomic bombs were developed just as strategists were finalizing and implementing theories of strategic bombardment, the use of aerial bombing against nonmilitary targets for the purpose of undermining the morale that provided popular support for an enemy's war efforts. This notion provided the rationale for the first use of atomic weapons in Japan. See Freedman, *The Evolution of Nuclear Strategy,* 4–6 and 14–22.

3. Although the weapons framing was both the dominant and the most important framing of nuclear explosives, they have also been framed as explosives for other purposes. The idea of peaceful nuclear explosives has only recently been largely overcome. The PNE framing saw nuclear explosives as powerful engineering tools, deploying the energy of a nuclear explosion for earthmoving on a large scale. Concerns over both the environmental effects of PNEs and possibilities of weapons tests being hidden as PNEs (as India did in 1974) have largely resulted in the delegitimation of the PNE idea.

4. Jonathan Schell, *The Fate of the Earth* (New York: Knopf, 1982), 3. Anatol Rapoport ("Editor's Introduction," in Carl von Clausewitz, *On War*, ed. Rapoport [London: Penguin, 1968]) has usefully characterized various philosophies of war in a way that makes sense of the metaphors Schell uses and is consonant with my arguments, as he argues that "the nature of war is itself to a large extent determined by how man conceives of it" (12). Rapoport suggests that there are three views of war—the political, the eschatological, and the cataclysmic: "The cataclysmic view pictures war as a catastrophe that befalls some portion of humanity or the entire human race" (16).

5. In some ways the influence of these strategists is not surprising, as RAND was closely tied to the U.S. Air Force. The leading works from these most influential nuclear theorists are Bernard Brodie, *Strategy in the Missile Age* (Princeton: Princeton University Press, 1959); Herman Kahn, *On Thermonuclear War* (Princeton: Princeton University Press, 1960); Kahn, *Thinking About the Unthinkable* (New York: Horizon, 1962); and Thomas Schelling, *The Strategy of Conflict* (New York: Oxford University Press, 1960).

6. *Acheson-Lilienthal Report,* 1–2. The Agreed Declaration to which it refers was agreed by the United States, Canada, and the United Kingdom on 15 November 1945 and set the terms of the committee's investigation.

7. The effect of the nuclear revolution in enabling mutual deterrence by removing the need to defeat an enemy in order to destroy it is now a standard feature of nuclear strategy debate. For an important, early statement of the argument, see Glenn H. Snyder, *Deterrence and Defence: Toward a Theory of National Security* (Princeton: Princeton University Press, 1961), 8–16.

8. See Michael Williams, "Rethinking the 'Logic' of Deterrence," *Alternatives* 17 (1) 1992, 67–93. Williams argues that these two positions result from the attempt to operationalize the pure concept of deterrence, that the contradiction between the two is an artifact of that operationalization and is thus inherent to the concept of deterrence. The debate is therefore necessarily circular.

9. Ibid., 77.

10. Robert Jervis, *The Illogic of American Nuclear Strategy* (Ithaca: Cornell University Press, 1984), 56–63.

11. Some strands of strategic theory tried to constitute nuclear weapons as just that. Even in the 1980s, however, when so-called war-fighting strategies came to dominate U.S. strategic debate, proponents of strategies of nuclear use still argued that the function of those strategies was to enhance deterrence. Once essential parity with the Soviet Union had been recognized by the U.S. strategic community, nuclear weapons were inseparable from deterrence.

12. Emmanuel Adler, "The Emergence of Cooperation: National Epistemic Communities and the International Evolution of the Idea of Nuclear Arms Control," *International Organization* 46 (1) 1992, 101–145.

13. Gerald Holton, ed., *Arms Control*, special issue of *Daedalus* 89 (4) 1960. For a discussion of the impact of this issue, see Robin Ranger, "The Four Bibles of Arms Control," in Susan Shepard, ed., *Books and the Pursuit of American Foreign Policy,* special issue of *Books Forum* 6, 1984, 416–432. A series of other key texts appeared at the same time, and together they form the founding canon of arms control theory: Donald Brennan, ed., *Arms Control, Disarmament, and National Security* (New York: Braziller, 1961); Thomas Schelling and Morton Halperin, with the assistance of Donald Brennan, *Strategy and Arms Control* (New York: Twentieth Century Fund, 1961); and Hedley Bull, *The Control of the Arms Race: Disarmament and Arms Control in the Missile Age* (New York: Praeger, 1961).

14. Adler, "Emergence of Cooperation," 107–116. The overlap between the two is seen in a number of ways, not least in the overlap of the people producing both sets of theory. The strategists who articulated and formalized deterrence strategy were also the ones who at the same time were elaborating theories of arms control. The most obvious instance is that of Thomas Schelling, who produced his classic strategy text, *Strategy of Conflict,* only a year before his arms control book, *Strategy and Arms Control.* These two—strategy and arms control—were seen by those developing the arguments as part of the same enterprise.

15. Thomas Schelling, testimony to U.S. Congress House Committee on Foreign Affairs, March 1969, quoted by Adler, "Emergence of Cooperation," 124, note 87.

16. Adler, "Emergence of Cooperation," 113.

17. In the preface to a reissue of *Strategy and Arms Control* in 1985, Schelling and Halperin single out the ABM treaty as "almost the ideal model of what we had proposed." Schelling and Halperin, *Strategy and Arms Control,* reissued with a new preface (New York: Pergamon-Brassey's, 1985), xi.

18. This line was originally backed up with a radio circuit. In 1971 the two countries agreed to replace it with a pair of satellite circuits, with the wire line retained as a backup.

19. ACDA Narrative, "Memorandum of Understanding Between the United States of America and the Union of Soviet Socialist Republics Regarding the Establishment of a Direct Communications Link (with Annex) [Hot Line Agreement]" (http://www.acda.gov/treaties/hotline1.htm).

20. Treaty Between the United States of America and the Union of Soviet Socialist Republics on the Limitation of Anti-Ballistic Missile Systems, signed 26 May 1972 (http://www.acda.gov/treaties/abm2.htm).

21. Treaty Between the United States of America and the Union of Soviet Socialist Republics on the Limitation of Strategic Offensive Arms, Together with Agreed Statements and Common Understandings Regarding the Treaty (SALT II), signed 18 June 1979 (http://www.acda.gov/treaties/SALT2-2.htm).

22. Ibid., Preamble (emphasis added).

23. ACDA Narrative, "Hot Line Agreement."

24. *Acheson-Lilienthal Report;* see in particular the three premises of the report, pp. 1–2.

25. The relationship between rational decisionmaking and accidents in deterrence theory is precisely what is at stake in the contemporary debate between proliferation optimists and pessimists. Optimists rely on the irrationality of starting a nuclear war to argue that "more may be better," whereas pessimists point to the possibilities of accidents and say that "more will be worse." For the leading statement of these two positions, see Scott Sagan and Kenneth Waltz, *The Spread of Nuclear Weapons: A Debate* (New York: Norton, 1995).

26. ABM Treaty, Preamble.

27. The classic discussion of escalation in nuclear strategy was provided by Herman Kahn in *On Escalation: Metaphors and Scenarios* (New York: Praeger, 1965).

28. For a detailed discussion of the balance of power as metaphor in the disciplinary history of contemporary international relations, see Chilton, *Security Metaphors*, 91–114.

29. This is not to say there have been no other instances of power balancing in international politics. David Hume argued that the balance of power was a feature of the classical world (see Hume, "Of the Balance of Power," in Charles Hendle, ed., *David Hume's Political Essays* [Indianapolis: Bobbs-Merril, 1953]). Herbert Butterfield opposed this view, suggesting that "the idea of the balance of power is associated with the modern history of our part of the world, and envisages the political units of the Continent as forming what used to be called 'the European states-system'" (Butterfield, "The Balance of Power," in Butterfield and Martin Wight, eds., *Diplomatic Investigations* [London: Allen and Unwin, 1967], 133.) Similarly, Hedley Bull provides examples from sixteenth-, seventeenth-, and eighteenth-century Europe of the balance-of-power mechanism (Bull, *The Anarchical Society: A Study of Order in World Politics* [London: Macmillan, 1977], 101–102).

30. Bull, *The Anarchical Society,* 104.

31. Kenneth Waltz, *Theory of International Politics* (New York: Random House, 1979), 118.

32. The two-pan scale is an image evoked by Morgenthau in his discussion of the balance of power (Morgenthau, *Politics Among Nations,* 193).

33. The relationship among three bodies under the influence of gravity—the famed three-body problem—is one of the most difficult in the history of Newtonian physics. Although two bodies will settle into a stable orbit, the addition of a third body introduces complex and possibly chaotic interactions among the three. Waltz uses the three-body problem to bolster his claim that a two-power system is the most stable: "The three-body problem has yet to be solved by physicists. Can political scientists or policy-makers hope to do better in charting the courses of three or more interacting states?" (*Theory of International Politics,* 192).

34. Bull, *The Anarchical Society,* 102 (emphasis added).

35. Martin Wight, "The Balance of Power," in Butterfield and Wight, eds., *Diplomatic Investigations,* 152. The dualism inherent in the concept of equipoise can be seen by tracing through its meanings. The *Oxford English Dictionary* defines equipoise with reference to counterbalance, which it further defines as "*a* weight or influence which balances *an*other" (emphasis added).

36. Waltz, *Theory of International Politics,* 192. In addition, see the rest of chapter 8 (161–193), to which this sentence forms a conclusion. Waltz claims that "chapter 8 will show why two is the best of small numbers. . . . Problems of national security in multi- and bipolar worlds do clearly show the advantages of having two great powers, and only two, in the system" (161).

37. The imaginary that produced the Cold War as a stable balance is very much a Western imaginary. The Soviet Union, by contrast, generally imagined the relationship in terms of the correlation of forces. This difference in the framing of the Cold War relationship was a central sticking point in years of arms control negotiations between the two sides. Maintaining a stable balance and manipulating the correlation of forces entail quite different results for negotiated arms control.

38. The CD was constituted in 1979, replacing the Conference of the Committee on Disarmament, which had replaced the Eighteen Nation Disarmament Conference in 1969, which in turn had replaced the Ten Nation Disarmament Conference in 1962. As of June 1996 the CD had expanded to 63 members. It is a matter of some contention among those members as to whether the CD is part of the UN.

39. This linkage is even reflected in the nuclear nonproliferation treaty, where in Article VI the parties undertake to negotiate "measures relating to a cessation of the nuclear arms race at an early date and to nuclear disarmament, and on a treaty on general and complete disarmament" NPT §VI.

40. *Acheson-Lilienthal Report,* 2.

41. This number seems somewhat apocryphal and is certainly elusive. Joseph Pilat reports the expectation as "over 20" (Joseph Pilat, "Introduction: The Nonproliferation Predicament," in Joseph Pilat, ed., *The Nonproliferation Predicament* [Oxford: Transaction, 1985], 1), but he provides no supporting documentation. William Potter (*Nuclear Power and Nonproliferation: An Interdisciplinary Perspective* [Cambridge, Mass.: Oelgeschalger, Gunn and Hain, 1982], 41, note 18) refers only to President Kennedy and puts the number at 10, supporting this with reference to "President Kennedy as quoted by Arthur Schlesinger . . . cited in Johnathan Medalia" and now made here! The highest number I could find was 20–30, also attributed to President Kennedy, this time by Hans Blix in a 1990 speech to the Graduate Institute of International Studies in Geneva and quoted by Tariq Rauf, "The NPT Article VI Bargain—A Retrospective," in Rauf, ed., *Regional Approaches to Curbing Nuclear Proliferation in the Middle East and South Asia,* Aurora Papers 16 (Ottawa: Canadian Centre for Global Security, 1992), 1, note 6.

42. Barnaby, *How Nuclear Weapons Spread,* 2. Typically, a nuclear energy reactor "burns" uranium—that is, it generates heat through the controlled fission of uranium. Uranium is also used in fission weapons, although it is enriched to a much different isotopic mix than for electricity generation. Generally, uranium in nuclear power reactors is enriched to 3–4 percent U-235, whereas nuclear weapons use uranium enriched to roughly 90 percent or more (this is termed highly enriched uranium). One of the by-products of this fission, however, is plutonium, the most effective fissile material for use in nuclear weapons.

43. "Address by President Eisenhower Before the United Nations General Assembly, December 8, 1953," reprinted in *Nuclear Proliferation Factbook.* Prepared for the Committee on International Relations and the Committee on Governmental Affairs, U.S. Congress, by the Congressional Research Service (Washington, D.C.: U.S. Government Printing Office, 1977), 7–13.

44. NPT, Articles I and II.

45. Article IV provides for the right of all states to research and develop nuclear technology for peaceful purposes and requires that states with the technology

make it available. Article V requires that states with nuclear explosive technology make such explosives available for peaceful purposes.

46. NPT, Article IV (ii), reads: "Parties to the Treaty in a position to do so shall also cooperate in contributing alone or together with other States or international organizations to the further development of the applications of nuclear energy for peaceful purposes, especially in the territories of non-nuclear-weapon States Party to the Treaty, with due consideration for the needs of the developing areas of the world."

47. NPT, Article VI.

48. "Protocol for the Prohibition of the Use in War of Asphyxiating, Poisonous and Other Gases, and of Bacteriological Methods of Warfare," Geneva, 17 June 1925.

49. "Convention on the Prohibition of the Development, Production and Stockpiling of Bacteriological (Biological) and Toxin Weapons and on Their Destruction," London, Moscow, and Washington, D.C., 10 April 1972.

50. Richard Price, "A Genealogy of the Chemical Weapons Taboo," *International Organization* 49 (1) 1995, 73–103. See also his book-length study of the same subject: Richard Price, *The Chemical Weapons Taboo* (Ithaca: Cornell University Press, 1997).

51. Price, "Genealogy," 74.

52. Frederic Brown, *Chemical Warfare: A Study in Restraints* (Princeton: Princeton University Press, 1968), 291–296.

53. Price, "Genealogy," 75.

54. Ibid., 102–103.

55. Richard Price and Nina Tannenwald, "Norms and Deterrence: The Nuclear and Chemical Weapons Taboos," in Peter J. Katzenstein, ed., *The Culture of National Security: Norms and Identity in World Politics* (New York: Columbia University Press, 1996), 143.

56. Matthew Meselson, ed., *Chemical Weapons and Chemical Arms Control* (New York: Carnegie Endowment for International Peace, 1978). The three chapters are titled "Defense Planning for Chemical Warfare," "Chemical Weapons for NATO?" and "Preventing Chemical Warfare."

57. Jozef Goldblat, "Chemical Disarmament: From the Ban on Use to a Ban on Possession," *Background Paper* 17 (Ottawa: Canadian Institute for International Peace and Security, February 1988).

58. Aspen Strategy Group, *Chemical Weapons and Western Security Policy* (Aspen: Aspen Institute, 1987), 3.

59. Price, "Genealogy," 95–98, details the importance of a discourse of civilization to the constitution of the CW taboo.

60. H. C. Englebrecht and F. C. Hanighen, *Merchants of Death* (New York: Dodd-Mead, 1934).

61. *The Covenant of the League of Nations (Including Amendments Adopted to December, 1924)*, Article 8.

62. Ibid., Article 23(4).

63. For a discussion of efforts by the League of Nations to control arms production and trade, see SIPRI, *The Arms Trade with the Third World* (New York: Humanities Press, 1971), 90–100.

64. Quoted in ibid., 95.

65. UNGA Resolution 46/36L, December 1991.

66. Anthony Sampson, *The Arms Bazaar: The Companies, the Dealers, the Bribes: From Vickers to Lockheed* (London: Hodder and Stoughton, 1977), 14.

67. Ibid., 24.

68. The following is a short list of book-length discussions of aspects of conventional arms production and transfer, each containing one or more of the phrases: Ian Anthony, Agnès Allebeck, and Herbert Wulf, *West European Arms Production: Structural Changes in the New Political Environment* (Stockholm: SIPRI, 1990); William Bajusz and David Louscher, *Arms Sales and the U.S. Economy* (Boulder: Westview, 1988); J. Boutwell, M. T. Klare, and L. W. Reed, eds., *Lethal Commerce: The Global Trade in Small Arms and Light Weapons* (Cambridge: American Academy of Arts and Sciences, 1995); Anne Hessing Cahn and Joseph Kruzel, *Controlling Future Arms Trade* (New York: McGraw-Hill, 1977); Cindy Cannizzo, ed., *The Gun Merchants: Politics and Policies of the Major Arms Suppliers* (New York: Pergamon, 1980); Basil Collier, *Arms and the Men: The Arms Trade and Governments* (London: Hamish Hamilton, 1980); Benjamin Cooling, ed., *War, Business and World Military-Industrial Complexes* (Port Washington, N.Y.: Kennikat, 1981); Michael Klare, *American Arms Supermarket* (Austin: University of Texas Press, 1984); David Mussington, *Arms Unbound: The Globalization of Defense Production,* CSIA Studies in International Security No. 4 (Cambridge: Center for Science and International Affairs, John F. Kennedy School of Government, Harvard University/Brassey's [U.S.], 1994); Andrew Pierre, *The Global Politics of Arms Sales* (Princeton: Princeton University Press, 1983); Ernie Regehr, *Arms Canada: The Deadly Business of Military Exports* (Toronto: James Lorimer, 1987); Sampson, *The Arms Bazaar;* Naoum Sloutzky, *Le Contrôle du Commerce International des Armes de Guerre* (Genève: Dotation Carnegle Pour la Paix Internationale, 1969).

69. Ian Black and David Fairhall, "Analysis: The Arms Trade: The Profits of Doom," *Guardian,* 16 October 1997, 17.

70. See, for example, Sampson, *The Arms Bazaar*. For similar work on other industries, for example, see the various recent works on Bill Gates and Microsoft, inter alia: James Wallace, *Hard Drive: Bill Gates and the Making of the Microsoft Empire* (New York: Wiley, 1992); James Wallace, *Overdrive: Bill Gates and the Race to Control Cyberspace* (Chichester, N.Y.: Wiley, 1997); Daniel Ichbiah, *The Making of Microsoft: How Bill Gates and His Team Created the World's Most Successful Software Company* (Rocklin, Calif.: Prima, 1991).

71. Black and Fairhall, "The Arms Trade," 17.

72. Keith Krause, *Arms and the State: Patterns of Military Production and Trade* (Cambridge: Cambridge University Press, 1993), 27. By the transfer of technology I Krause means the transfer of the weapons without the designs (technology II) or the capacity of basic scientific knowledge or technical expertise (technology III).

73. David Hencke and John Aglionby, "Indonesian Arms Deal Undercuts Cook's Line," *Guardian,* 9 October 1997.

74. Black and Fairhall, "The Arms Trade" (emphasis added).

75. An assessment of this effort published in 1982 concluded: "His guidelines did provide criteria to judge requests for arms, but in practice arms sales were not an 'exceptional' implement of foreign policy, nor did the dollar ceiling result in reduced arms sales. The conventional arms transfer talks, which were to complement the effort at unilateral restraint, also fell short of their objective of limiting the arms sales of the other major suppliers." Roger P. Labrie, John G. Hutchines, and Edwin W. A. Peura, with Diana H. Richman, *U.S. Arms Sales Policy: Background and Issues* (Washington, D.C.: American Enterprise Institute, 1982), 11.

76. Ibid., 17 (emphasis added).

Chapter 4

1. The CD and its precursors had been discussing a Chemical Weapons Convention since 1968. The Biological and Toxin Weapons Convention emerged from these negotiations, was opened for signature in 1972, and entered into force in 1975. Article IX of the BTWC calls on the states party to negotiate in good faith toward a Convention on Chemical Weapons.

2. Chemical Weapons Convention, Article I. For a text of the CWC and its schedules, see http://www.opcw.nl:80/ptshome.htm, the official Internet site of the Organization for the Prohibition of Chemical Weapons. For a more user-friendly version, see http://www.dfait-maeci.gc.ca/nndi-agency/cwc/english/cwc.html. For a discussion of the CWC and its features, see Edward Spiers, *Chemical and Biological Weapons: A Study of Proliferation* (London: Macmillian, 1994), 130–134.

3. For Schedule 2 chemicals, the threshold at which a state must report production ranges between 1 kg and 1 tonne per year, with a threshold at which facilities must be inspected set at 10 times the declaration threshold. For Schedule 3 chemicals, production must be declared at 30 tonnes, with inspection set at 200 tonnes per year.

4. Chemical Weapons Convention, Article IX.8 (emphasis added).

5. States party may report any suspected violations to the UN Security Council and are required to cooperate with the council in any investigation it chooses to carry out (BTWC, §§V–VI). Both provisions are also contained in the UN Charter (*Charter of the United Nations,* Articles 39–40). On the verification of the BTWC, see Andrzej Karkoska, "The Convention on Biological Weapons (1972)," in Sur, ed., *Verification of Current Disarmament and Arms Limitation Agreements,* 209–229.

6. SIPRI, *World Armaments and Disarmament: SIPRI Yearbook 1982* (London: Taylor and Francis for SIPRI, 1982), 322.

7. SIPRI, *SIPRI Yearbook 1987: World Armaments and Disarmament* (Oxford: Oxford University Press for SIPRI, 1987), 389.

8. See, inter alia, *SIPRI Yearbook* and the *Arms Control Reporter* for the period. For instance, in 1984 the *Arms Control Reporter* noted under its list of outstanding issues: "The U.S. has suggested a special on-site inspection procedure 'anywhere, anytime' without right of refusal. The East has expressed its complete disapproval of this notion." *Arms Control Reporter* 5-84, 704.A.5.

9. Counting launchers involved balancing the number of missiles and bombers on each side, warheads the number of actual nuclear explosive charges, yields the total megatonnage, and throw weight the payload capacity of the launchers. The debate over throw weight became particularly vigorous around the U.S. Star Wars proposals, because additional payload could be used to fire decoys along with warheads and overwhelm strategic defenses.

10. "Treaty Between the United States of America and the Russian Federation on Further Reduction and Limitation of Strategic Offensive Arms" (START II), Article 1.1.

11. *SIPRI Yearbook 1987,* 388.

12. *Arms Control Reporter* 5-85, 704.B.124.

13. Conference on Disarmament, *Document CD/PV.370.*

14. See SIPRI, *World Armaments and Disarmaments: SIPRI Yearbook 1986* (Oxford: Oxford University Press for SIPRI, 1986), 460–462; *SIPRI Yearbook 1987,* 388–389; and Conference on Disarmament, *Document CD/CW/WP.128.*

15. Paul de Man, "The Epistemology of Metaphor," *Critical Inquiry* 5, 1978, 23 (emphasis added).

16. Elsewhere I have argued that cell proliferation can be seen as an originating location of the proliferation metaphor as applied to nuclear weapons. (See Mutimer, "Reimagining Security," 200–204.) Upon reflection this argument seems flawed, as the specialized study of cancer is hardly the "familiar" in terms of which the "unfamiliar"—the spread of nuclear weapons—would be imagined. I now suggest rather that both cell biologists and nuclear strategists have appropriated the same familiar—the proliferation that produces children—to understand their respective objects. Looking to cell proliferation here gives me a means to highlight the entailments of such an appropriation, rather than argue a genealogy of nuclear proliferation through cell proliferation and cancer. I am indebted to Andrew Latham for his trenchant criticisms of the earlier formulation.

17. Andrew Murray and Tim Hunt, *The Cell Cycle: An Introduction* (New York: Freeman,1993), 1.

18. The similarity is unlikely to be entirely coincidental or simply to have derived from the two discourses using the same metaphorical language. Nuclear proliferation has entered widely into popular discourse and so is likely to have been evoked as cell biologists spoke of proliferation. Similarly, medical metaphors, particularly cancer, have been fairly common in post–World War II strategic discourse.

19. Barnaby, *How Nuclear Weapons Spread,* 2.

20. Chemical Weapons Convention, Article I. The text of the article reads: "Each State Party to this Convention undertakes never under any circumstances: (a) To develop, produce, otherwise acquire, stockpile or retain chemical weapons, or transfer, directly or indirectly, chemical weapons to anyone; (b) To use chemical weapons; (c) To engage in any military preparations to use chemical weapons; (d) To assist, encourage or induce, in any way, anyone to engage in any activity prohibited to a State Party under this Convention."

21. NPT, Articles I and II.

22. NPT, Article III, sets out the requirements for NNWSs party to safeguard their nuclear industries. The safeguard agreements between the IAEA and the NNWSs party are modeled on INFCIRC/153 and follow the wording of that model agreement very closely. For a discussion of the safeguards procedure, including the voluntary safeguards agreements signed with the NWSs, see von Baekmann, "The Treaty on the Non-Proliferation of Nuclear Weapons (NPT) (1968)," 167–176.

23. NPT, Article IV. The text of the article reads:

> 1. Nothing in this Treaty shall be interpreted as affecting the inalienable right of all the Parties to the Treaty to develop research, production and use of nuclear energy for peaceful purposes without discrimination and in conformity with articles I and II of this Treaty.
>
> 2. All the Parties to the Treaty undertake to facilitate, and have the right to participate in, the fullest possible exchange of equipment, materials and scientific and technological information for the peaceful uses of nuclear energy. Parties to the Treaty in a position to do so shall also cooperate in contributing alone or together with other States or international organizations to the further development of the applications of nuclear energy for peaceful purposes, especially in the territories of non-nuclear-weapon States Party to the Treaty, with due consideration for the needs of the developing areas of the world.

24. Efforts made have also been made to bolster the nuclear nonproliferation regime by strengthening and supplementing the NPT and its attendant supplier

groups. In particular, a treaty banning all nuclear testing has been negotiated. The safeguards system has been strengthened, and negotiations are ongoing for a treaty banning the further production of fissile material for weapons purposes. Although these are important to the proliferation control agenda, they are not directly relevant to my argument, so I will not discuss them in any detail.

25. The Canadian government, for example, has run a series of workshops for customs officials of Central European and former Soviet states designed to explain the techniques of export control.

26. See, for example, the chapters collected in Brad Roberts, ed., *Biological Weapons: Weapons of the Future* (Washington, D.C.: Center for Strategic and International Studies, 1993).

27. States Party to the BTWC, "Final Declaration: Special Conference of the States Party to the BTWC," 1994, §38, *BWC/SPCONF/1*.

28. See John Harvey, "Regional Ballistic Missiles and Advanced Strike Aircraft: Comparing Military Effectiveness," *International Security* 17 (2) 1992, 41–83.

29. External Affairs and International Trade Canada, "Missile Technology: Looking Beyond Supply-Side Control," *Disarmament Bulletin* 21, 1993, 5.

30. Lynn E. Davis, "Statement at Confirmation Hearing," *U.S. Department of State Dispatch* 4 (12) 1993, 170 (emphasis added).

31. The current register requests only that states submit their imports and exports of major weapons systems while providing for the voluntary provision of information on domestic procurement and holdings. An ongoing review is aimed at making procurement and holding an integral part of the register.

32. The 28 States, "New Multilateral Export Control Arrangement," press statement issued after the High Level Meeting of 28 States, Wassenaar (11 and 12 September 1995), §1 and §4.

33. The phrase is part of the formal title of the treaty: "Convention on Prohibitions or Restrictions on the Use of Certain Conventional Weapons Which May Be Deemed to Be Excessively Injurious or to Have Indiscriminate Effects," *UN Treaty Series*, Registration Number 22495.

34. On the importance of civilization to restrictions on the use of chemical weapons, see Price, "Genealogy," 95–98.

35. Canada, Department of Foreign Affairs and International Trade, "A Note from Minister Axworthy," *AP Mine Ban: Progress Report,* No. 1, February 1997 (http://www.dfait-maeci.gc.ca/english/foreignp/disarm/mines/report1).

36. The final list of signatories from the conference has been published by the Canadian government at: http://www.mines.gc.ca/conpar-e.htm.

37. "Convention on the Prohibition of the Use, Stockpiling, Production and Transfer of Anti-personnel Mines and on Their Destruction" [Ottawa Convention], 18 September 1997, Article 1.

38. For the comparable text, see note 20 (this chapter). Article 1 of the CWC does have a number of words not found in the Ottawa Convention. Some of these concern the destruction of chemical weapons production facilities and the prohibition of preparations for chemical warfare that are not particularly relevant to land mines. More interesting, the CWC obliges states party to destroy chemical weapons found on the land of other states. A comparable obligation in the Ottawa Convention would be remarkable, as it would oblige parties to clear their minefields. The convention does call on states party to clear the minefields under their jurisdiction but does not make them liable for mine clearance in other countries.

39. Ottawa Convention, Article 8.5.3.

40. For alternative readings of the land mines ban but ones that share a number of theoretical commitments with this work, see Keith Krause and Andrew

Latham, "Constructing Non-Proliferation and Arms Control: The Norms of Western Practice," in Krause, ed., *Culture and Security: Multilateralism, Arms Control
and Security Building*. Special issue of *Contemporary Security Policy* 19 (1) 1998,
42–45; and Richard Price, "Reversing the Gun Sights: Transnational Civil Society
Targets Land Mines," *International Organization* 52 (3) 1998, 613–644. Krause
and Latham argue that the land mines ban was made possible by a shift in the construction of the West as a civilization after the Cold War and a consequent recon-
sideration of inhumane weapons against the renewed standards of civilization.
Price argues that nongovernmental organizations were crucial in working to set
agendas and teach states about land mines, thereby producing the Ottawa Convention. These accounts do not necessarily contradict the one I have advanced in this
work but rather can be read as revealing possibilities created by the conjunctions
of altered framings and practices. Such an account would recognize the role of the
"proliferation" framing in providing the conditions of possibility for dramatic action on various forms of weapons—regimes similar to the NPT and the CWC can
be considered for any weapon identified as a problem. The practices to which Price
points, however, and the discursive resources highlighted by Krause and Latham
are, in turn, crucial to understanding why antipersonnel land mines in particular received this treatment.

41. Brad Roberts, "1995 and the End of the Post–Cold War Era," *Washington
Quarterly* 18 (1) 1995, 6–7.

42. Ibid., 6.

43. Black and Fairhall, "The Arms Trade," 17.

44. For a useful review of the military as modernizer literature, see Nicole
Ball, *Security and Economy in the Third World* (Princeton: Princeton University
Press, 1988), 3–15.

45. On the end of history, see Francis Fukayama, *The End of History and the
Last Man* (New York: Free Press, 1992). Capitalism, or more commonly economic
liberalism, is seen as an essential part of the liberal peace so popular with scholars
and U.S. policymakers.

Chapter 5

1. Shyman Bhatia, "Saddam's Doomsday Arsenal Uncovered," (London) *Observer*, 2 November 1997, 1.

2. Rolf Ekéus, "The United Nations Special Commission on Iraq," in *SIPRI
Yearbook 1992: World Armaments and Disarmament* (Oxford: Oxford University
Press for SIPRI, 1992), 509 (emphasis added).

3. Bhatia, "Saddam's Doomsday Arsenal Uncovered," 1.

4. Krauthammer, "Unipolar Moment," 30.

5. *SIPRI Yearbook 1992*, 403 (emphasis added).

6. See Campbell, *Politics Without Principle*, for an account of Iraq's sudden
transformation to "enemy," which is central to the story of its altered place in
the arms trade. For the U.S. position immediately before the invasion, see pp. 45–
48.

7. See Roger Tooze, "Prologue: States, Nationalisms and Identities—Thinking
in IR Theory," in Jill Krause and Neil Renwick, eds., *Identities in International Relations* (London: Macmillan, 1996), xvi–xx. As Tooze notes, "It is *this specific political identity* (i.e., state = nation) that has dominated the development of thinking

about international relations, at least for the past fifty years. It is this collective identity which has been one of the principal starting points for the subject of International Relations (IR) and the corpus of theory associated with IR" (xvii) (italics in the original).

8. R. B. J. Walker, *Inside/Outside: International Relations as Political Theory* (Cambridge: Cambridge University Press, 1993), 162.

9. William Connolly, *Identity/Difference: Democratic Negotiation of Political Paradox* (Ithaca: Cornell University Press, 1991), 64.

10. On the importance of naming in the construction of identity, see Judith Butler, *Excitable Speech: A Politics of the Performative* (London: Routledge, 1997), particularly pp. 30–31.

11. Connolly, *Identity/Difference,* 9–10.

12. Ibid., 36–48.

13. See Campbell, *Writing Security,* for a discussion of the constitution of the American self through the articulation of the danger posed by the Communist other.

14. For a useful discussion of this form of analysis, see Marysia Zalewski and Cynthia Enloe, "Questions About Identity in International Relations," in Ken Booth and Steve Smith, eds., *International Relations Theory Today* (Cambridge: Polity, 1995), 279–305. For a collection of essays on various forms of identity and identity politics in international relations from varied perspectives, see Krause and Renwick, *Identities in International Relations.* For research that explicitly links questions of identity to problems of security, see Ole Wœver, Barry Buzan, Morten Kelstrup, and Pierre Lemaitre, *Identity, Migration and the New Security Agenda in Europe* (London: Pinter, 1993). For an excellent study that uses deconstruction to ask questions of identity and security, although without invoking security directly, see David Campbell, *National Deconstruction: Violence, Identity and Justice in Bosnia* (Minneapolis: University of Minnesota Press, 1998).

15. This literature also spans a number of different approaches. See Alexander Wendt, "Anarchy Is What States Make of It: The Social Construction of Power Politics," *International Organization* 46 (2) 1992, 391–325; Wendt, *Social Theory of International Politics* (Cambridge: Cambridge University Press, forthcoming); Katzenstein, ed., *The Culture of National Security;* Eric Ringmar, *Identity, Interest and Action: A Cultural Explanation of Sweden's Intervention in the Thirty Years War* (Cambridge: Cambridge University Press, 1996); Thomas J. Biersteker and Cynthia Weber, eds., *State Sovereignty as Social Construct* (Cambridge: Cambridge University Press, 1996); and Iver Neumann, *Russia and the Idea of Europe: A Study in Identity and International Relations* (London: Routledge, 1996). The best of this work problematizes both the singular form of collective identity and the identity of the state. See, in particular, Campbell, *Writing Security.*

16. The constructed nature of nation and state identity does allow us to problematize being as well as recognition. The Islamic revolution in Iraq's neighbor Iran, for example, altered the nature of the state and nation, as had the revolution in Russia 60 years earlier. Again, both of these examples are outside the field of vision of the realist-inspired theory of international relations, as they are entirely domestic events that left the nation and state intact as international actors. For realism, some states change governments by election, others by revolution, and others not at all—and none of it matters.

17. For a discussion of the use of World War II metaphors in general and the analogy with Hitler in particular, see Campbell, *Politics Without Principle,* 21–28.

18. Canada, "Post-Hostilities Activities."

19. "The Wassenaar Arrangement on Export Controls for Conventional Arms and Dual-Use Goods and Technologies: Initial Elements" (as adopted by the Plenary of 11–12 July 1996). The crucial parts of the text read:

II. Scope

1. Participating States will meet on a regular basis to ensure that transfers of conventional arms and transfers in dual-use goods and technologies are carried out responsibly and in furtherance of international and regional peace and security.

2. To this end, Participating States will exchange, on a voluntary basis, information that will enhance transparency, will lead to discussions among all Participating States on arms transfers, as well as on sensitive dual-use goods and technologies, and will assist in developing common understandings of the risks associated with the transfer of these items. On the basis of this information they will assess the scope for co-ordinating national control policies to combat these risks. The information to be exchanged will include any matters which individual Participating States wish to bring to the attention of others, including, for those wishing to do so, notifications which go beyond those agreed upon.

3. The decision to transfer or deny transfer of any item will be the sole responsibility of each Participating State. All measures undertaken with respect to the arrangement will be in accordance with national legislation and policies and will be implemented on the basis of national discretion.

• • •

III. Control Lists

1. Participating States will control all items set forth in the List of Dual-Use Goods and Technologies and in the Munitions List . . . with the objective of preventing unauthorised transfers or re-transfers of those items.

20. COCOM, the precursor to the Wassenaar Arrangement, maintained three lists: the Industrial List, the Munitions List, and the Atomic Energy List. The first of these has become the list of Dual-Use Goods and Technologies and together with the Munitions List has been incorporated into Wassenaar, which did not pick up the Atomic Energy List. Canada's lists also include two groups unrelated to issues of proliferation, at least directly: a Miscellaneous List, which covers various odd controls, and a list concerned with controlling chemicals for the purpose of producing illicit drugs. Government of Canada, *A Guide to Canada's Export Controls* (Ottawa: Department of Foreign Affairs and International Trade, 1994). The updated guide is available online at http://www.dfait-maeci.gc.ca/~eicb/export/milit_tech-e.htm.

21. "Wassennaar Arrangement," §I.3.

22. Ibid., §I.4.

23. Exporter Reports, tabulated in *Basic Reports,* No. 16, 12 November 1997, 5–11.

24. Russia and China are also able to export missile technology and have done so. The MTCR has wooed both countries, and although they have not joined they have agreed to abide by the guidelines.

25. The 28 States, "New Multilateral Export Control Arrangement," §2 (emphasis added).

26. United States Security Council, "Statement by the President of the Security Council on Behalf of the Members of the Council on the Responsibility of the Security Council in the Maintenance of International Peace and Security," S/23500, 31 January 1992.

27. See Michel Foucault, *Discipline and Punish: The Birth of the Prison* (New York: Vintage, 1979), for an account of the construction of the "normal" as opposed to the "criminal," produced and policed in part by the discipline of criminology, and Foucault, *Madness and Civilisation* (New York: Pantheon, 1965), for his account of the "normal" as opposed to the "insane" and its policing by psychiatry.

28. For a discussion of the relationship among the Kurds and other sub- and transnational social groups in the Iran-Iraq War, see W. Thom Workman, *The Social Origins of the Iran-Iraq War* (Boulder: Lynne Rienner, 1994).

29. For a discussion of the complexity of the security environment as seen by India, see Andrew Latham, "Constructing National Security: Culture and Identity in Indian Arms Control and Disarmament Practice," in Krause, ed., *Culture and Security*, 138–141.

30. Raju Thomas, "The Growth of India's Military Power: From Sufficiency to Nuclear Deterrence," in Ross Babbage and Sandy Gordon, eds., *India's Strategic Future* (New York: St. Martin's, 1992), 38. See also ibid., 141–145.

31. For a discussion of the conservative political implications of the proliferation discourse, see my "Reimagining Security," 210–212.

32. Krauthammer, "Unipolar Moment," 23.

33. The chair at the time was Senator Sam Nunn, a longtime supporter of the military in Congress. Cited in Michael Klare, *Rogue States and Nuclear Outlaws: America's Search for a New Foreign Policy* (New York: Hill and Wang, 1995), 14.

34. Ibid., 11.

35. Ibid., 26.

36. Ibid., 34.

37. U.S. Secretary of Defense Richard Cheney, Statement to the House Armed Services Committee, 19 March 1991, cited in ibid., 131.

38. See Campbell, *Politics Without Principle,* 42–48, for a discussion of the Glaspie meeting.

39. U.S. Secretary of State Warren Christopher, "The Strategic Priorities of American Foreign Policy: Statement Before the Senate Foreign Relations Committee," Washington, D.C., 4 November 1993. *U.S. Department of State Dispatch* 4 (47), 22 November 1993.

40. John Harris, "Will Jones Case Finally Dent Clinton's Ratings Armor?" *International Herald Tribune,* 20 January 1998, 3.

41. Krauthammer, "Unipolar Moment," 30 (emphasis added).

42. For a useful review of the so-called proliferation pessimist position that uses this argument, see David J. Karl, "Proliferation Pessimism and Emerging Nuclear Powers," *International Security* 21 (3) 1996–97, 87–119. As Karl notes, there is a newer version of pessimism, exemplified in the work of Scott Sagan, which denies the maturity of the old nuclear powers and focuses instead on the difficulties they had in maintaining control. See Scott Sagan, "More Will Be Worse," in Waltz and Sagan, *The Spread of Nuclear Weapons.*

43. "Citations to Rogue Nation, Rogue State, or Rogue Regime," Proliferation Watch, Senate Committee on Governmental Affairs, March–April 1994, 2. Cited in Klare, *Rogue States,* 277.

Chapter 6

1. NPT, Article X.2.

2. Roberts, "1995," 15–16.

3. NPT, Article VI.

4. For discussions of the importance of the comprehensive test ban to the review conferences, see M. I. Shaker, "The Third NPT Review Conference: Issues
and Prospects," in David Dewitt, ed., *Nuclear Non-Proliferation and Global Security* (London: Croom Helm, 1987), 3–6; and David Fischer, "The NPT Review
Conference, Geneva, 27 August to 21 September 1985: A Retrospective," in Dewitt, ed., *Nuclear Non-Proliferation and Global Security,* 217. M. I. Shaker was
the Egyptian representative and president of the review conference; David Fischer
is former director-general of the IAEA. Fischer writes, for instance, "By far, the
most profound [of three difficult and divisive issues] was the lack of progress in
nuclear arms control called for by Article VI of the treaty; in particular, the resistance of the United States . . . to negotiating a Comprehensive Test Ban (CTB)
treaty" (217).

5. "Final Document of the Third Review Conference of the Parties to the
Treaty on the Non-Proliferation of Nuclear Weapons," 25 September 1985,
NPT/CONF.III/I Annex I, reprinted in Dewitt, ed., *Nuclear Non-Proliferation and
Global Security*, 251.

6. Eric Arnett, "The Comprehensive Nuclear Test Ban," in SIPRI *Yearbook
1995: Armaments, Disarmament and International Security* (Oxford: Oxford University Press for SIPRI, 1995), 697. Arnett notes that previous negotiations had
been held among the United States, the United Kingdom, and the USSR in 1958–
1963 and 1977–1980. The CD procedures for negotiating a treaty involve mandating an ad hoc committee, which engages in substantive negotiations and produces
a text that is then approved by the CD as a whole. Mandating an ad hoc committee for negotiation of a CTBT was therefore a very important step.

7. "Remarks of the Honorable John D. Holum, Director, U.S. Arms Control
and Disarmament Agency, 4 August 1994" (Washington, D.C.: ACDA Office of
Public Information, 1994).

8. One of the most interesting proposals was put forward by Costa Rica,
which argued that the NPT could be extended by renewing it in its entirety—including Article X.2. This would mean that in another 25 years the states party
would be faced with exactly the same choice. Other proposals tended to be variations on the possibility of fixed periods, producing a rolling extension with the
NPT renewed every 5 years.

9. "Letter Dated 14 September 1994 from the Head of the Delegation of Indonesia," NPT/CONF.1995/PC.III/13, §§3–5. The key paragraphs read:

> 3. The Non-Aligned Countries value the Non-Proliferation Treaty as
> a key instrument to channel international efforts to halt vertical and hor-
> izontal proliferation of nuclear weapons. Notwithstanding the important
> role of the Treaty in the maintenance of international security, it should
> be recognized that the Treaty has fundamental shortcomings that have be-
> come the bone of contention between NWSs and NNWSs Parties to the
> NPT ever since it came into being, thus eroding the perceived value of
> the Treaty.
>
> 4. The preparations for the NPT Conference in 1995 provide an ex-
> cellent opportunity towards the realisation of the objectives enshrined in
> the Treaty.
>
> 5. The cessation of the nuclear arms race, nuclear disarmament and
> general disarmament as a whole, continue to be the main objectives of
> the Treaty.

10. Prakash Shah, "Nuclear Non-Proliferation Implications and the NPT Review: An Indian Perspective," paper presented to the international workshop

Nuclear Disarmament and Non-Proliferation: Issues for International Action, Tokyo, 15–16 March 1993, 3.

11. See Latham, "Constructing National Security," particularly p. 149, for India's consistent rejection of "proliferation" in favor of "disarmament."

12. "Letter Dated 14 September," §3.

13. Recall Thomas Schelling's testimony to the U.S. Congress in 1969: "Whatever the prospects for successful negotiations with the Soviet Union during the coming months and years, on the subject of strategic weapons, there could not be a greater contrast between *the serious and businesslike prospects for realistic negotiations in 1969 and all the fantasy and pretense about 'general and complete disarmament'* that characterized the beginning of our decade." In Adler, "Emergence of Cooperation," 124 (emphasis added).

14. "Letter Dated 14 September," §§12–13.

15. For a leading statement of how problems do not a security agenda make, see Robert Dorff, "A Commentary on *Security Studies for the 1990s* as a Model Core Curriculum," *International Studies Notes* 19 (3) 1994, 21–31. For a response to Dorff from the perspective of critical security study, see Krause and Williams, "From Strategy to Security," 35–36.

16. On security as a speech act, see Ole Wœver, "Securitization and Desecuritization," in Ronnie D. Lipschutz, ed., *On Security* (New York: Columbia Universtiy Press, 1995), 46–86.

17. It is an open question whether a guns and butter trade-off exists at all. One study in which I was involved concluded that "there is no simple and straightforward trade-off in government priorities between military and other social welfare spending. Neither richer nor poorer states have a discernable tendency to trade off higher military expenditures against social welfare spending." Nevertheless, we also noted: "Even if there is *no* evidence that military spending exerts a negative impact on economic growth, there are opportunity costs of these choices . . . and armed forces consume resources which could in principle be used for other purposes." Keith Krause, Kenneth Epps, William Weston, and David Mutimer, *Constraining Conventional Proliferation: A Role for Canada* (Ottawa: Department of Foreign Affairs and International Trade, 1996), 110–111.

18. "Discover India—Brought to You by the Ministry of External Affairs" (http://www.meadev.gov.in/science/nucl.htm) (emphasis added).

19. See Barnaby, *How Nuclear Weapons Spread*, 2.

20. "Discover India."

21. "Statute of the International Atomic Energy Agency, Done at the Headquarters of the United Nations, on 26 October 1956," *UN Treaty Series* No. 3988, Article II.

22. Ibid., §§ 1–2.

23. NPT, Article IV.

24. Krause, *Arms and the State,* 13–14. At this point in his argument Krause cites Clive Trebilcock, who found arms production produced "a battery of stimulating effects" within the industrializing economies of late nineteenth-century Europe.

25. David Mussington, "Verifying End-Use Restrictions on Dual-Use Technology Transfers: Toward a Technology Transparency Hierarchy," in David Mutimer, ed., *Moving Beyond Supplier Controls in a Mature Technology Environment* (Toronto: York Centre for International and Strategic Studies, 1995), 40.

26. Ibid., 41.

27. Some leading examples of this literature are Hans Daalder, *The Role of the Military in the Emerging Countries* (The Hague: Mouton, 1962); Morton Janowitz,

The Military in the Political Development of New Nations: An Essay in Comparative Analysis (Chicago: University of Chicago Press, 1964); John Johnson, *The Military and Society in Latin America* (Stanford: Stanford University Press, 1964); John Johnson, ed., *The Role of the Military in Underdeveloped Countries* (Princeton: Princeton University Press, 1962); and Marion J. Levy, *Modernization and the Structure of Society: An International Setting* (Princeton: Princeton University Press, 1962).

28. For a review and update of the Nunn-Lugar program, which encompasses cooperative threat reduction, conversion of fissile materials, and attempts to keep Russian nuclear scientists in Russia, see Jason D. Ellis and Todd Perry, "Nunn-Lugar's Unfinished Agenda," *Arms Control Today* 27 (7) 1997, 14–22; and "Nunn-Lugar Threat Reduction Programs," *Coalition to Reduce Nuclear Dangers: Issue Brief* 2 (10) March 1998. Http://www.clw.org/pub/clw/coalition/brief10.htm.

29. Los Alamos National Laboratory. Http://www.lanl.gov/external/science/index.html.

30. Los Alamos National Laboratory. Http://www.lanl.gov/external/welcome/.

31. "UC Prime Contract, Appendix M: Technology Commercialization." Http://ext.lanl.gov/orgs/citpo/TCO/appendm.htm describes the purposes of the Technology program as:

> (1) The transfer of new and emerging technologies between the Laboratory and private industry to enhance the Laboratory's ability to meet mission requirements and improve the industrial competitiveness of the United States, and
> (2) The development of improved mechanisms for the utilization of Laboratory technologies to stimulate new business startups, attract entrepreneurs, create alternative job opportunities, and attract businesses and capital to the region while also continuing to serve the nation as a whole.

32. Bonn International Center for Conversion, *Conversion Survey 1997: Global Disarmament and Disposal of Surplus Weapons* (Oxford: Oxford University Press, 1997), 43.

33. The White House, *A National Security Strategy of Engagement and Enlargement* (Washington, D.C.: U.S. Government Printing Office, 1996), 27.

34. Ibid., 3.

35. Ibid., 26.

36. Ibid., 27.

37. Ibid.

Chapter 7

1. Eric Arnett, "The Comprehensive Nuclear Test-Ban Treaty," in SIPRI, *SIPRI Yearbook 1997: Armaments, Disarmament and International Security* (Oxford: Oxford University Press for SIPRI, 1997), 403.

2. G. Allen Greb and Warren Heckrotte, "The Long History: The Test Ban Debate," *Bulletin of the Atomic Scientists,* August–September 1983, 36.

3. Benjamin S. Loeb, "Test Ban Proposals and Agreements: The 1950s to the Present," in Richard Dean Burns, ed., *Encyclopedia of Arms Control and Disarmament,* Vol. 2 (New York: Scribner, 1993), 828.

4. See Chapter 3, note 38.

5. PNEs are the use of nuclear explosions for some ostensibly peaceful purpose—the most commonly discussed is earthmoving. Since the verification of a

test ban of any kind will be performed primarily through seismology, allowing PNEs while banning nuclear tests makes little sense. The Indian test in 1974, for example, is claimed to have been a test of a peaceful nuclear explosive.

6. Jack F. Evernden, "Politics, Technology, and the Test Ban," *Bulletin of the Atomic Scientists,* March 1985, 12.

7. Arms Control Association, *Arms Control and National Security* (Washington, D.C.: Arms Control Association, 1989), 116.

8. Ibid.

9. This is not to say that these problems were necessarily as central as they appeared. The United States knew the Soviet Union (at least before Gorbachev) would refuse to agree to intrusive on-site inspections and so was able to use its verification stand to prevent an agreement.

10. Jozef Goldblat, "Multilateral Arms Control Efforts," in *SIPRI Yearbook 1987,* 391–392.

11. Jozef Goldblat, "Multilateral Arms Control Efforts," in *SIPRI Yearbook 1988: World Armaments and Disarmament* (Oxford: Oxford University Press for SIPRI, 1988), 366.

12. White House, *National Security Strategy of Engagement and Enlargement,* 21.

13. Both the term *blatantly obstructive role* and the characterization of India's new policy as a reversal are from Arnett, "The Comprehensive Nuclear Test-Ban Treaty," 404.

14. Gregory E. van der Vink, David Simpson, Christel Hennet, Jeffrey Park, and Terry Wallace, *Nuclear Testing and Nonproliferation: The Role of Seismology in Deterring the Development of Nuclear Weapons.* Prepared at the Request of the Senate Committee on Governmental Affairs and the House Committee on Foreign Affairs of the United States Congress (Arlington, Va.: IRIS Consortium, 1994), II-18–19.

15. "Report of the Conference on Disarmament to the General Assembly of the United Nations," CD/1436, 12 September 1996, Section I, §20.

16. Ibid. (emphasis added).

17. Annex 2 reads: "List of States Pursuant to Article XIV: List of States members of the Conference on Disarmament as at 18 June 1996 which formally participated in the work of the 1996 session of the Conference and which appear in Table 1 of the International Atomic Energy Agency's April 1996 edition of 'Nuclear Power Reactors in the World,' and of States members of the Conference on Disarmament as at 18 June 1996 which formally participated in the work of the 1996 session of the Conference and which appear in Table 1 of the International Atomic Energy Agency's December 1995 edition of 'Nuclear Research Reactors in the World': Algeria, Argentina, Australia, Austria, Bangladesh, Belgium, Brazil, Bulgaria, Canada, Chile, China, Colombia, Democratic People's Republic of Korea, Egypt, Finland, France, Germany, Hungary, India, Indonesia, Iran (Islamic Republic of), Israel, Italy, Japan, Mexico, Netherlands, Norway, Pakistan, Peru, Poland, Romania, Republic of Korea, Russian Federation, Slovakia, South Africa, Spain, Sweden, Switzerland, Turkey, Ukraine, United Kingdom of Great Britain and Northern Ireland, United States of America, Viet Nam, Zaire."

18. The conventional interpretation of the entry-into-force restrictions is that the formula chosen was an attempt to require that the so-called threshold states (India, North Korea, Iraq, Israel, and Pakistan) must ratify for the CTBT to enter into force, without naming them directly. Although this is almost certainly the case, such an argument does not contradict the one I am advancing. First, the threshold states are the primary targets of proliferation control efforts. On the other hand, the

formula that was finally agreed is enabled by the "proliferation" discourse only in terms of "proliferation" can states with nuclear energy and research facilities meaningfully be singled out as the heart of a regime designed to control nuclear explosions.

19. At the end of the 1980s the Congressional Research Service prepared a report on "all aspects of the nuclear testing issues." This comprehensive survey of the issues surrounding nuclear testing was organized into six substantive chapters. Of these only one concerned anything other than the U.S.-Soviet nuclear relationship, and of that, only half of it concerned nuclear proliferation; the rest treated the effects of a CTBT on the other three NWSs. Clearly, at the end of the 1980s a CTBT was not part of a nonproliferation agenda. See Jonathan Medalia, Paul Zinsmeister, and Robert Civiak, eds., *Nuclear Weapons and Security: The Effects of Test Ban Treaties* (Boulder: Westview, 1991).

20. The possibility of developing new weapons will depend largely on the effectiveness of computer simulations of nuclear tests—and, as important, the military's willingness to trust that effectiveness.

21. Hugh Gusterson, *Nuclear Rites: A Weapons Laboratory at the End of the Cold War* (Berkeley: University of California Press, 1996), provides a rather different reading of the opposition to a test ban within weapons laboratories. He argues that the social practices of the weapons labs have produced a "regime of truth" in Foucault's sense, which privileges testing as the final source of expertise on nuclear weapons. Therefore it is not so much that testing is necessary to certify the reliability of old weapons but that only by participating in tests can a weapons scientist gain the authority to pronounce on reliability.

22. E. H. Carr, *The Twenty Years' Crisis 1919–1939,* 2d ed. (London: Macmillan, 1946), 51–53. The identification of Carr as a founding realist is the traditional construction of the discipline, but it is by no means the only interpretation of Carr. See, for example, Andrew Linklater, "The Transformation of Political Community: E. H. Carr, Critical Theory and International Relations," *Review of International Studies* 23 (3) 1997, 321–338, who attempts to reclaim Carr for critical IR theory. For a critical examination of the disciplinary lore and Carr's place in it, see Jim George, *Discourses of Global Politics: A Critical (Re)Introduction to International Relations* (Boulder: Lynne Rienner, 1994), 77–83.

23. Arnold Wolfers, "'National Security' as an Ambiguous Symbol," in Robert Art and Robert Jervis, eds., *International Politics: Anarchy, Force, Political Economy, and Decision Making,* 2d ed. (New York: HarperCollins, 1985), 42.

24. Morgenthau, *Politics Among Nations,* 5.

25. Ibid. (emphasis added).

26. Ibid., 10, 127–169, and 146–147.

27. Waltz, *Theory of International Politics,* 134.

28. Wolfers, "'National Security,'" 42.

29. Stephen Krasner, "Structural Causes and Regime Consequences: Regimes as Intervening Variables," in Krasner, ed., *International Regimes* (Ithaca: Cornell University Press, 1983), 5.

30. Robert Keohane, "Theory of World Politics: Structural Realism and Beyond," in Keohane, *International Institutions and State Power: Essays in International Relations Theory* (Boulder: Westview, 1989), 54–55.

31. Weldes, "Constructing National Interests," 279.

32. Stephen Krasner, "Regimes and the Limits of Realism: Regimes as Autonomous Variables," in Krasner, ed., *International Regimes,* 361.

33. Keohane, "Theory of World Politics," 62 (emphasis added).

34. Morgenthau writes that "political realism believes that politics, like society in general, is governed by objective laws" (*Politics Among Nations,* 4). On the acceptance of this proposition by neorealists and neoliberals, see Waltz, *Theory of International Politics,* 1–17; John Mearsheimer, "Back to the Future: Instability in Europe After the Cold War," *International Security* 15 (1) 1990, 9–10; and Robert Keohane, "Neoliberal Institutionalism: A Perspective on World Politics," in Keohane, *International Institutions and State Power,* 7–9.

35. Wendt, "Anarchy," 392–395.

36. Ibid., 398. See also Alexander Wendt, "Collective Identity Formation and the International State," *American Political Science Review* 88 (2) 1994, 385–396.

37. Wendt, "Anarchy," 393–394. Wendt notes there that "Constructivism's potential contribution to a strong liberalism has been obscured, however, by recent epistemological debates between modernists and post-modernists, in which Science disciplines Dissent for not defining a conventional research program, and Dissent celebrates its liberation from Science." Wendt firmly marks himself in the modernist camp.

38. See both "Anarchy" and "Collective Identity." In the first, Wendt writes, "My objective in this article is to build a bridge between these two traditions (and, by extension, between the realist-liberal and rationalist-reflectivist debates)" ("Anarchy," 394). In the latter article Wendt sets out his arguments about identity and interest in terms of an alternative hypothesis to the realist and liberal hypotheses, which can then be tested in an empirical manner ("Collective Identity," 391). Weldes accepts Wendt's constructivist move but argues that he retains the realist conception of the "black box" state. She also appears more willing than Wendt to accept the epistemological implications of his arguments. See Weldes, "Constructing National Interests," 279–284.

39. Weldes, "Constructing National Interests," 280.

40. Ibid., 282.

41. "Ottawa Convention," Preamble.

42. "Wassenaar Arrangement," §I.1.

43. See "Alliance Policy Framework on Proliferation of Weapons of Mass Destruction," issued at the Ministerial Meeting of the North Atlantic Council held in Istanbul, Turkey, on 9 June 1994. Press Release M-NAC-1(94)45, 9 June 1994, §1. In the framework the alliance states: "Heads of State and Government of NATO countries at the 1994 Brussels Summit stressed that proliferation of WMD and their delivery means poses a threat to *international security and is a matter of concern to the Alliance*" (emphasis added).

44. The leading statement of the debate between pessimists and optimists is Waltz and Sagan, *The Spread of Nuclear Weapons.* For a selection of interventions in the debate, see "The Kenneth Waltz–Scott Sagan Debate: The Spread of Nuclear Weapons: Good or Bad?" six articles plus responses from Waltz and Sagan, *Security Studies* 4 (4) 1995, 693–810; Bradley Thayer and Steven Lee, "The Kenneth Waltz–Scott Sagan Debate II," *Security Studies* 5 (1) 1995, 149–170; Karl, "Proliferation Pessimism and Emerging Nuclear Powers," 87–119; Peter Feaver, Scott Sagan, and David Karl, "Proliferation Pessimism and Emerging Nuclear Powers," *International Security* 22 (2) 1997, 185–207; John Mearsheimer, "The Case for a Ukrainian Nuclear Deterrent," *Foreign Affairs* 72 (3) 1993, 50–66; Steven Miller, "The Case Against a Ukrainian Nuclear Deterrent," *Foreign Affairs* 72 (3) 1993, 67–80; Martin van Creveld, *Nuclear Proliferation and the Future of Conflict* (New York: Free Press, 1993); Scott Sagan, ed., *Civil-Military Relations and Nuclear Weapons* (Stanford: Stanford University Center for International Security and Arms

Control, 1994); Zachary Davis and Benjamin Frankel, eds., *The Proliferation Puzzle: Why Nuclear Weapons Spread (and What Results)* (London: Frank Cass, 1993); Lewis Dunn, *Containing Nuclear Proliferation,* Adelphi Paper 263 (London: International Institute for Strategic Studies [IISS], 1991); and Karl Kaiser, "Non-Proliferation and Nuclear Deterrence," *Survival* 31 (2) 1989, 123–136.

45. The most famous statement of this case is by John Mearsheimer, "Back to the Future," 5–56. Mearsheimer was drawing on an earlier argument by Kenneth Waltz, *The Spread of Nuclear Weapons: More May Be Better,* Adelphi Paper 171 (London: IISS, 1981), revised and reprinted as "More May Be Better" in Sagan and Waltz, *The Spread of Nuclear Weapons.*

46. "Wassenaar Arrangement," §I.3 (emphasis added).

47. Ibid., §§I.1, I.3.

48. Ibid., §I.4.

49. Ibid., §I.3 (emphasis added).

50. Waltz, *Theory of International Politics,* 134.

51. "Fact Sheet: Middle East Arms Control Initiative," 3.

52. I think my work has fallen prey to this problem, particularly my "Reimagining Security: The Metaphors of Proliferation." I am indebted to Andreas Behnke for useful discussion of this problem.

53. President Clinton, "Confronting the Challenges of a Broader World," Address to the UN General Assembly, New York City, September 27, 1993. *Department of State Dispatch* 4 (39) 1993. Http://dosfan.lib.uic.edu/ERC/briefing/dispatch/1993/html/Dispatchv4no39.html.

54. Davis, "Statement at Confirmation Hearing," 170.

55. Klare, *Rogue States,* 28.

56. Ibid., 11.

57. The classic statement of the bureaucratic politics model is Graham Allison, *Essence of Decision: Explaining the Cuban Missile Crisis* (Boston: Little, Brown, 1971). Allison and Morton Halperin then refined the model in "Bureaucratic Politics: A Paradigm and Some Policy Implications," in G. John Ikenberry, ed., *American Foreign Policy: Theoretical Essays* (Glenview: Scott, Foresman, 1989), 378–409.

58. Klare, *Rogue States,* 11.

59. Krause, *Arms and the State,* 15.

60. Walker, *Inside/Outside,* particularly 159–169.

61. Thomas Biersteker and Cynthia Weber, "The Social Construction of State Sovereignty," in Biersteker and Weber, eds., *State Sovereignty as Social Construct,* 12.

62. Mark Suchman and Dana Eyre, "Military Procurement as Rational Myth: Notes on the Social Construction of Weapons Proliferation," *Sociological Forum* 7 (1) 1992, 150.

63. Ibid.

64. UK Ministry of Defence, "Supporting Essay One: The Strategic Defence Review Process," one of 11 essays provided as a public guide to the review process, which was to be open and public in nature. Http://www.mod.uk/policy/sdr/essay01.htm, §3–4 (emphasis added).

65. UK Ministry of Defence, "Supporting Essay Two: The Policy Framework," one of 11 essays provided by the MOD as a public guide to the review process, which was to be open and public in nature. Http://www.mod.uk/policy/sdr/essay02.htm, §5 (emphasis added). The second of these interests was

Britain's place as a European state whose security is indivisible from that of other European Union and NATO members. The third is the centrality of international trade to UK security. The fourth is that Britain still has global responsibilities, both in a globally spread citizenry and in a series of overseas territories. The fifth of the paragraphs sets out the British values that are to be promoted and protected by the UK's defense policy, guaranteeing security by promoting international stability, freedom, and economic development (§§6–9).

66. On the importance of export to the maintenance of a defense-industrial base, see Krause, *Arms and the State*, 26–32 and 136–142; on the special position of the superpowers during the Cold War, see pp. 99–126.

67. Dana Eyre and Mark Suchman, "The Proliferation of Conventional Weapons: An Institutional Theory Approach," in Katzenstein, ed., *The Culture of National Security*, 86.

Chapter 8

1. UN Security Council Resolution 1154 (1998), Adopted by the Security Council at its 3,858th meeting on 2 March 1998, S/RES/1154 (1998), 2 March 1998, §3.

2. The repetition of these crises is remarkable. I first drafted this concluding chapter in spring 1998, just as Resolution 1154 was being passed. I wrote these first few paragraphs to reflect the crisis of winter 1998, when UN inspectors were barred from entering the presidential palaces. I revised the manuscript in autumn 1998 and as part of that exercise I changed these first few paragraphs to refer to the autumn 1998 crisis, sparked by Iraq's withdrawal of cooperation in August of that year. I have had to change barely a word of the account in this updating.

3. "U.S. Says 85% of Iraqi Targets Were Hit," *New York Times*, 22 December 1998, http://www.nytimes.com/library/world/mideast/122298iraq-military.html.

4. UN Security Council Resolution 687 (1991), Adopted by the Security Council at its 2,981st meeting, on 8 April 1991, S/RES/687 (1991), 8 April 1991, §9.

5. The UNSCOM inspections began with seven inspections conducted by the IAEA to investigate the Iraqi nuclear program. Six reports were issued in respect to those seven inspections; they have been followed by 22 UNSCOM reports up to October 1997.

6. UN Security Council, "Report of the Secretary-General on the Activities of the Special Commission Established by the Secretary-General Pursuant to Paragraph 9 (b) (i) of Resolution 687 (1991)," S/1997/774, 6 October 1997, §123.

7. Ibid., §124.

8. Ibid., §125 (emphasis added).

9. UN Security Council, "Report of the Secretary-General on the Activities of the Special Commission Established by the Secretary-General Pursuant to Paragraph 9 (b) (i) of Resolution 687 (1991)," S/1996/848, 11 October 1997, §94.

10. A listing of the inspections can be found at the end of the report of activity for the period December 1995–April 1996: UN Security Council, "Report of the Secretary-General on the Activities of the Special Commission Established by the Secretary-General Pursuant to Paragraph 9 (b) (i) of Resolution 687 (1991)," S/1996/258, 11 April 1996, 28–34, and at the end of each subsequent report.

11. UN Security Council Summit, "Final Declaration." Reported in *New York Times*. "Summit at the UN: Security Council Summit Declaration: 'New Risks for Stability and Security,'" 1 February 1992.

12. UN Security Council, "Consolidated Report on the First Two IAEA Inspections Under Security Council Resolution 687 (1991) of Iraqi Nuclear Capabilities," S/22788, 1991, §2.

13. UN Security Council, "Plan for Future Ongoing Monitoring and Verification of Iraq's Compliance with Relevant Parts of Section C of Security Council Resolution 687 (1991)," S/22871/Rev.1, 2 October 1991, §1.

14. Ibid., Annex I, §1.

15. UN Security Council, S/1997/774, §97.

16. It is worth noting that the United States considers itself less bound than some others by these norms, routinely assuming the extraterritorial applicability of U.S. law.

17. UN Security Council, S/22871/Rev.1, §17 (emphasis added).

18. For a discussion of the South African program, see Darryl Howlett and John Simpson, "Nuclearisation and Denuclearisation in South Africa," *Survival* 35 (3) 1993, 154–173.

19. Vannunu's story was told by the *Sunday Times* in 1986 ("Revealed: The Secrets of Israel's Nuclear Arsenal," *Sunday* [London] *Times,* 5 October 1986), for which he was sentenced to 18 years in prison. For a discussion of Israel's nuclear program, see Barnaby, *How Nuclear Weapons Spread*, 80–85.

20. *Globe and Mail* (Toronto), 9 December 1998.

21. "Sharif Sets Terms for Signing CTBT," *Hindu,* 28 September 1998, 1, http://www.hinduonline.com/daily/980925/01/01250004.htm; "U.S. Welcomes Remarks from PM on CTBT," *Hindu,* 28 September 1998, 1, http://www.hinduonline.com/daily/980926/01/01260005.htm.

22. "CTBT: UN Adopts Indian Sponsored Resolution," *Deccan Herald* (Bangalore), 15 November 1998, http://www.deccanherald.com/deccanherald/nov15/ctbt.htm.

23. "George Denies Deal on CTBT," *Hindustan Times* (New Delhi), 26 October 1998, http://www.hindustantimes.com/nonfram/261098/detFRO02.htm.

24. "Vajpayee Hits Out at International N-Regime," *Hindustan Times,* 16 September 1998, http://www.hindustantimes.com/nonfram/160998/detNat02.htm.

25. "India Seeks changes in Hi-Tech Transfer over CTBT," *Hindustan Times,* 17 September 1998, http://www.hindustantimes.com/nonfram/170998/detFRO01.htm.

26. "George Denies Deal on CTBT." See also "We Proved Our Worth with N-Tests," *Times of India,* 29 October 1998, http://www.timesofindia.com/today/29indi13.htm: "Dr. A. P. J. Abdul Kalam, scientific adviser to the defence minister, dispelled on Monday doubts over India's status [as] a nuclear weapon power. 'We do not need more nuclear tests to prove our worth because the number of nuclear tests required for becoming a nuclear power depends on a country's technological capability. By conducting multiple tests simultaneously, something which no other country has done, we have proved our technological worth.'"

27. Strobe Talbott, "U.S. Diplomacy in South Asia: A Progress Report," Transcript as delivered, provided by the Brookings Institution, http://www.brook.edu/comm/transcripts/19981112a.htm.

28. Ibid.

29. "France Ready to Accept Nuclear India," *Hindu,* 30 October 1998, 1, http://www.hinduonline.com/daily/981030/01/01300005.htm. See also "Returns

from the French Connection," *Indian Express,* 29 October 1998, http://www.
indian-express.com/ie/daily/19981029/30250934.html.

30. "India Plans to Sign Nuclear-Test Ban," *Globe and Mail,* 25 September
1998, A10. The negotiations between the United States and India are secret, and so
the reports are not official and have not been acknowledged by either government.

Chapter 9

1. Foucault, "Practicing Criticism," 155.
2. Gusterson, *Nuclear Rites,* 222.

Bibliography

Abraham, Itty. "Pakistan-India and Argentina-Brazil: Stepping Back from the Nuclear Threshold?" *Occasional Paper No. 15*. Washington, D.C.: Stimson Center, 1993.

"Address by President Eisenhower Before the United Nations General Assembly, December 8, 1953," reprinted in *Nuclear Proliferation Factbook*. Prepared for Committee on International Relations and the Committee on Governmental Affairs, U.S. Congress, by the Congressional Research Service. Washington, D.C.: GPO, 1977.

Adler, Emmanuel. "The Emergence of Cooperation: National Epistemic Communities and the International Evolution of the Idea of Nuclear Arms Control." *International Organization* 46 (1) 1992, 101–145.

Advisory Council on Peace and Security. *Towards a Multi-Faceted Non-Proliferation Policy*. The Hague: Advisory Council on Peace and Security, 1992.

Albright, David. "A Proliferation Primer." *Bulletin of the Atomic Scientists* 49, 1993, 14–23.

Albright, David, Frank Berkhout, and William Walker. *World Inventory of Plutonium and Highly Enriched Uranium*. Stockholm: SIPRI, 1992.

Allan, Charles T. "Extended Conventional Deterrence: In from the Cold and Out of the Nuclear Fire?" *Washington Quarterly* 17 (3) 1994, 203–233.

Allebeck, Agnès Courades. "Arms Trade Regulations." In *SIPRI Yearbook 1989*, 319–338.

Allentuck, Jack. *Challenge Inspections in Arms Control Treaties: Any Lessons for Strengthening NPT Verification*. Report no. BNL-46941. Upton, N.Y.: Brookhaven National Laboratory, 1992.

"Alliance Policy Framework on Proliferation of Weapons of Mass Destruction." Issued at the Ministerial Meeting of the North Atlantic Council held in Istanbul, Turkey, on 9 June 1994. Press Release M-NAC-1(94)45.

Allison, Graham. *Essence of Decision: Explaining the Cuban Missile Crisis*. Boston: Little, Brown, 1971.

Allison, Graham, and Morton Halperin. "Bureaucratic Politics: A Paradigm and Some Policy Implications." In G. John Ikenberry, ed. *American Foreign Policy: Theoretical Essays*. Glenview: Scott, Foresman, 1989, 378–409.

Anthony, Ian, Agnès Allebeck, and Herbert Wulf. *West European Arms Production: Structural Changes in the New Political Environment*. Stockholm: SIPRI, 1990.

Anthony, Ian, ed. *Arms Export Regulations*. Oxford: Oxford University Press, 1991.

Arms Control Association. *Arms Control and National Security*. Washington, D.C.: Arms Control Association.

Arnett, Eric. "The Comprehensive Nuclear Test Ban." In *SIPRI Yearbook 1995*, 697–718.

———. "The Comprehensive Nuclear Test-Ban Treaty." In *SIPRI Yearbook 1997*, 403–436.

Aspen Strategy Group. *Chemical Weapons and Western Security Policy*. Aspen: Aspen Institute, 1987.

Avenhaus, R. *Safeguards System Analysis*. New York: Plenum, 1986.

Babbage, Ross, and Sandy Gordon, eds. *India's Strategic* Future. New York: St. Martin's, 1992.

Bailey, Kathleen C. *Strengthening Nuclear Non-Proliferation*. Boulder: Westview, 1993.

Bajusz, William, and David Louscher. *Arms Sales and the U.S. Economy*. Boulder: Westview, 1988.

Ball, Nicole. *Security and Economy in the Third World*. Princeton: Princeton University Press, 1988.

Barnaby, Frank. *How Nuclear Weapons Spread: Nuclear-Weapon Proliferation in the 1990s*. London: Routledge, 1994.

Beardsley, T. "Devilish Details: Businesses and Arms Controllers Square Off on Export Restrictions." *Scientific American* 270 (5) 1994, 108 and 110.

Benson, Lucy Wilson. "Turning the Supertanker: Arms Transfer Restraint." *International Security* 3 (4) 1979, 3–17.

Betts, Richard K. "The Tragicomedy of Arms Trade Control." *International Security* 5 (1) 1980, 80–110.

Biersteker, Thomas J., and Cynthia Weber. "The Social Construction of State Sovereignty." In Biersteker and Weber, eds. *State Sovereignty as Social Construct*, 1–21.

———, eds. *State Sovereignty as Social Construct*. Cambridge: Cambridge University Press, 1996.

Bitzinger, Richard. *The Globalization of Arms Production: Defense Markets in Transition*. Washington, D.C.: Defense Budget Project, 1993.

Blackwill, Robert D., and Albert Carnesale. *New Nuclear Nations: Consequences for U.S. Policy*. New York: Council on Foreign Relations, 1993.

Blechman, Barry, and Janne Nolan. *The U.S. Soviet Conventional Arms Transfer Negotiations*. FPI Case Studies 3. Baltimore: Foreign Policy Institute, School of Advanced International Studies, Johns Hopkins University, January 1987.

Blix, Hans. "Verification of Nuclear Nonproliferation: The Lesson of Iraq." *Washington Quarterly* 15 (4) 1992, 57–65.

Bonn International Center for Conversion. *Conversion Survey 1997: Global Disarmament and Disposal of Surplus Weapons*. Oxford: Oxford University Press, 1997.

Booth, Ken. "Security and Emancipation." *Review of International Studies* 17(4) 1991, 315–326.

Boulding, Kenneth E. *The Image*. Ann Arbor: University of Michigan Press, 1956.

Boutwell, J., M. T. Klare, and L. W. Reed, eds. *Lethal Commerce: The Global Trade in Small Arms and Light Weapons*. Cambridge: American Academy of Arts and Sciences, 1995.

Bowman, Steve R., Richard F. Grimmett, Robert D. Shuey, and Zachary Davis. *Weapons Proliferation and Conventional Arms Transfers: The Outlook in Mid-1992.* CRS Report for Congress, 92-994 ENR. Washington, D.C.: Congressional Research Service, 31 December 1992.

Brennan, Donald, ed. *Arms Control, Disarmament, and National Security.* New York: Braziller, 1961.

Brodie, Bernard. *Strategy in the Missile Age.* Princeton: Princeton University Press, 1959.

Brown, Frederic. *Chemical Warfare: A Study in Restraints.* Princeton: Princeton University Press, 1968.

Brzoska, Michael. "Third World Arms Control: Problems of Verification." *Bulletin of Peace Proposals* 14 (2) 1983, 165–173.

———. "The Arms Trade—Can It Be Controlled?" *Journal of Peace Research* 24 (4) 1987, 327–331.

Brzoska, Michael, and Frederic Pearson. *Arms and Warfare.* Columbia: University of South Carolina Press, 1994.

Bukharin, Oleg. "Weapons to Fuel." *Science & Global Security* 4 (2) 1994, 179–188.

Bukharin, Oleg, and Helen Hunt. "The U.S.-Russian HEU Agreement: Internal Safeguards to Prevent the Diversion of HEU." *Science and Global Security* 4 (2) 1994, 189–212.

Bull, Hedley. *The Control of the Arms Race: Disarmament and Arms Control in the Missile Age.* New York: Praeger, 1961.

———. *The Anarchical Society: A Study of Order in World Politics.* London: Macmillan, 1977.

Bundy, McGeorge. *Danger and Survival.* New York: Random House, 1988.

Bundy, McGeorge, William J. Crowe Jr., and Sidney Drell. *Reducing Nuclear Danger: The Road Away from the Brink.* New York: Council on Foreign Relations, 1993.

Bunn, George. "Viewpoint: The NPT and Options for Its Extension in 1995." *Nonproliferation Review* 1 (2) 1994, 52–60.

Bunn, George, and Roland M. Timerbaev. "Avoiding the 'Definition' Pitfall to a Comprehensive Test Ban." *Arms Control Today* 23 (4) 1993, 15–18.

———. "Security Assurances to the Non-Nuclear Weapon States." *Nonproliferation Review* 1 (1) 1993, 11–20.

———. *Nuclear Verification Under the NPT: What Should It Cover—How Far May It Go?* PPNN Study No. 5. Southampton: Programme for the Promotion of Nuclear Nonproliferation, 1994.

Bunn, George, and Charles N. Van Doren. *Two Options for the 1995 NPT Extension Conference Revisited.* Washington, D.C.: Lawyers Alliance for World Security, 1992.

Bunn, George, Charles N. Van Doren, and David Fischer. *Options and Opportunities: The NPT Extension Conference of 1995.* PPNN Study No. 2. Southampton: Programme for the Promotion of Nuclear Nonproliferation, 1992.

Burck, Gordon, and Charles Flowertree. *International Handbook on Chemical Weapons Proliferation.* New York: Greenwood, 1991.

Bush, George. "Bush Proposes Arms Control Initiative for the Middle East." Text of a speech by President George Bush to the Air Force Academy. *EUR304,* 29 May 1991.

Butler, Judith. *Bodies That Matter: On the Discursive Limits of Sex.* London: Routledge, 1993.

———. *Excitable Speech: A Politics of the Performative.* London: Routledge, 1997.

Butterfield, Herbert. "The Balance of Power." In Herbert Butterfield and Martin Wight, eds. *Diplomatic Investigations.* London: Allen and Unwin, 1967, 132–148.

Buzan, Barry, Ole Wœver, and Jaap de Wilde. *Security: A New Framework for Analysis.* Boulder: Lynne Rienner, 1998.

Cahn, Anne Hessing, and Joseph Kruzel. *Controlling Future Arms Trade.* New York: McGraw-Hill, 1977.

Calogero, F., M. L. Goldberger, and S. P. Kapitza, eds. *Verification—Monitoring Disarmament.* Boulder: Westview, 1991.

Cameron, Deborah. "Naming of Parts: Gender, Culture, and Terms for the Penis Among American College Students." *American Speech* 67 (4) 1992.

Campbell, David. *Writing Security: United States Foreign Policy and the Politics of Identity.* Manchester: Manchester University Press, 1992.

———. *Politics Without Principle: Sovereignty, Ethics and the Narratives of the Gulf War.* Boulder: Lynne Rienner, 1993.

———. *National Deconstruction: Violence, Identity and Justice in Bosnia.* Minneapolis: University of Minnesota Press, 1998.

Canada, Department of Foreign Affairs and International Trade. "A Note from Minister Axworthy." *AP Mine Ban: Progress Report,* No. 1, February 1997. Http://www.dfait-maeci.gc.ca/english/foreignp/disarm/mines/report1.

Cannizzo, Cindy. "Prospects for the Control of Conventional Arms Transfers." In Cannizzo, ed. *The Gun Merchants,* 187–195.

———. "Trends in Twentieth Century Arms Transfers." In Cannizzo, ed. *The Gun Merchants,* 1–17.

———, ed. *The Gun Merchants: Politics and Policies of the Major Arms Suppliers.* New York: Pergamon, 1980.

Carasales, Julio. "Nuclear Cooperation: One of the Pillars of the Argentine-Brazilian Relationship." *Disarmament* 15 (3) 1992, 109–122.

Carr, E. H. *The Twenty Years' Crisis, 1919–1939.* 2d ed. London: Macmillan, 1946.

Chalmers, Malcolm, and Owen Greene. *Implementing and Developing the United Nations Register of Conventional Arms.* Peace Research Report No. 32 and Bradford Arms Register Studies No. 1. Bradford, Yorkshire, UK: Bradford, 1993.

———. *The United Nations Register of Conventional Arms: An Initial Examination of the First Report.* Bradford Arms Register Studies No. 2. Bradford: Bradford, 1993.

———. *Background Information: An Analysis of Information Provided to the UN on Military Holdings and Procurement Through National Production in the First Year of the Register of Conventional Arms.* Bradford Arms Register Studies No. 3. Bradford: Bradford, 1994.

Chalmers, Malcolm, Owen Greene, Edward Laurence, and Herbert Wulf, eds. *Developing the UN Register of Conventional Arms.* Bradford Arms Register Studies No. 4. Bradford: Bradford, 1994.

Chilton, Paul. *Security Metaphors: Cold War Discourse from Containment to Common House.* New York: Peter Lang, 1996.

Clements, Kevin. "Limiting the Production and Spread of Landmines." *Pacific Research,* February 1994, 3–6.

Cohen, S. P., ed. *Nuclear Proliferation in South Asia.* Boulder: Westview, 1991.

Collier, Basil. *Arms and the Men: The Arms Trade and Governments.* London: Hamish Hamilton, 1980.

Congressional Research Service. *Changing Perspectives on U.S. Arms Transfer Policy.* A report to the Subcommittee on International Security and Scientific Affairs, Committee on Foreign Affairs, House of Representatives, 97th Congress, 1st session. Washington, D.C.: U.S. Government Printing Office, 1981.

Connolly, William. *Identity/Difference: Democratic Negotiation of Political Paradox.* Ithaca: Cornell University Press, 1991.

Cooling, Benjamin, ed. *War, Business and World Military-Industrial Complexes.* Port Washington, N.Y.: Kennikat, 1981.

Daalder, Hans. *The Role of the Military in the Emerging Countries.* The Hague: Mouton, 1962.

Davis, Lynn E. "Statement at Confirmation Hearing." *U.S. Department of State Dispatch* 4 (12) 1993, 170.

Davis, Zachary, and Warren H. Donnelly. *The Nuclear Nonproliferation Treaty: Preparations for a Vote on Its Extension.* Issue Brief. Washington, D.C.: Congressional Research Service, 1994.

Davis, Zachary, and Benjamin Frankel, eds. *The Proliferation Puzzle: Why Nuclear Weapons Spread (and What Results).* London: Frank Cass, 1993.

Dean, Jonathan. "The Final Stage of Nuclear Arms Control." *Washington Quarterly,* 17 (4) 1994, 31–52.

Deger, Saadet, and Robert West, eds. *Defense, Security and Development.* New York: St. Martin's, 1987.

de Man, Paul. "The Epistemology of Metaphor." *Critical Inquiry* 5, 1978, 13–30.

Dewitt, David, ed. *Nuclear Non-Proliferation and Global Security.* London: Croom Helm, 1987.

Domenici, Pete. "Countering Weapons of Mass Destruction." *Washington Quarterly* 18 (1) 1995, 145–152.

Dorff, Robert. "A Commentary on *Security Studies for the 1990s* as a Model Core Curriculum." *International Studies Notes* 19 (3) 1994, 23–31.

Doty, Roxanne. "Foreign Policy as Social Construction: A Post-positivist Analysis of U.S. Counterinsurgency Policy in the Philippines." *International Studies Quarterly* 37 (3) 1993, 297–320.

———. "Aporia: A Critical Exploration of the Agent-Structure Problematique in International Relations Theory." *European Journal of International Relations* 3 (3) 1997, 365–392.

Dowry, Alan. "Sanctioning Iraq: The Limits of the New World Order." *Washington Quarterly* 17 (3) 1994, 179–198.

Dunay, Pal. *The CFE Treaty: History, Achievements and Shortcomings.* PRIF Reports No. 24. Frankfurt: Peace Research Institute Frankfurt, October 1991.

Dunn, Lewis. *Containing Nuclear Proliferation.* Adelphi Paper 263. London: International Institute for Strategic Studies, 1991.

———. "Rethinking the Nuclear Equation: The United States and the New Nuclear Powers." *Washington Quarterly* 17 (1) 1994, 5–25.

Ekéus, Rolf. "The United Nations Special Commission on Iraq." In *SIPRI Yearbook 1992,* 509–530.

Ellis, Jason D., and Todd Perry. "Nunn-Lugar's Unfinished Agenda." *Arms Control Today* 27 (7) 1997, 14–22.

Englebrecht, H. C., and F. C. Hanighen. *Merchants of Death.* New York: Dodd-Mead, 1934.

Evernden, Jack F. "Politics, Technology, and the Test Ban." *Bulletin of the Atomic Scientists,* March 1985, 9–12.

External Affairs and International Trade Canada. "Post-Hostilities Activities." *Backgrounder,* 8 February 1991.

———. "Missile Technology: Looking Beyond Supply-Side Control." *The Disarmament Bulletin* 21, 1993, 5.

Eyre, Dana, and Mark Suchman. "The Proliferation of Conventional Weapons: An Institutional Theory Approach." In Katzenstein, ed. *The Culture of National Security,* 79–113.

Fearon, James. "Counterfactuals and Hypothesis Testing in Political Science." *World Politics* 43 (2) 1991, 169–195.

Feaver, Peter, Scott Sagan, and David Karl. "Proliferation Pessimism and Emerging Nuclear Powers." *International Security* 22 (2) 1997, 185–207.

Fetter, Steve. *Toward a Comprehensive Test Ban.* Cambridge: Ballinger, 1988.

———. "Ballistic Missiles and Weapons of Mass Destruction." *International Security* 16 (1) 1991, 5–42.

———. "Nuclear Archaeology: Verifying Declarations of Fissile Material Production." *Science and Global Security* 3 (3–4) 1993, 237–259.

Fischer, David. "The NPT Review Conference, Geneva, 27 August to 21 September 1985: A Retrospective." In Dewitt, ed. *Nuclear Non-Proliferation and Global Security,* 217–232.

———. *Stopping the Spread of Nuclear Weapons: The Past and the Prospects.* London: Routledge, 1992.

Fischer, David, Ben Sanders, Lawrence Scheinman, and George Bunn. *A New Nuclear Triad: The Non-Proliferation of Nuclear Weapons, International Verification, and the International Atomic Energy Agency.* PPNN Study no. 3. Southampton: Programme for the Promotion of Nuclear Nonproliferation, 1992.

Fluornoy, Michele A., ed. *Nuclear Weapons After the Cold War: Guidelines for U.S. Policy.* New York: HarperCollins, 1993.

Foucault, Michel. *Madness and Civilisation.* New York: Pantheon, 1965.

———. *Discipline and Punish: The Birth of the Prison.* New York: Vintage, 1979.

———. "Practicing Criticism." In Lawrence Kritzman, ed. *Michel Foucault, Politics, Philosophy, Culture: Interviews and Other Writings 1977–1984.* London: Routledge, 1988, 152–156.

Freedman, Lawrence. *Arms Production in the United Kingdom: Problems and Prospects.* London: Royal Institute of International Affairs, 1978.

———. *The Evolution of Nuclear Strategy.* London: Macmillan, 1981.

Fry, M. P., N. P. Keatinge, and J. Rotblat, eds. *Nuclear Non-Proliferation and the Non-Proliferation Treaty.* Berlin: Springer Verlag, 1990.

Fukayama, Francis. *The End of History and the Last Man.* New York: Free Press, 1992.

Gaertner, Heinz. *Challenges of Verification: Smaller States and Arms Control.* Boulder: Westview, 1989.

Garnett, John. "Strategic Studies and Its Assumptions." In John Baylis, Ken Booth, John Garnett, and Phil Williams, eds. *Contemporary Strategy I: Theories and Concepts.* London: Holmes and Meier, 1987, 3–29.

Garrity, Patrick J., and Steven A. Maaranen. *Nuclear Weapons in the Changing World.* New York: Plenum, 1993.

Gebhard, Paul. "Not by Diplomacy or Defence Alone: The Role of Regional Security Strategies in U.S. Proliferation Policy." *Washington Quarterly* 18 (1) 1995, 167–179.

General Accounting Office. *Nuclear Nonproliferation and Safety: Challenges Facing the International Atomic Energy Agency.* Washington, D.C.: U.S. Government Printing Office, 1993.

George, Jim. *Discourses of Global Politics: A Critical (Re)Introduction to International Relations.* Boulder: Lynne Rienner, 1994.

Giddens, Anthony. *The Constitutution of Society: Outline of the Theory of Structuration.* Berkeley: University of California Press, 1984.

Gill, Bates. *The Challenge of Chinese Arms Proliferation: U.S. Policy for the 1990s.* Carlisle, Pa.: U.S. Army War College, 1993.

Gill, Bates, and J. N. Mak, eds. *Arms, Transparency and Security in South-East Asia.* Oxford: Oxford University Press for SIPRI, 1997.

Goatly, Andrew. *The Language of Metaphors.* London: Routledge, 1997.

Goldblat, Jozef. "Multilateral Arms Control Efforts." In *SIPRI Yearbook 1987,* 383–408.

———. "Chemical Disarmament: From the Ban on Use to a Ban on Possession." *Background Paper* 17. Ottawa: Canadian Institute for International Peace and Security, February 1988.

———. "Multilateral Arms Control Efforts." In *SIPRI Yearbook 1988,* 347–371.

———. "Issues Facing the 1995 NPT Extension Conference." *Security Dialogue* 23, December 1992, 25–32.

———. *The Non-Proliferation Treaty: How to Remove the Residual Threats.* Research Paper No. 13. Geneva: UN Institute for Disarmament Research, 1992.

Goldblat, Jozef, and David Cox, eds. *Nuclear Weapon Tests: Prohibition or Limitation?* Oxford: Oxford University Press, 1988.

Government of Canada. *A Guide to Canada's Export Controls.* Ottawa: Department of Foreign Affairs and International Trade, 1994.

Gray, Chris Hables. *Postmodern War: The New Politics of Conflict.* London: Routledge, 1997.

Gray, Colin. "Traffic Control for the Arms Trade." *Foreign Policy* 6, 1972, 153–169.

———. "Arms Control Does Not Control Arms." *Orbis* 37 (3) 1993, 333–348.

Greb, G. Allen, and Warren Heckrotte. "The Long History: The Test Ban Debate." *Bulletin of the Atomic Scientists,* August–September 1983, 36–42.

Gronlund, Lisbeth, and David Wright. *Beyond Safeguards: A Program for More Comprehensive Control of Weapon-Usable Fissile Material.* Washington, D.C.: Union of Concerned Scientists, May 1994.

Gülcher, E. *Tackling the Flow of Arms: An International Survey of Initiatives and Campaigns Against Arms Transfers.* Geneva: International Peace Bureau, 1992.

Gusterson, Hugh. *Nuclear Rites: A Weapons Laboratory at the End of the Cold War.* Berkeley: University of California Press, 1996.

Hartung, William. *And Weapons for All.* New York: HarperCollins, 1994.

Harvey, John. "Regional Ballistic Missiles and Advanced Strike Aircraft: Comparing Military Effectiveness." *International Security* 17 (2) 1992, 41–83.

Holsti, K. J. *The Dividing Discipline: Hegemony and Diversity in International Theory.* Winchester, Mass.: Allen and Unwin, 1985.

Holton, Gerald, ed. *Arms Control.* Special issue of *Daedalus* 89 (4) 1960.

Hopkins, John C., and Weixing Hu. *Strategic Views from the Second Tier: The Nuclear Weapons Policies of France, Britain, and China*. La Jolla: University of California Institute on Global Conflict and Cooperation, 1994.

Howlett, Darryl, and John Simpson. "The NPT and the CTBT: Linkages, Options, and Opportunities." *Arms Control* 13 (1) 1992, 85–107.

———. *Nuclear Non-Proliferation: A Reference Handbook*. Harlow, UK: Longman, 1992.

———. "Nuclearisation and Denuclearisation in South Africa." *Survival* 35 (3) 1993, 154–173.

Human Rights Watch Arms Project and Physicians for Human Rights. *Landmines: A Deadly Legacy*. New York: Human Rights Watch, 1993.

Hume, David. "Of the Balance of Power." In Charles Hendel, ed. *David Hume's Political Essays*. Indianapolis: Bobbs-Merril, 1953, 142–144.

Ichbiah, Daniel. *The Making of Microsoft: How Bill Gates and His Team Created the World's Most Successful Software Company*. Rocklin, Calif.: Prima, 1991.

Inventory of International Non-Proliferation Organizations and Regimes. Monterey: Monterey Institute of International Studies, 1994.

Janowitz, Morton. *The Military in the Political Development of New Nations: An Essay in Comparative Analysis*. Chicago: University of Chicago Press, 1964.

Jervis, Robert. *The Illogic of American Nuclear Strategy*. Ithaca: Cornell University Press, 1984.

Johnson, John. *The Military and Society in Latin America*. Stanford: Stanford University Press, 1964.

———, ed. *The Role of the Military in Underdeveloped Countries*. Princeton: Princeton University Press, 1962.

Johnson, Teresa Pelton. "Writing for *International Security*: A Contributors' Guide." *International Security* 16 (2) 1991, 171–180.

Kahn, Herman. *On Thermonuclear War*. Princeton: Princeton University Press, 1960.

———. *Thinking About the Unthinkable*. New York: Horizon, 1962.

———. *On Escalation: Metaphors and Scenarios*. New York: Praeger, 1965.

Kaiser, Karl. "Non-Proliferation and Nuclear Deterrence." *Survival* 31 (2) 1989, 123–136.

Karkosa, Andrzej. "The Convention on Biological Weapons (1972). In Sur, ed. *Verification of Current Disarmament and Arms Limitation Agreements*, 209–229.

Karl, David J. "Proliferation Pessimism and Emerging Nuclear Powers." *International Security* 21 (3) 1996–1997, 87–119.

Katzenstein, Peter J., ed. *The Culture of National Security: Norms and Identity in World Politics*. New York: Columbia University Press, 1996.

Kay, David. "Denial and Deception Practices of WMD Proliferators: Iraq and Beyond." *Washington Quarterly* 18 (1) 1995, 85–105.

Kearns, Graham. *Arms for the Poor: President Carter's Policies on Arms Transfer to the Third World*. Canberra: Australian National University, 1980.

"The Kenneth Waltz–Scott Sagan Debate: The Spread of Nuclear Weapons: Good or Bad?" *Security Studies* 4 (4) 1995, 693–810.

Keohane, Robert. *International Institutions and State Power: Essays in International Relations Theory*. Boulder: Westview, 1989.

———. "Neoliberal Institutionalism: A Perspective on World Politics." In Keohane, *International Institutions and State Power*, 1–20.

———. "Theory of World Politics: Structural Realism and Beyond." In Keohane, *International Institutions and State Power*, 35–73.

Khan, S. A., ed. *Nuclear War, Nuclear Proliferation and Their Consequences*. Oxford: Clarendon, 1986.

Kidder, Ray E. "How Much More Nuclear Testing Do We Need?" *Arms Control Today* 22 (9) 1992, 11–14.

Kirk, Elizabeth J., W. Thomas Wander, and Brian D. Smith, eds. *Trends and Implications for Arms Control, Proliferation, and International Security in the Changing Global Environment*. Washington, D.C.: American Association for the Advancement of Science.

Klare, Michael. *American Arms Supermarket*. Austin: University of Texas Press, 1984.

———. *Rogue States and Nuclear Outlaws: America's Search for a New Foreign Policy*. New York: Hill and Wang, 1995.

Klein, Bradley. *Strategic Studies and World Order: The Global Politics of Deterrence*. Cambridge: Cambridge University Press, 1994.

Krasner, Stephen. "Regimes and the Limits of Realism: Regimes as Autonomous Variables." In Krasner, ed. *International Regimes*, 355–368.

———. "Structural Causes and Regime Consequences: Regimes as Intervening Variables." In Krasner, ed. *International Regimes*, 1–21.

———, ed. *International Regimes*. Ithaca: Cornell University Press, 1983.

Krause, Jill, and Neil Renwick, eds. *Identities in International Relations*. London: Macmillan, 1996.

Krause, Keith. "Constructing Regional Security Régimes and the Control of Arms Transfers." *International Journal* 45 (2) 1990, 386–423.

———. *Arms and the State: Patterns of Military Production and Trade*. Cambridge: Cambridge University Press, 1993.

Krause, Keith, ed. *Culture and Security: Multilateralism, Arms Control and Security Building*. Special issue of *Contemporary Security Policy* 19 (1) 1998.

Krause, Keith, Kenneth Epps, William Weston, and David Mutimer. *Constraining Conventional Proliferation: A Role for Canada*. Ottawa: Department of Foreign Affairs and International Trade, 1996.

Krause, Keith, and Andrew Latham. "Constructing Non-Proliferation and Arms Control: The Norms of Western Practice." *Contemporary Security Policy* 19 (1) 1998, 23–54.

Krause, Keith, and Michael Williams. "From Strategy to Security: Foundations of Critical Security Studies." In Krause and Williams, eds. *Critical Security Studies*, 33–59.

———, eds. *Critical Security Studies: Concepts and Cases*. Minneapolis: University of Minnesota Press, 1997.

Krauthammer, Charles. "The Unipolar Moment." *Foreign Affairs* 70 (1) 1991, 23–33.

Kunzendorff, Volker. *Verification in Conventional Arms Control*. London: Brassey's, 1989.

Labrie, Roger P., John G. Hutchines, Edwin W. A. Peura, with Diana H. Richman. *U.S. Arms Sales Policy: Background and Issues*. Washington, D.C.: American Enterprise Institute, 1982.

Lakoff, George. *Women, Fire and Dangerous Things: What Categories Reveal About the Mind*. Chicago: University of Chicago Press, 1987.

Lakoff, George, and Mark Johnson. *Metaphors We Live By*. Chicago: University of Chicago Press, 1980.

Lamaziere, Georges, and Roberto Jaguaribe. "Beyond Confidence Building: Brazilian-Argentine Nuclear Cooperation." *Disarmament* 15 (3) 1992.

Lamb, F. K. "Monitoring Yields of Underground Nuclear Tests Using Hydrodynamic Methods." In Schroeer and Hafemeister, eds. *Nuclear Arms Technologies in the 1990s.*

Lamb, John M., and Jennifer L. Moher. *Conventional Arms Transfers: Approaches to Multilateral Control in the 1990s.* Ottawa: Canadian Centre for Arms Control and Disarmament, 1992.

Latham, Andrew. "Constructing National Security: Culture and Identity in Indian Arms Control and Disarmament Practice." In Krause, ed. *Culture and Security,* 129–158.

Laurance, Edward, Siemon Wezeman, and Herbert Wulf. *Arms Watch: SIPRI Report on the First Year of the UN Register of Conventional Arms.* SIPRI Research Report No. 6. Oxford: Oxford University Press for SIPRI, 1993.

Lennon, Alexander. "The 1995 NPT Extension Conference." *Washington Quarterly* 17 (4) 1994, 205–227.

Leonard, James F. *Strengthening the Non-Proliferation Treaty in the Post–Cold War World.* Working Paper No. 1. Washington, D.C.: Washington Council on Non-Proliferation, 1992.

Leventhal, Paul, and Sharon Tanzer, eds. *Averting a Latin American Nuclear Arms Race.* New York: St. Martin's, 1992.

Levy, Marion J. *Modernization and the Structure of Society: An International Setting.* Princeton: Princeton University Press, 1962.

Lindsey, George. *Modernization of Weapons and Qualitative Problems of Arms Control.* Ottawa: Canadian Institute for International Peace and Security, 1992.

Linklater, Andrew. "The Transformation of Political Community: E. H. Carr, Critical Theory and International Relations." *Review of International Studies* 23 (3) 1997, 321–338.

Loeb, Benjamin S. "Test Ban Proposals and Agreements: The 1950s to the Present." In Richard Dean Burns, ed. *Encyclopedia of Arms Control and Disarmament,* Vol. 2. New York: Scribner, 1993, 827–846.

Mazarr, Michael J. "Nuclear Weapons After the Cold War." *Washington Quarterly* 15 (3) 1992, 185–201.

Mazarr, Michael J., and Alexander T. Lennon. *Toward a Nuclear Peace: The Future of Nuclear Weapons.* New York: St. Martin's, 1994.

McFate, P., S. Graybeal, G. Lindsey, and D. M. Kilgour. *Constraining Proliferation: The Contribution of Verification Synergies.* Arms Control Verification Studies No. 5. Ottawa: Non-Proliferation, Arms Control and Disarmament Division of the Canadian Department of External Affairs, 1993.

Mearsheimer, John. "Back to the Future: Instability in Europe After the Cold War." *International Security* 15 (1) 1990, 5–56.

———. "The Case for a Ukrainian Nuclear Deterrent." *Foreign Affairs* 72 (3) 1993, 50–66.

Medalia, Jonathan, P. Zinsmeister, and Robert Civiak, eds. *Nuclear Weapons and Security: The Effects of Alternative Test Ban Treaties.* Boulder: Westview, 1991.

Meselson, Matthew, ed. *Chemical Weapons and Chemical Arms Control.* New York: Carnegie Endowment for International Peace, 1978.

Miller, Steven. "The Case Against a Ukrainian Nuclear Deterrent." *Foreign Affairs* 72 (3) 1993, 67–80.

Millot, Marc Dean. "Facing the Emerging Reality of Regional Nuclear Adversaries." *Washington Quarterly* 17 (3) 1994, 41–71.

Molander, Roger C., and Peter A. Wilson. "On Dealing with the Prospect of Nuclear Chaos." *Washington Quarterly* 17 (3) 1994, 19–39.

Monahan, Bill. "Giving the Non-Proliferation Treaty Teeth: Strengthening the Special Inspection Procedures of the International Atomic Energy Agency." *Virginia Journal of International Law* 33, Fall 1992, 161–196.

Moore, James W. *Conventional Arms Control and Disarmament in Europe: A Model of Verification System Effectiveness.* Ottawa: Arms Control and Disarmament Division, External Affairs and International Trade Canada, 1990.

Morgenthau, Hans. *Politics Among Nations,* 5th ed. New York: Knopf, 1978.

Murray, Andrew, and Tim Hunt. *The Cell Cycle: An Introduction.* New York: Freeman, 1993.

Mussington, David. *Arms Unbound: The Globalization of Defense Production.* CSIA Studies in International Security No. 4. Cambridge: Center for Science and International Affairs, John F. Kennedy School of Government, Harvard University/Brassey's (U.S.), 1994.

———. "Understanding Contemporary International Arms Transfers." *Adelphi Paper* 291. London: International Institute for Strategic Studies, 1994.

———. "Verifying End-Use Restrictions on Dual-Use Technology Transfers." In Mutimer, ed. *Moving Beyond Supplier Controls,* 31–56.

Mutimer, David. "Reimagining Security: The Metaphors of Proliferation." In Krause and Williams, eds. *Critical Security Studies,* 187–221.

———. "Reconstituting Security: The Practices of Proliferation Control." *European Journal of International Relations* 4 (1) 1998, 99–129.

———, ed. *Control but Verify: Verification in the New Nonproliferation Agenda.* Toronto: York Centre for International and Strategic Studies, 1994.

———. *Moving Beyond Supplier Controls in a Mature Technology Environment.* Toronto: York Centre for International and Strategic Studies, 1995.

Nardin, Terry. *Law, Morality and the Relations of States.* Princeton: Princeton University Press, 1983.

Neff, Thomas. "Integrating Uranium from Weapons into the Civil Fuel Cycle." *Science and Global Security* 3 (3-4) 1993, 215–222.

Neufeld, Mark. "Interpretation and the 'Science' of International Relations." *Review of International Studies* 19 (3) 1993, 39–61.

Neuman, Stephanie, and Robert Harkavy, eds. *Arms Transfers in the Modern World.* New York: Praeger, 1979.

Neumann, Iver. *Russia and the Idea of Europe: A Study in Identity and International Relations.* London: Routledge, 1996.

Nolan, Janne. "The Conventional Arms Trade: Prospects for Control." *Working Paper* No. 42. Canberra: Australian National University, 1988.

———. "The Global Arms Market After the Gulf War: Prospects for Control." *Washington Quarterly* 14 (3) 1991, 125–138.

———. *Trappings of Power: Ballistic Missiles in the Third World.* Washington, D.C.: Brookings Institution, 1991.

Nolan, Janne, ed. *Global Engagement: Cooperation and Security in the 21st Century.* Washington, D.C.: Brookings Institute, 1994.

Non-Seismic Technologies in Support of a Nuclear Test Ban. Ottawa: Verification Research Unit, Canada, Department of External Affairs, 1993.

NPT Review and Extension Conference. "Principles and Objectives for Nuclear Non-Proliferation and Disarmament." NPT/CONF.1995/L.5, 1995.

Nuclear Non-Proliferation and Safeguards. Paris and La Grange Park, Ill.: Atlantic Institute for International Affairs and American Nuclear Society, 1981.

"Nunn-Lugar Threat Reduction Programs." *Coalition to Reduce Nuclear Dangers: Issue Brief* 2 (10) March 1998. Http://www.clw.org/pub/clw/coalition/brief10.htm.

Ohlson, Thomas, ed. *Arms Transfer Limitations and Third World Security.* Oxford: Oxford University Press, 1988.

Ozaga, D. A. *A Chronology of MTCR Development.* Monterey: Monterey Institute for International Studies, November 1993.

Pearson, Frederic. "U.S. Arms Transfer Policy: The Feasibility of Restraint." *Arms Control* 2 (1) 1981, 25–65.

———. "The Question of Control in British Defence Sales Policy." *International Affairs* (London) 59, 1983, 211–238.

———. *The Global Spread of Arms: Political Economy of International Security.* Boulder: Westview, 1994.

Permanent Five Members of the UN Security Council. "Statement of the Five Countries." Press Release. Paris, 9 July 1991.

Pierre, Andrew. "International Restraints on Conventional Arms Transfers." In Sharp, ed. *Opportunities for Disarmament,* 47–60.

———. *The Global Politics of Arms Sales.* Princeton: Princeton University Press, 1983.

———, ed. *Arms Transfers and American Foreign Policy.* New York: New York University Press, 1979.

Pilat, Joseph F., and Walter Kirchner. "The Technological Promise of Counterproliferation." *Washington Quarterly* 18 (1) 1995, 153–166.

Pilat, Joseph, ed. *The Nonproliferation Predicament.* Oxford: Transaction, 1985.

Pilat, Joseph F., and Robert E. Pendley, eds. *Beyond 1995: The Future of the NPT Regime.* New York: Plenum, 1990.

Potter, William. *Nuclear Power and Nonproliferation: An Interdisciplinary Perspective.* Cambridge: Oelgeschalger, Gunn and Hain, 1982.

Price, Richard. "A Genealogy of the Chemical Weapons Taboo." *International Organization* 49 (1) 1995, 73–103.

———. *The Chemical Weapons Taboo.* Ithaca: Cornell University Press, 1997.

———. "Reversing the Gun Sights: Transnational Civil Society Targets Land Mines." *International Organization* 52 (3) 1998, 613–644.

Price, Richard, and Nina Tannenwald. "Norms and Deterrence: The Nuclear and Chemical Weapons Taboos." In Katzenstein, ed. *The Culture of National Security,* 114–152.

Quester, George. "No-First-Use and Nonproliferation: Redefining Extended Deterrence." *Washington Quarterly* 17 (2) 1994, 103–114.

Quester, George H., and Victor Utgoff. "U.S. Arms Reductions and Nuclear Nonproliferation: The Counterproductive Possibilities." *Washington Quarterly* 16 (1) 1993, 129–140.

Ramberg, Bennett, ed. *Arms Control Without Negotiation: From the Cold War to the New World Order.* Boulder: Lynne Rienner, 1993.

Ranger, Robin. "The Four Bibles of Arms Control." In Susan Shepard, ed. *Books and the Pursuit of American Foreign Policy.* Special issue of *Books Forum* 6, 1984, 416–432.

Rapoport, Anatol. "Editor's Introduction." In Carl von Clausewitz, *On War.* Rapoport, ed. London: Penguin, 1968, 11–80.

Rathjens, George. "Rethinking Nuclear Proliferation." *Washington Quarterly* 18 (1) 1995, 181–193.

Rauf, Tariq, ed. *Regional Approaches to Curbing Nuclear Proliferation in the Middle East and South Asia.* Aurora Papers No. 16. Ottawa: Canadian Centre for Global Security, 1992.

Redick, John. "Argentina-Brazil Nuclear Non-Proliferation Initiatives." *PPNN Issue Review,* No. 3, January 1994.

Redick, John, Julio Carasales, and Paulo Wrobel. "Argentine-Brazilian Nuclear Rapprochement." *Washington Quarterly* 18 (1) 1995, 107–122.

Regehr, Ernie. *Arms Canada: The Deadly Business of Military Exports.* Toronto: James Lorimer, 1987.

Reiss, Mitchell. "The Last Nuclear Summit?" *Washington Quarterly* 17 (3) 1994, 5–15.

"Remarks of the Honorable John D. Holum, Director, U.S. Arms Control and Disarmament Agency, 4 August 1994." Washington, D.C.: ACDA Office of Public Information, 1994.

A Report on the International Control of Atomic Energy (Acheson-Lilienthal Report). Prepared for the Secretary of State's Committee on Atomic Energy. Washington, D.C.: U.S. Government Printing Office, 16 March 1946. Department of State Publication 2498. Http://www.learnworld.com/ZNW/LWText.Acheson-Lilienthal.html.

Riga, Thierry. "Une approche coopérative de la non-prolifération nucléaire: L'exemple de l'Argentine et du Brésil." *UNIDIR Research Papers,* No. 29. Geneva: UN Institute for Disarmament Research, 1994.

Ringmar, Eric. *Identity, Interest and Action: A Cultural Explanation of Sweden's Intervention in the Thirty Years War.* Cambridge: Cambridge University Press, 1996.

Rioux, Jean François, ed. *Limiting the Proliferation of Weapons: The Role of Supply-Side Strategies.* Ottawa: Carleton University Press, 1992.

Roberts, Brad. "From Nonproliferation to Antiproliferation." *International Security* 18 (1) 1993, 139–173.

———. "1995 and the End of the Post–Cold War Era." *Washington Quarterly* 18 (1) 1995, 5–25.

———, ed. *Biological Weapons: Weapons of the Future.* Washington, D.C.: Center for Strategic and International Studies, 1993.

Saferworld Foundation. *Regulating Arms Exports: A Programme for the European Community.* London: Saferworld Foundation, 1991.

Sagan, Scott. "The Perils of Proliferation: Organization Theory, Deterrence Theory, and the Spread of Nuclear Weapons." *International Security* 18 (4) 1994, 66–107.

———. "More Will Be Worse." In Scott Sagan and Kenneth Waltz, *The Spread of Nuclear Weapons: A Debate.* New York: Norton, 1995, 47–91.

———. "Why Do States Build Nuclear Weapons? Three Models in Search of a Bomb." *International Security* 21 (3) 1996–1997, 54–86.

———, ed. *Civil-Military Relations and Nuclear Weapons.* Stanford: Stanford University Center for International Security and Arms Control, 1994.

Scott Sagan and Kenneth Waltz. *The Spread of Nuclear Weapons: A Debate.* New York: Norton, 1995.

Sampson, Anthony. *The Arms Bazaar: The Companies, the Dealers, the Bribes: From Vickers to Lockheed.* London: Hodder and Stoughton, 1977.

Sanders, Ben. "Non-Proliferation Diplomacy: Preparing for 1995." *Security Dialogue* 24, June 1993, 221–231.

Schear, J. A., ed. *Nuclear Weapons Proliferation and Nuclear Risks.* Aldershot: Gower, 1984.

Scheinman, Lawrence. *Assuring the Nuclear Non-Proliferation Safeguards System.* Washington, D.C.: Atlantic Council, 1992.

———. "Lessons from Post-War Iraq for the International Full-Scope Safeguards Regime." *Arms Control Today* 22 (4) 1993, 3–6.

Scheinman, Lawrence, and David Fischer. "Managing the Coming Glut of Nuclear Weapon Materials." *Arms Control Today* 22 (3) 1992, 7–12.

Schell, Jonathan. *The Fate of the Earth.* New York: Knopf, 1982.

Schelling, Thomas. *The Strategy of Conflict.* New York: Oxford University Press, 1960.

Schelling, Thomas, and Morton Halperin. *Strategy and Arms Control.* Reissued with a new preface. New York: Pergamon-Brassey's, 1985.

Schelling, Thomas, and Morton Halperin, with Donald Brennan. *Strategy and Arms Control.* New York: Twentieth Century Fund, 1961.

Schiffrin, Deborah. *Approaches to Discourse.* Oxford: Blackwell, 1994.

Schroeer, Dietrich, and David Hafemeister, eds. *Nuclear Arms Technologies in the 1990's: Washington, D.C., 1988.* New York: American Institute of Physics, 1988.

Secretary-General of the United Nations. "Study on Ways and Means of Promoting Transparency in International Transfers of Conventional Arms." Report of the Secretary-General to the United Nations General Assembly, *A/46/301,* 9 September 1991.

———. "Verification in All Its Aspects, Including the Role of the United Nations in the Field of Verification." Report of the Secretary-General to the United Nations General Assembly, *A/50/377,* 22 September 1995.

Shah, Prakash. "Nuclear Non-Proliferation Implications and the NPT Review: An Indian Perspective." Paper presented to the international workshop Nuclear Disarmament and Non-Proliferation: Issues for International Action. Tokyo, 15–16 March 1993.

Shaker, M. I. "The Third NPT Review Conference: Issues and Prospects." In Dewitt, ed. *Nuclear Non-Proliferation and Global Security,* 3–12.

———. "The 1995 NPT Extension Conference: A Rejoinder." *Security Dialogue* 23 (4) 1992, 33–36.

Sharp, Jane M. O., ed. *Opportunities for Disarmament.* Washington, D.C.: Carnegie Endowment for International Peace, 1978.

Shuey, Robert. *Missile Proliferation: A Discussion of U.S. Objectives and Policy Options.* Report 90-120F. Washington, D.C.: Congressional Research Service, 1990.

Simpson, John. "The Nuclear Non-Proliferation Regime: Options and Opportunities." *Disarmament* 16 (2) 1993, 21–38.

———. "Nuclear Non-Proliferation in the Post–Cold War Era." *International Affairs* (London) 70, January 1994, 17–39.

Sims, Nicholas. *International Organization for Chemical Disarmament.* SIPRI Chemical and Biological Warfare Studies No. 8. Oxford, University Press: Oxford University Press for SIPRI, 1987.

SIPRI (Stockholm Peace Research Institute). *The Arms Trade with the Third World.* New York: Humanities Press, 1971.

———. *World Armaments and Disarmament: SIPRI Yearbook 1982.* Oxford: Taylor and Francis, 1982.

———. *World Armaments and Disarmament: SIPRI Yearbook 1986.* Oxford: Oxford University Press for SIPRI, 1986.

———. *SIPRI Yearbook 1987: World Armaments and Disarmament.* Oxford: Oxford University Press, 1987.

———. *SIPRI Yearbook 1988: World Armaments and Disarmament.* Oxford: Oxford University Press, 1988.

———. *SIPRI Yearbook 1992: World Armaments and Disarmament.* Oxford: Oxford University Press, 1992.

————. *SIPRI Yearbook 1995: World Armaments and Disarmament*. Oxford: Oxford University Press, 1995.

————. *SIPRI Yearbook 1997: World Armaments and Disarmament*. Oxford: Oxford University Press, 1997.

Sloutzky, Naoum. *Le Contrôle du Commerce International des Armes de Guerre*. Genève: Dotation Carnegie Pour la Paix Internationale, 1969.

Snyder, Glenn H. *Deterrence and Defence: Toward a Theory of National Security*. Princeton: Princeton University Press, 1961.

Sokolski, Henry. "Will There Be an Arms Trade Intelligence Deficit?" *Annals of the American Academy of Political and Social Science* 535, 1994, 158–162.

Spector, Leonard S. "Repentant Nuclear Proliferants." *Foreign Policy* 88, Fall 1992, 21–37.

Spiers, Edward M. *Chemical and Biological Weapons: A Study of Proliferation*. London: Macmillan, 1994.

Stanley, Ruth. "Cooperation and Control: The New Approach to Nuclear Nonproliferation in Argentina and Brazil." *Arms Control* 13 (2) 1992, 191–213.

States Party to the BTWC. "Final Declaration: Special Conference of the States Party to the BTWC." *BWC/SPCONF/1*, 1994.

Strulak, Tadeusz. "The Nuclear Suppliers Group." *Non-Proliferation Review* 1, 1993, 2–10.

Subrahmanyam, K. "An Equal-Opportunity NPT." *Bulletin of the Atomic Scientists* 49, June 1993, 37–39.

Suchman, Mark, and Dana Eyre. "Military Procurement as Rational Myth: Notes on the Social Construction of Weapons Proliferation." *Sociological Forum* 7 (1) 1992, 137–161.

Sur, Serge, ed. *Verification of Current Disarmament and Arms Limitation Agreements: Ways, Means and Practices*. Aldershot: Dartmouth for UNIDIR, 1991.

Talbott, Strobe. "U.S. Diplomacy in South Asia: A Progress Report." Transcript as delivered, provided by the Brookings Institute. Http://www.brook.edu/comm/transcripts/19981112a.htm.

Tanner, Fred, ed. *From Versailles to Baghdad: Post-War Armament Control of Defeated States*. Geneva: United Nations Institute for Disarmament Research, 1992.

Taylor, Charles. *Philosophy and the Human Sciences*. Cambridge: Cambridge University Press, 1985.

Taylor, Trevor. "The Evaluation of Arms Transfer Control Proposals." In Cannizzo, ed. *The Gun Merchants*, 167–186.

Thayer, Bradley, and Steven Lee. "The Kenneth Waltz–Scott Sagan Debate II." *Security Studies* 5 (1) 1995, 149–170.

Thomas, Raju. "The Growth of India's Military Power: From Sufficiency to Nuclear Deterrence." In Babbage and Gordon, eds. *India's Strategic Future*, 35–66.

Timerbaev, Roland. "Strengthening the NPT Regime: A CTBT and Cut-Off of Fissionable Material." *Disarmament* 16 (2) 1993, 97–108.

Tooze, Roger. "Prologue: States, Nationalisms and Identities." In Krause and Renwick, eds. *Identities in International Relations*, xvi–xx.

28 States, The. "New Multilateral Export Control Arrangement." Press statement issued after the High Level Meeting of 28 States, Wassenaar, 11 and 12 September 1995.

UK Ministry of Defence. "Supporting Essay One: The Strategic Defence Review Process." Http://www.mod.uk/policy/sdr/essay01.htm.

————. "Supporting Essay Two: The Policy Framework." Http://www.mod.uk/policy/sdr/essay02.htm.

United Nations. "Transparency in International Arms Transfers." *UN Disarmament Topical Papers,* No. 3. New York: United Nations, 1990.

United Nations General Assembly. "General and Complete Disarmament: International Arms Transfers: Study on Ways and Means of Promoting Transparency in International Transfers of Conventional Arms." *A/46/301,* 9 September 1991.

―――. "General and Complete Disarmament: Transparency in Armaments: Report to the Register on Conventional Arms." *A/47/342,* 14 August 1992.

―――. "New Dimensions of Arms Regulation and Disarmament in the Post–Cold War Era: Report of the Secretary-General of the United Nations, Mr. Boutros Boutros-Ghali, on the Occasion of Disarmament Week, 27 October 1992." *A/C.1.47/7,* 23 October 1992.

United Nations Security Council. "Consolidated Report on the First Two IAEA Inspections Under Security Council Resolution 687 (1991) of Iraqi Nuclear Capabilities." *S/2278,* 1991.

―――. "Statement by the President of the Security Council on Behalf of the Members of the Council on the Responsibility of the Security Council in the Maintenance of International Peace and Security." *S/23500,* 31 January 1991.

―――. "Plan for Future Ongoing Monitoring and Verification of Iraq's Compliance with Relevant Parts of Section C of Security Council Resolution 687 (1991)." *S/22871/Rev.1,* 2 October 1991.

―――. "Report on the Seventh IAEA On-Site Inspection in Iraq Under Security Council Resolution 687 (1991)." *S/23215,* 11–22 October 1991.

―――. "Report of the Secretary-General on the Activities of the Special Commission Established by the Secretary-General Pursuant to Paragraph 9 (b) (i) of Resolution 687 (1991)." *S/1996/258,* 11 April 1996.

―――. "Report of the Secretary-General on the Activities of the Special Commission Established by the Secretary-General Pursuant to Paragraph 9 (b) (i) of Resolution 687 (1991)." *S/1997/774,* 6 October 1997.

―――. "Report of the Secretary-General on the Activities of the Special Commission Established by the Secretary-General Pursuant to Paragraph 9 (b) (i) of Resolution 687 (1991)." *S/1996/848,* 11 October 1997.

U.S. Arms Control and Disarmament Agency. "Memorandum of Understanding Between the United States of America and the Union of Soviet Socialist Republics Regarding the Establishment of a Direct Communications Link (with Annex)." ACDA Narrative. Http://www.acda.gov/treaties/hotline1.htm.

U.S. Congress, Office of Technology Assessment. *Arming Our Allies: Cooperation and Competition in Defense Technology.* Washington, D.C.: U.S. Government Printing Office, 1990.

―――. *Proliferation of Weapons of Mass Destruction: Assessing the Risks.* OTA-ISC-559. Washington, D.C.: U.S. Government Printing Office, 1993.

―――. *Export Controls and Nonproliferation Policy.* OTA-ISS-596. Washington, D.C.: U.S. Government Printing Office, 1994.

U.S. Department of State. "Fact Sheet: Middle East Arms Control Initiative." *Department of State Dispatch,* 3 June 1991.

―――. Secretary of State Warren Christopher. "The Strategic Priorities of American Foreign Policy: Statement Before the Senate Foreign Relations Committee." Washington, D.C., 4 November 1993. *U.S. Department of State Dispatch* 4 (47) 22 November 1993.

van Creveld, Martin. *Nuclear Proliferation and the Future of Conflict.* New York: Free Press, 1993.

van der Vink, Gregory E., and Christopher E. Paine. "The Politics of Verification: Limiting the Testing of Nuclear Weapons." *Science and Global Security* 3 (3-4) 1993, 261–288.

van der Vink, Gregory E., David Simpson, Christel Hennet, Jeffrey Park, and Terry Wallace. *Nuclear Testing and Nonproliferation: The Role of Seismology in Deterring the Development of Nuclear Weapons.* Prepared at the request of the Senate Committee on Governmental Affairs and the House Committee on Foreign Affairs of the United States Congress. Arlington, Va.: IRIS Consortium, 1994.

van Ham, Peter. *Managing Non-Proliferation Regimes in the 1990s.* London: Pinter, 1993.

von Baekmann, Adolf. "The Treaty on the Non-Proliferation of Nuclear Weapons (NPT) (1968)." In Sur, ed. *Verification of Current Disarmament and Arms Limitation Agreements,* 167–189.

Walker, R. B. J. *Inside/Outside: International Relations as Political Theory.* Cambridge: Cambridge University Press, 1993.

Wallace, James. *Hard Drive: Bill Gates and the Making of the Microsoft Empire.* New York: Wiley, 1992.

———. *Overdrive: Bill Gates and the Race to Control Cyberspace.* Chichester, N.Y: Wiley, 1997.

Walt, Stephen M. "The Renaissance of Security Studies." *International Studies Quarterly* 35 (2) 1991, 211–239.

Waltz, Kenneth. *Theory of International Politics.* New York: Random House, 1979.

———. "The Spread of Nuclear Weapons: More May Be Better." *Adelphi Paper No. 171.* London: International Institute for Strategic Studies, 1981.

Wander, W. Thomas, Eric Arnett, and Paul Bracken, eds. *The Diffusion of Advanced Weaponry: Technologies, Regional Implications, and Responses.* Washington, D.C.: American Association for the Advancement of Science, 1994.

Watt, F. "Strengthening the United Nations Arms Trade Register." *Issues Action Briefing Paper,* No. 19. Ottawa: World Federalists of Canada, 1995.

Wœver, Ole. "Securitization and Desecuritization." In Ronnie D. Lipschutz, ed. *On Security.* New York: Columbia University Press, 1995, 46–86.

Wœver, Ole, Barry Buzan, Morten Kelstrup, and Pierre Lemaitre. *Identity, Migration and the New Security Agenda in Europe.* London: Pinter, 1993.

Weldes, Jutta. "Constructing National Interests." *European Journal of International Relations* 2 (3) 1996, 275–318.

Wendt, Alexander. "Anarchy Is What States Make of It: The Social Construction of Power Politics." *International Organization* 46 (2) 1992, 391–425.

———. "Collective Identity Formation and the International State." *American Political Science Review* 88 (2) 1994, 385–396.

———. *Social Theory of International Politics.* Cambridge: Cambridge University Press, forthcoming.

White House. *National Drug Control Strategy.* Washington, D.C.: Government Printing Office, 1990.

———. *A National Security Strategy of Engagement and Enlargement.* Washington, D.C.: Government Printing Office, 1996.

Wight, Martin. "The Balance of Power." In Butterfield and Wight, eds. *Diplomatic Investigations,* 149–175.

Williams, Michael. "Rethinking the 'Logic' of Deterrence." *Alternatives* 17, 1992, 67–93.

Williamson, R., ed. *The Arms Trade Today: Arms Transfers and Proliferation—A CCIA Consultation.* Geneva: World Council of Churches' Commission of the Churches on International Affairs, 1993.

Wilmshurst, W. J. "The Adequacy of IAEA Safeguards for the 1990s." In Fry, Keatinge, and Rotblat, eds. *Nuclear Non-Proliferation and the Non-Proliferation Treaty.*

Wolfers, Arnold. "'National Security' as an Ambiguous Symbol." In Robert Art and Robert Jervis, eds. *International Politics: Anarchy, Force, Political Economy, and Decision Making.* 2d ed. New York: HarperCollins, 1985, 42–54.

Workman, W. Thom. *The Social Origins of the Iran-Iraq War.* Boulder: Lynne Rienner, 1994.

Wulf, Herbert. "Arms Transfer Control: The Feasibility and the Obstacles." In Deger and West, eds. *Defense, Security and Development,* 190–206.

Yuan, Jing-Dong. "Non-Proliferation Export Controls in the 1990s." *Martellow Papers* No. 7. Kingston: Centre for International Relations, Queen's University, 1994.

Zalewski, Marysia, and Cynthia Enloe. "Questions About Identity in International Relations." In Ken Booth and Steve Smith, eds. *International Relations Theory Today.* Cambridge: Polity, 1995, 279–305.

Index

ABM. *See* Antiballistic missile treaty
ACDA. *See* Arms Control and
Disarmament Agency
Acheson, Dean, 30
Acheson-Lilienthal report, 30–31,
170(n1), 171(n6)
Adler, Emmanuel, 34
Agnew, Harold, 120
Agreed Declaration, 32–33, 171(n6)
Annan, Khofi, 143–144
Antiballistic missile treaty (ABM), 34,
163, 172(nn17,20)
Armament Year Book (League of
Nations), 47
Arms. *See* Weapons; Weapons,
biological; Weapons, chemical;
Weapons, nuclear
*Arms and the State: Patterns of
Military Production and Trade*
(Krause), 50
Arms control, 30–31; ABM and SALT,
34–36; chemical and biological
weapons, 43–45, 53–55, 177(n1);
conventional weapons, 46–51; export
control, 83–84; national interests
and, 134–135; nuclear strategy and,
171(n14); proliferation prevention,
132. *See also* Balance of power;
Proliferation control; Verification;
Weapons
Arms Control and Disarmament
Agency (ACDA), 35, 163
Arms production. *See under* Weapons
Australia Group, 83, 84, 163; in a
disarmament practice, 106–107;

formation of, 65; proliferation
prevention, 132; as supplier group
for BW, 67

Balance of power, 173(nn29,32); arms
control compliance verification,
55–58; in a disarmament image,
104–107; emergence and labeling of
rogue states, 91–97; Iraqi invasion of
Kuwait, 95–96; multiple-states
instability, 37–43, 89–91,
173(nn33,35), 174(n36); USSR
perspective, 174(n37)
Barnaby, Frank, 41, 61
Baruch, Bernard, 170(n1)
Baruch Plan, 30
Batzel, Roger, 120
Biological and Toxin Weapons
Convention (BTWC), 163; formation
of, 177(n1); nonproliferation claims
in, 131(table); NPT extension, 99;
proliferation control, 67–68;
verification and, 5
Biological weapons. *See* Weapons,
biological
Biologism, 170(n29)
Blair, Tony, 138
Body, material, 23–25, 170(n34)
Boeing Corporation, 49
Bonn International Centre for
Conversion, 113–114
Booth, Ken, 13–14
Boulding, Kenneth, 17–18
Brodie, Bernard, 32
Brookings Institution, 153

213

optimists and pessimists, 132–133, 183(n42); policy position, 158–159
Proliferation control, 63–73; appropriateness of, 155–156; elements of, 66(table), 72(table); national interests and, 133–134; two-tiered practices, 64(table)

RAND Corporation, 32, 171(n5)
Reagan, Ronald, 51, 120–121
Realism, 12–13, 128–130
Regime theory, 127–128
Register of Conventional Arms (UN), ix, 47–48, 68–69, 86, 131, 179(n31)
Resolution 687 (UN), viii, 78, 144
Review and Extension Conference, NPT, 100–101
Roberts, Brad, 73
Rogue doctrine, 92–93
Rogue states, ix; in a disarmament image, 104–107; India as potential rogue, 108–109; Iraq's emergence as, 77–79, 92–93, 95–97; as U.S. military strategy, 91–97, 135–136
Russia, 112–113, 182(n24), 186(n28). *See also* Union of Soviet Socialist Republics

Sagan, Scott, 183(n42)
SALT. *See* Strategic arms limitation treaty
Sampson, Anthony, 48
Schell, Jonathan, 31
Schelling, Thomas, 32, 185(n13)
Security, international, 168(n9); criticism of proliferation as threat, 11–13; examination of, 130–131; institutions and actors concerned with, 13–14; link to economics, 114–116; as national interest, 127; post–Cold War threat blank, 92–93; in a proliferation image, 61, 135–141, 156; subjective quality of, 107–108. *See also* Stability
Security Metaphors (Chilton), 19–20
Security studies, 14–17, 169(n11)
Shaker, M. I., 184(n4)
SIPRI. *See* Stockholm International Peace Research Institute
SIPRI Yearbook 1987, 57
Six Nations Initiative, 121
Social relations, 169(n15)
Society, image and practice, 18–19
South Asia, 90
Sovereignty: military as necessity for, 137–141; norms of, 148–149, 192(n16)
St. Germain Convention, 47
Stability, as norm, 89–91
START. *See* Strategic arms reduction treaty
State: absorption of personal identity, 79–83; action in terms of practice, 18–19; as actor in international security, 14–15; as locus of identity, 81–82
Statistical Year-Book of the League of Nations, 47
Stockholm International Peace Research Institute (SIPRI), 55, 165
Strategic arms limitation treaty (SALT), 34–37, 45, 56–57, 165, 173(n21); proliferation prevention, 132
Strategic arms reduction treaty talks (START), 45, 56–57, 165
Strategic Defense Initiative (SDI), 165
Strategic studies, 14–15
Strategy, nuclear: arms control and, 171(n14); of deterrence, 31–33, 172(n11); MAD, 171(n7)
Suchman, Mark, 137, 140
Supplier groups, 83–84, 96–97, 155–156; in a disarmament image, 106–107, 118; member countries, 84–86, 87(table); national interests and, 133–134; proliferation prevention, 132; technology recipients, 133–134

Talbott, Strobe, 153
Tannenwald, Nina, 45
Taylor, Charles, 18
Technology, 133–134; denying access to, 152; in a development image, 107–110; in a disarmament image, 103–107; as element of CTBT, 124–125; management of production and flow, 6–7; military vs. civilian applications, 111–114; movement vs. arms production, 156–157; national

About the Book

The proliferation of all kinds of weapons (nuclear, chemical, biological, and even conventional) is emerging as a focal point for international security. This book shows how both the language used to talk about weapons proliferation and the practices adopted to respond to it define the problem in ways that promote policy responses doomed to failure.

Examining the metaphors that have been gathered into the proliferation discourse—in terms of the nature of the problems they construct, the various interests they create, and the identity of the actors that are constituted—Mutimer makes a seminal contribution to both critical IR and policy debates.

David Mutimer is assistant professor in the Department of Political Science at York University (Canada).